Praise for

Breakthroughs in Technical Analysis
New Thinking from the World's Top Minds
Edited by David Keller

"Mr. Keller went to great lengths to collect diverse methodology in technical analysis from around the globe. For over forty years I have seen interest in technical analysis wane and wax as markets change and practitioner skills change. *Breakthroughs in Technical Analysis* offers commentary from the leading experts in the newest quantitative methodologies as well as old reliable techniques. I recommend the book to established professionals as well as bright newcomers."
   PHILIP J. ROTH, CMT
   Chief Technical Market Analyst, Miller Tabak & Co., LLC
   Past President and Board Member of the Market Technicians Association

"Navigating financial markets can be a hazardous exercise. In *Breakthroughs in Technical Analysis*, Dave Keller has assembled contributions from an experienced crew of established technicians and market timers to ease the journey and demystify the arcane world of technical analysis. The book features a number of approaches (as diverse as DeMark and Ichimoku), which challenge conventional wisdom and are sure to form an invaluable part of your trading arsenal, whether you're technically or fundamentally oriented."
   JASON PERL
   Global Head of Fixed Income, Foreign Exchange and
   Commodities Technical Strategy, UBS Investment Bank

"The concepts and experiences shared by the ten global contributors in David Keller's book embody the precept that supply and demand for technical analysis is indeed a universal language. These varied topics are very timely and extremely useful in trading and investing in all markets around the world."
   RALPH J. ACAMPORA, CMT
   Managing Director, Director of Technical Research
   Knight Equity Markets, LP

Breakthroughs
in
Technical
Analysis

Also available from
BLOOMBERG PRESS

New Insights on Covered Call Writing: The Powerful Technique
That Enhances Return and Lowers Risk in Stock Investing
by Richard Lehman and Lawrence G. McMillan

Tom Dorsey's Trading Tips: A Playbook for Stock Market Success
by Thomas J. Dorsey and the DWA Analysts

Wall Street Secrets for Tax-Efficient Investing:
From Tax Pain to Investment Gain
by Robert N. Gordon with Jan M. Rosen

New Thinking in Technical Analysis:
Trading Models from the Masters
edited by Rick Bensignor

Option Strategies for a Directionless Market:
Trading with Butterflies, Iron Butterflies, and Condors
by Anthony J. Saliba
(November 2007)

Technical Analysis Tools: Creating a Profitable Trading System
by Mark Tinghino
(December 2007)

A complete list of our titles is available at
www.bloomberg.com/books

Breakthroughs
in
Technical
Analysis

New Thinking from the
World's Top Minds

———

Edited by David Keller

Bloomberg Press

New York

This publication contains the authors' opinions and is designed to provide accurate and authoritative information. It is sold with the understanding that the authors, publisher, and Bloomberg L.P. are not engaged in rendering legal, accounting, investment-planning, or other professional advice. The reader should seek the services of a qualified professional for such advice; the authors, publisher, and Bloomberg L.P. cannot be held responsible for any loss incurred as a result of specific investments or planning decisions made by the reader.

First edition published 2007
1 3 5 7 9 10 8 6 4 2

Library of Congress Cataloging-in-Publication Data

Breakthroughs in technical analysis : new thinking from the world's top minds / edited by David Keller.
   p.cm.
   Summary: "Breakthroughs in Technical Analysis explains the new trading methods used by the world's top technicians, encompassing in one volume the investing approaches of ten proven practitioners. More important, some of these techniques have never left their country's borders before and are not known or used in other parts of the world."--Provided by publisher.
   Includes index.
   ISBN 978-1-57660-242-3 (alk. paper)
   1. Investment analysis. I. Keller, David, date.

HG4529.B725 2007
332.63'2042 --dc22   2007021051

Acquired by Sophia Efthimiatou
Edited by Mary Ann McGuigan and Janet Coleman

Contents

About the Contributors

David Bowden is the founder of Safety in the Market, one of Australia's longest-running investment training organizations. Through his courses and seminars and with a clientele that spans the globe, Bowden has trained many people to understand the markets and trade them with safety. Bowden began his trading career in 1985 by studying and researching the methods of W.D. Gann, a legend in the world of stock and commodity traders. Using Gann's unique style of forecasting and technical analysis, Bowden quickly established an impressive track record with his market forecasts. He called the market top for 1987, to the day. Catching the eye of many fellow traders and associates, he was thrust into the world of trading education in 1988. In 1995, Bowden authored the first nationally accredited Diploma of Technical Analysis course.

Constance Brown, CMT, founded the global investment company Aerodynamic Investments Inc. (www.aeroinvest.com) after working for more than twenty years as an institutional trader in New York City. She continues to actively trade from her equestrian estate in South Carolina and advises numerous financial institutions and banks around the world via the Internet. She now has more than seventy students who have moved on to manage assets themselves or work for major institutions. Seminars and lectures are viewed as an important part of contributing to the further development of technical analysis. Brown's second book, *Technical Analysis for the Trading Professional* (McGraw-Hill, 1999), was selected by the Market Technicians Association (MTA) as required reading to prepare for CMT Level 3, the final examination that awards professionals the industry's Chartered Market Technician (CMT) accreditation. She is also a member of the American Association of Professional Technical Analysts (AAPTA). Brown currently has six books in print.

Tom DeMark is the president of Market Studies Inc., a provider of proprietary market timing indicators to Bloomberg and other financial services companies. He also serves as a consultant to multibillion-dollar hedge funds. Currently, DeMark is special consultant to Steve Cohen and SAC Capital. Previously, he was special adviser to Leon Cooperman and Omega Advisors and executive vice president of Tudor. DeMark was also chairman of Logical Information Machines (LIM), a supplier of high-technology software services for sophisticated market research. He is a former partner of Charlie DiFrancesca, the largest trader on CBOT. From 1982 to 1988, DeMark was president of DeMark Investment Advisory, Inc., a consultancy to large fund managers, including Goldman Sachs, Loews Corp., Union Carbide, Citibank, Morgan Bank, IBM, Minnesota Mining, Steinhardt Partners, Soros, Trust Company of the West, and Atlantic Richfield. DeMark's systems and indicators have been the subject of numerous feature articles in many highly regarded and widely read financial magazines and papers, and he has appeared regularly on television and radio, as well as at seminars, both domestically and internationally. He is also the author of three best-selling books, *The New Science of Technical Analysis* (John Wiley & Sons, 2001), *New Market Timing Techniques* (John Wiley & Sons, 1997), and *DeMark on Day Trading Options* (McGraw-Hill, 1999).

Jeremy du Plessis, CMT, FSTA, is head of technical analysis at Updata PLC, based in London. He is a member of the Market Technicians Association (MTA) and the American Association of Professional Technical Analysts (AAPTA) in the United States, as well as a fellow of the Society of Technical Analysts (STA) in the United Kingdom. Du Plessis sets the syllabus for the point-and-figure module of the International Federation of Technical Analysts (IFTA) certificate and lectures on point and figure for the STA. A regular speaker on point and figure at international conferences and seminars, du Plessis has dedicated the past twenty-five years to the field of technical analysis and in particular to developing technical analysis software. In 1983, the company he founded, Indexia Research Limited, released one of the first PC-based technical analysis systems available, with point and figure as its cornerstone. Du Plessis's book *The Definitive Guide to Point and Figure* (Harriman House, 2005) is regarded by many as the bible of point and figure analysis.

Nicole Elliott is Mizuho Corporate Bank's senior analyst in London and covers the foreign exchange, interest rate, commodity markets, and equity indexes. Elliott has worked in the City of London for twenty-five years. Technical Analysis has always been the backbone of her trading methodology, in sales and as an analyst within the Treasury departments of major international banks. She is a member of the Society of Technical Analysts and a graduate of the London School of Economics.

Robin Griffiths is one of the world's most senior technical analysts, having published technical research for forty years and coauthored three books. He has been head of asset allocation at Rathbone Brothers PLC since 2002, overseeing $20 billion of investments, and is adviser to two hedge funds, ECU Fund and Rathpeacon. From 1986 to 2002, he was chief technical strategist at HSBC James Capel. Prior to that, Griffiths was technical analyst and Japan specialist at Grieveson Grant (1983–1986); technical analyst and partner at W.I. Carr in Hong Kong, Tokyo, and London (1971–1983); and equity broker at Phillips and Drew (1966–1971). Griffiths is a member of the Market Technicians Association; former chairman of the International Federation of Technical Analysts (1994–1997); and former chairman (1990–1993) and now fellow of the British Society of Technical Analysts.

Ted Hearne is a private trader and the president of a consulting firm with expertise in market analysis, trading software, mass psychology, and economic behavior. Hearne has been an active trader and student of the markets for two decades. In 1991, he became acquainted with point-and-line theory and in 1993 met Charles Drummond, with whom shortly thereafter he formed a business and writing partnership. Together over the last ten years they have created a landmark body of theoretical and educational writings about the trading methodology now known as Drummond Geometry. Major writings include work on the Pldot.com Web site and The Lessons, an extensive instructional series about market structure, market analysis, and trading practice. Hearne's Web site is www.tedtick.com.

Robin Mesch, founder and CEO of Robin Mesch Associates, enables professional traders and money managers to consistently maximize profitability and optimize their portfolios using her proprietary trading models and software. Mesch is a pioneer and educator in the field of technical analysis and market theory. She has been building market models for more than twenty years and has been profiled in numerous books such as Bloomberg's *New Thinking in Technical Analysis*; *Bulls, Bears and Millionaires*; *The Outer Game of Trading*; *The Day Trader's Advantage*; *The Tao of Trading*; and *Women of the Pits.*

Bernie Schaeffer is chairman and CEO of Schaeffer's Investment Research, Inc. and author of *The Option Advisor: Wealth-Building Techniques Using Equity and Index Options* (Wiley, 1997). He has edited the *Option Advisor* newsletter since its inception in 1981, and it has since grown to be the nation's leading options newsletter. Schaeffer is widely recognized as an expert on equity and index options, investor sentiment, and market timing. *Timer Digest* has been monitoring him since 1984 and ranks him as the No. 2 Gold Timer for the past ten years running and the No. 5 Bond Timer for the past ten years. In 2003, Aaron Task of TheStreet.com selected Schaeffer as the market "Guru of the Year." Schaeffer is the proud recipient of the 2004 Traders' Library Trader's Hall of Fame Award for his numerous contributions to the field of trading. In addition, Schaeffer received the Best of the Best Award from the Market Technicians Association for his contributions to sentiment/psychological analysis.

Yosuke Shimizu is the general manager of the investment information department at Monex, Inc., which he joined in 2003. His work is devoted to investor education through the explanation and analysis of market activities for individual investors. Shimizu is also well known for his practical technical analysis techniques acquired through his sales and trading experiences at major securities firms. Previously, he worked at Daiwa Securities. Shimizu is a member of the Security Analysts Association of Japan and the Nippon Technical Analysts Association. He holds a BA in law from Keio University.

Acknowledgments

This book was a collaboration of many people, each lending their expertise to create a final product in which we can all take pride. I would like to thank the following individuals for their specific contributions:

My wife Carrie, for challenging me, encouraging me, and sharing this journey.

My family, for always reminding me to "relax and let it flow."

The hardworking people at Bloomberg Press: Sophia Efthimiatiou for her enthusiasm and careful planning, Mary Ann McGuigan and Janet Coleman for their tireless work in editing the content, and the production team: Mary Macher, Dru-Ann Chuchran, and JoAnne Kanaval.

Steve Araki of *Bloomberg Markets* magazine for his gracious help with the Japanese translation.

The ten contributors who took time out of the trading day to lend us powerful insight into market dynamics.

And finally, the technical analysts and traders I have met over the years, who have taught me to always be a student of the markets.

Introduction

One day back in early 2001, I called an equity salesperson in Chicago to ask whether he would be interested in meeting to discuss some technical analysis techniques. He quickly declined, calling technical analysis a "voodoo science" and arguing that it was fundamental analysis that truly drives the markets.

Two years later, I received a call from that same salesperson. He had had a major change of heart. He invited me to visit him so that we could talk about technical analysis. I wondered what had made him change his mind. He said that his clients had started observing charts, and that if he wanted to keep their business he had to learn how to speak their language.

Traveling around the United States and Canada to discuss technical analysis with traders, fund managers, analysts, and investors, I have come to two conclusions: Market participants today are using technical analysis more than ever before, and most of them are struggling to identify which techniques they should be applying to their markets of interest.

Every year, I find myself spending increasingly more time talking to portfolio managers who are using a hybrid of fundamental and technical analysis to identify potential investments. As a result, I get more and more calls from salespeople and sales traders, all scrambling to understand how to incorporate technical analysis into their conversations.

Here's how I introduce technical analysis to those newly converted to the technical approach: Fundamental analysis tells you the "what" and the "why," whereas technical analysis tells you the "when" and the "how." Analyzing a company's financial statements, the broad economic picture, and other fundamental factors helps investors identify which securities should be moving based on market environment. But when you look at a price chart, you're peeking into the minds of millions of traders to gauge their collective psychology. What's more, you're studying trends and momentum to see how traders have reacted to historical events and news flow. That's why investing without looking at a chart puts you at a major disadvantage.

One of the questions I pose at the beginning of seminars is "Does technical analysis work because people use it, or do people use it because it works?" The first part of that question positions technical analysis as a self-fulfilling prophecy—if enough people expect a certain price movement and make trades in anticipation of that movement, then the price will move as a result of their own actions. The second part suggests that there is in fact value in technical analysis as a method of breaking down investor sentiment and market psychology over time.

All of the authors in this book have developed certain techniques that have helped them to successfully trade and analyze various global markets. This book is designed to bring their ideas together and help you draw on their experiences and incorporate their concepts into your own trading.

In planning the book, I realized that although more and more investors had broadened their approach to allow for international markets, the existing technical analysis literature was still quite localized. In meeting with technical analysts and traders from around the world and from organizations such as the Market Technicians Association, I've learned that each region has its own experts who have successfully tailored their technical strategies to the local markets.

The goal for the book was to assemble some of the top minds in the field from all parts of the world and have them share their insights into how price and volume analysis can help investors identify profitable trading opportunities. The end result is a powerful illustration of how interrelated the financial markets really are; it's also a testament to the global reach of technical analysis as a language of the markets.

Each chapter in *Breakthroughs in Technical Analysis* is intended to stand independently. You can study a single chapter, and then apply those concepts to your own charts and markets before you move on to another. Keep in mind that although the author may be writing about, say, Australian index futures or U.S. Treasury spreads, the concepts discussed can be readily applied to *any* market, and often on different time periods than those discussed in the chapter.

We start with Ted Hearne's discussion of a technique called "Drummond Geometry" as applied to the foreign exchange markets. You'll find it's a great breakdown of how open/high/low/close data can be used to identify support and resistance, meaning levels at which the price tends to reverse. His examples demonstrate the value of studying different time frames (that is, daily, weekly, monthly, etc.) to see how short-term price moves fit into the long-term trend.

Tom DeMark goes to great lengths to analyze price trends and ways in which markets reverse direction. In his chapter, DeMark discusses one of his market-timing techniques, TD Combo™. Although many traders have worked with TD Sequential™, one of DeMark's other indicators, this chapter shows when and why TD Combo's more conservative approach to trend exhaustion can help an investor identify low-risk trading opportunities. He also presents methods to tweak both these techniques to make them more aggressive, methods that can often give an early warning of a trend reversal.

Nicole Elliott breaks down a traditional Japanese technique called Ichimoku Kinko Hyo, in which price data is used to create a series of indicators to measure the strength of a trend, as well as potential support and resistance areas. This trend-following technique is used heavily by Japanese investors and has grown in popularity in the United States and Europe. Many people who see this technique for the first time are overwhelmed by the amount of information the chart provides. Elliot does an exceptional job of cutting through that noise to explain the true value of Ichimoku charts.

Yosuke Shimizu takes us through the world of candlestick analysis from a Japanese perspective. Many of you may have heard of or even used patterns with peculiar names such as "abandoned baby" or "hanging man." Shimizu-san explains why these names are used and how they can add great value to your investment approach. His chapter, translated from Japanese, provides original insight into why traders have used these techniques for centuries, in a language that evokes the spirit of the region.

We return to a U.S. perspective with Constance Brown, who in her chapter shares with us her powerful charting acumen. Incorporating Gann analysis, Fibonacci retracements, and her own proprietary indicators, she has developed a sophisticated methodology for trading market moves more effectively. Brown graciously includes the formula behind her unique indicator, the Composite Index, and demonstrates how to efficiently combine technical approaches.

David Bowden takes us to the Australian markets through his own trading experiences using Gann analysis—a series of technical indicators that are often misunderstood because of their mystical nature. Walking us through his successes and failures in anticipating tops and bottoms, Bowden's discussion of the cyclical nature of the markets is a rare treat. Reading this chapter, you'll rediscover the value of the relationship between time and price and its importance in market fluctuation.

Traditional equity investors are increasingly including options in their portfolios as a way of managing risk and of raising returns by the power of leverage. In his chapter, Bernie Schaeffer gives a well-written overview of options strategies and then moves on to analyzing volatility to identify profitable options plays. If you've been considering incorporating options into your investment approach, you'll want to read this chapter first.

From Europe, we have Jeremy du Plessis with a chapter on point and figure charts, which are frequently used in futures and commodities exchanges. Du Plessis shows how these charts have evolved to better identify support and resistance levels, breakout points, and price objectives for any market. He wraps up with a discussion on applying conventional technical indicators to point and figure charts, a concept that even longtime point-and-figure devotees will find compelling.

Robin Mesch is one of the leading experts on Market Profile™, a method of analyzing the distribution of trades throughout the day to identify where supply and demand will come into play. Investors who use this technique are familiar with how price action often forms a bell curve by the end of the day. Mesch describes how to apply this technique to price spreads, showing how anyone trading security pairs can effectively gauge when a spread is poised to widen or tighten.

We conclude with Robin Griffiths's presentation of cycle-related investment strategies, from multiyear and seasonal cycles in the global equity markets to stop-losses, scaling trades, and money-management techniques. He presents his ten commandments for trading, a solid guide to intelligently tackling the game.

The title *Breakthroughs in Technical Analysis: New Thinking from the World's Top Minds* truly captures what we tried to accomplish in bringing the insights of these experts together. The ten contributors are among the leading technical analysts in the world, and they all demonstrate specific techniques they've used with great success over time. Some of our contributors present new techniques that they've developed or refined in the last couple years. Others take methodologies that have been used for decades and show how they can be adapted to today's global financial markets. Regardless of their geographical location, professional background, or preferred trading strategies, these experts make one central theme clear in every chapter: Technical analysis is a vital component of any trader's tool kit. An informed investor is defined by his ability to incorporate all available market data into his daily trading routine, and, most important, he has to take into account the investor psychology inherent in price charts.

We believe this book is a useful resource for identifying techniques that can add tremendous value to your investment strategy, and we're convinced that you'll enjoy reading it, too.

—David Keller, CMT
February 21, 2007
New York

Breakthroughs
in
Technical
Analysis

CHAPTER 1

Drummond Geometry: Picking Yearly Highs and Lows in Interbank Forex Trading

TED HEARNE

What if you could predict the yearly high and the yearly low in a major currency? If, at the start of the year, you could have a definite idea where the high will form in the Japanese yen or the Canadian dollar or the euro? Or if you knew where the market was headed many months ahead of time? Making an educated, accurate forecast of next year's high and low in every currency is surely the dream of every trader—a fantasy of omniscience and unlimited power over the markets.

In trading, as in war or building suspension bridges or performing transplant surgery or creating a new auto design or any complex undertaking, success is a function of many different elements—a combination of having the proper tools, the necessary knowledge, and the appropriate personal characteristics. If you would like to be one of the few who make accurate, high-probability, long-term forecasts about market highs and lows, then read on, because there are some little-known tools and a coherent body of knowledge that can help you.

Drummond Geometry

The practice of technical analysis has a few commonly accepted assumptions. Drummond Geometry builds on these with its own unique point of view:

1. Charts have patterns that can be identified and will reoccur.
2. Similar chart patterns exist in different time frames.
3. Prices in a given time frame will center on a consensus value, and when price moves away from that consensus, it will tend to revert to a mean. But this mean itself will be moving and changing as the market unfolds.
4. Support and resistance are real phenomena, and can be measured, predicted, and projected.
5. Time frame charts are interrelated, move simultaneously, and can be visualized as existing within each other.
6. Historical price charts of freely traded financial markets are the visual

representation of human crowd psychology in action.

7.   Support and resistance in different time frames react to price in predictable ways. The shorter time frames will react first, and then progressively longer time frames kick in.

These statements are simple, but when logically applied to the broadest context, using a coherent set of analytic tools, the implications are staggering. The trading theories and methodology I discuss here are based on the writings of Charles Drummond, the legendary Canadian trader who is emerging as one of the major market theorists of the twentieth century. He is not only a major theorist but also a hugely successful private trader who has the personal track record to back up the theory.

Drummond's substantial body of writings, privately published and distributed under nondisclosure agreements to his growing body of students, constitutes a major step forward in technical analysis. Many aspects of the work remain proprietary and not accessible in a public medium, but some of the main principles and underlying concepts, as well as their application to the long-term Forex markets, are free to be discussed in forums such as this chapter.

The methodology has come to be known as Drummond Geometry and consists of three main elements, or components:

- The identification of resistance and support and their projection into the future
- A description of the market's current state and its next anticipated state
- Multiple time period analysis, coordinating the first two elements in two, three, four, or more time frames

In Drummond Geometry, these three elements are combined into a coherent whole with specific rules for entries and exits, a methodology for monitoring and evaluating market moves, and a way to project viable turning points and targets within each time frame.

Projecting Resistance and Support

The idea of resistance and support is a key concept of technical analysis. Resistance is when buying peters out and selling increases, stopping and reversing an upward move; support is the reverse, when selling abates and buying begins, forcing price upward. Conventional technical analysis looks backward at where resistance and support have been located in the past and suggests that the

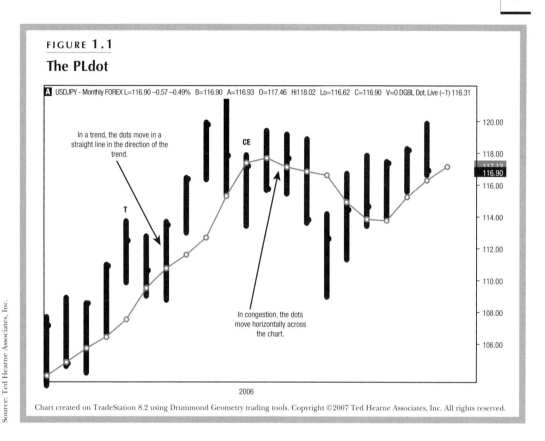

FIGURE **1.1**

The PLdot

A USDJPY - Monthly FOREX L=116.90 –0.57 –0.49% B=116.90 A=116.93 O=117.46 Hi118.02 Lo=116.62 C=116.90 V=0 DGBL Dot, Live (–1) 116.31

In a trend, the dots move in a straight line in the direction of the trend.

CE

T

In congestion, the dots move horizontally across the chart.

2006

same levels will be used in the future.

Drummond Geometry takes a different approach. Although it constructs these levels out of conventional tools such as moving averages and trend lines, it projects constantly evolving resistance and support areas into the future and watches how price reacts to these levels as the market moves forward.

The core building block of Drummond Geometry is a short-term moving average called "the PLdot" (see **Figure 1.1**). The PLdot was developed in response to the search for a tool that would distinguish between trend and congestion and run in a straight line sloped upward or downward in a trend but that would quickly and responsively indicate changes in market situation. The tool was empirically derived, and investigations resulted in the moving average known as the "Drummond Dot," or the PLdot.

The PLdot (PL stands for point and line) is a short-term moving average based on three price bars of data, which captures the trend/nontrend activity of the time frame that is being charted. The PLdot from the last three bars is plotted as a dot, or line, on the space where the next bar will appear.

The PLdot has a simple formula: the average of the average of the high, low, and close of the last three bars.

$$PLdot = \frac{\{Avg[H(1),L(1),C(1)] + Avg[H(2),L(2),C(2)] + Avg[H(3),L(3),C(3)]\}}{3}$$

The PLdot can be applied to any chart of any commodity, future, or stock. The first thing to note is that the dot is always there. It is a polestar in a constantly shifting universe, something that bears a constant relationship with the immediate past, capturing the recent energy of the hour, of the day, or of whatever period the trader is looking at.

What is so special about this particular moving average, the PLdot, that sets it apart from other moving averages? The characteristics of the dot prove to be useful in analysis. It moves across the chart horizontally in congestion, and when a trend develops, it immediately changes into a straight line slanted in the direction of the trend with very little lag. It is extraordinarily sensitive to trending markets; very quick to register the change of a market out of congestion into trend and sensitive to a trend that is ending, as well.

The PLdot captures the heart of market activity on the last three bars. In Drummond Geometry, this point would be thought of as the center of energy and represents the consensus of the crowd. But additional tools are needed to gauge the strength of moves away from this consensus. For this, other moving averages are added. To give the methodology greater muscle, Drummond added a simple envelope system constructed of a constant mathematical relationship based on the components of the dot. The resulting structure is illustrated in **Figure 1.2.**

Unlike many envelope systems, the objective here is not to contain all price activity within the envelope but to offer a constant, or a matrix, against which market moves can be measured. This turns out to be of great value when trying to tailor trading techniques to different market conditions.

The envelope system is also useful as a constant against which to measure the strength of recent and current market energy. When the market is in congestion, price tends to oscillate from one side of the envelope to another; thus, the trader has a pretty good idea of where the buying and selling zones will be placed in the market. But when the market is in a strong trend, the envelope functions dif-

FIGURE **1.2**

The PLdot and Envelope in Trends and Congestion

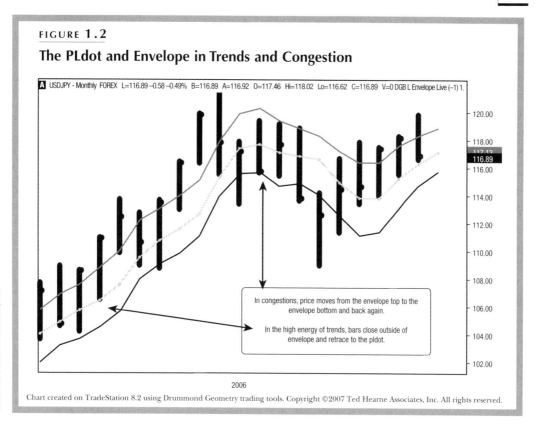

Chart created on TradeStation 8.2 using Drummond Geometry trading tools. Copyright ©2007 Ted Hearne Associates, Inc. All rights reserved.

ferently. The PLdot can be seen as "pushing" price in a trend, and the envelope top or bottom will be broken in the direction of the trend, with price bars often closing outside the envelope, and the envelope itself functioning as support or resistance. Price retracements in a trend will not move to the opposite side of the envelope but instead tend to stop at the level of the PLdot. In a strong trend, the bars will close outside of the envelope until the trend pauses or has finished, at which point they will move back inside the envelope.

Both the PLdot and the envelope are useful elements in determining support and resistance levels, but by themselves they are not sufficient. To these elements, Drummond analysis adds a series of short-term, two-bar trend lines that flag areas where price is likely to terminate. In the full methodology, there are a significant number of these lines; here just a few are shown.

In **Figure 1.3**, we can see how these short-term trend lines contribute to the definition of nearby support and resistance areas (shown by a gray box) and the further out support and resistance areas (shown by a black-outlined box). Note also

Source: Ted Hearne Associates, Inc.

FIGURE **1**.3

Short-Term Trend Lines

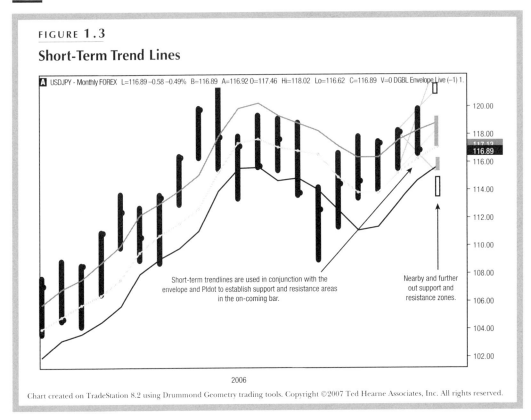

A USDJPY - Monthly FOREX L=116.89 –0.58 –0.49% B=116.89 A=116.92 O=117.46 Hi=118.02 Lo=116.62 C=116.89 V=0 DGBL Envelope Live (–1) 1.

Short-term trendlines are used in conjunction with the envelope and Pldot to establish support and resistance areas in the on-coming bar.

Nearby and further out support and resistance zones.

2006

that these lines, along with the PLdot and the envelope, are projected into the near-term future, so that the trader always knows where the support and resistance areas are that the market is moving into. The trader does not focus on areas that existed in the past but is always oriented toward the developing future.

If we apply these elements to a chart, we see the full envelope system together with the support and resistance zones established by the envelope, the dot, and the short-term trend lines, with these tools all projected into the future, onto the bar that has not yet formed. This setup constitutes the basic chart framework for any single time frame in Drummond Geometry. In **Figure 1.4**, we can see this full set of tools applied to a chart. Note the resistance and support areas plotted on top of each bar, along with the envelope and the PLdot. The price bars are plotted using a heavyweight "fat" bar so that the resistance and support tools can be plotted on top of them without obliterating the price bars themselves. The critical point is that these elements are projected forward into the future so that the trader always sees them coming up at him, on the right-hand side of the chart

FIGURE **1.4**

Computer-Generated "Nearby Support" and Resistance Areas

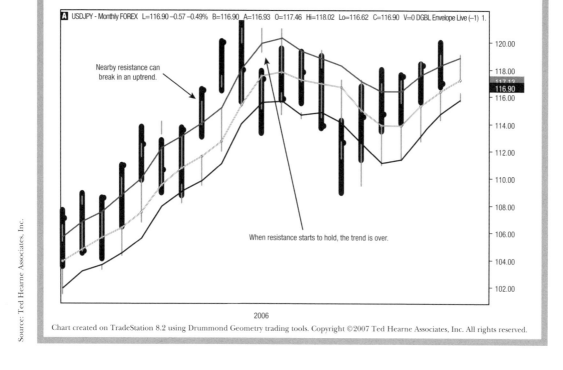

A | USDJPY - Monthly FOREX L=116.90 −0.57 −0.49% B=116.90 A=116.93 O=117.46 Hi=118.02 Lo=116.62 C=116.90 V=0 DGBL Envelope Live (−1) 1.

Nearby resistance can break in an uptrend.

When resistance starts to hold, the trend is over.

2006

Chart created on TradeStation 8.2 using Drummond Geometry trading tools. Copyright ©2007 Ted Hearne Associates, Inc. All rights reserved.

as time ticks forward and market activity unfolds.

Now let's stop and consider these few components of the first major section of Drummond Geometry. We have the definition of support and resistance; we have a means of monitoring market energy (placement and movement within and outside of the envelope system), a means of determining current market direction and future shifts in that direction (dot direction and slope), and a means of determining where price energy will terminate (where price is likely to stop for a given bar). All of these elements are extremely valuable to the trader. But as helpful as these tools are, by themselves they are not enough for success.

Predicting the State of the Market

Now let's look at the second leg of this three-legged stool. We need to know what the market is doing *now*, and we need to know what we expect the market to do *next*. We need to understand and predict the "state" of the market.

In essence, we must establish the market's internal decision-making tree for possible future actions. It's as if we could step inside the mind of the market, determine its present state of mind, and then determine the choices that are available to it for the immediate future. Applying a bit of logic, we can see that there are only a limited number of actions that the market can take. If the market is in a trend, for example, it has a very simple choice ahead of it. It can do only one of two things: continue that trend or enter congestion. If the market is in congestion, it can do only two things: continue that congestion or start to exit congestion into another trend. If you can develop clear and unambiguous definitions of trend and congestion, then determining the market's present type of trading and its next anticipated type of trading is a matter of quick and simple analysis. Knowing that the next type of trading will be one of two choices means that the trader can focus attention on the specific characteristics of the anticipated next type of trading and thus have a clear understanding of whether the pattern is actually occurring. And if it is not, then the trader knows that the alternate choice is occurring. This makes monitoring market action much more efficient and effective because the checkpoints and checklists to be watched are clear and easily identified.

Types of Trading

In Drummond Geometry there are only five types of trading:

- Trend
- Congestion entrance
- Congestion action
- Congestion exit
- Trend reversal

Each type is clearly defined: trend trading, for example, describes a situation in any given period when three successive price bars close on the same side of the PLdot. Thus, looking at the market at any point, we know whether that market is in a trend or not. Congestion entrance trading is characterized by the following: the market has been in a trend—that is, at least the last three bars have closed on one side of the PLdot—but the next bar closes on the opposite side of the PLdot. In Figure 1.1, the bar marked *T* (fifth bar from the left on the chart) defines the start of a trend because it is the third bar in a row that closes above the PLdot. The market remains in a trend until it reaches the bar marked *CE*, which is the first close on the opposite side of the PLdot; at that point, the market is in congestion entrance trading. Similar, unambiguous definitions cover congestion action, congestion exit, and trend reversal trading. These unambiguous definitions put traders in the driver's seat, because they can watch for exactly the action that will be required to change the basic orientation or "state" of market action. The trader can monitor for precisely those elements that are expected to occur.

Multiple Time Period Analysis

The first two major elements of Drummond Geometry—the definition of future support and resistance and the definition of the anticipated market state, or next type of trading—give traders a leg up, because with them they can start to identify the potential turning points at support and resistance levels as the market moves forward. To these major elements Drummond Geometry adds the concepts of "dot push" and "dot refresh," which describe movement away from the dot and market movement returning to the dot, respectively. We can say that dots push trends, support and resistance areas terminate trends, and the market moves from one type of trading to another type of trading in a regular, predictable manner.

In Figure 1.4, we can see how the dots push a strong trend upward and that as the market moves upward, the dots act as support for the trend, the price bars close over the top of the envelope, and the price bars can break nearby resistance and move into the resistance areas further out. When the trend stops, nearby resistance becomes strong and holds, and the dots start to move sideways as the market churns through its congestion areas, oscillating between the nearby support and resistance areas, which tend to hold and not break.

These are excellent advances, but they are still not enough to provide a successful, reliable, and consistent approach to trading. To ensure success, we need one more major enhancement, and that constitutes the third leg of this three-legged stool of Drummond Geometry.

It is not enough to know where support and resistance lie in the near future. We must also know whether that support or resistance will be strong or weak. If it is strong, it will hold, causing the market to change direction and turn back; if it is weak, it will break and give way, letting the market proceed farther in the same direction.

Determining the relative strength of support or resistance is a bit of a dilemma because there is nothing on the conventional single time period chart that can tell a trader if resistance or support will be strong or weak. And yet this is often the most important information a trader could have, because it commonly is the determining factor in deciding direction. If a trader has a firm handle on direction, then many of the other challenges fall into place and steady success is achievable. So if there is nothing that can be derived from conventional charting to provide this information, it must come from another source. In Drummond Geometry, that source is the chart of the same symbol viewed in a larger time resolution—a longer time frame—than the trading chart.

If, for example, the market has been trending upward in an hourly chart and the trader thinks it may turn around and enter congestion, he may indeed be correct. But without additional information there is no way to confirm this suspicion until after the market has made its move. However, if the trader places the hourly chart and its projected future support and resistance within the matrix of the daily chart's projected support and resistance areas, the context becomes clear. If the trader can see that hourly resistance has reached the anticipated daily resistance and daily resistance is anticipated to be strong based on the daily's position within the weekly and monthly matrix, then he can take action

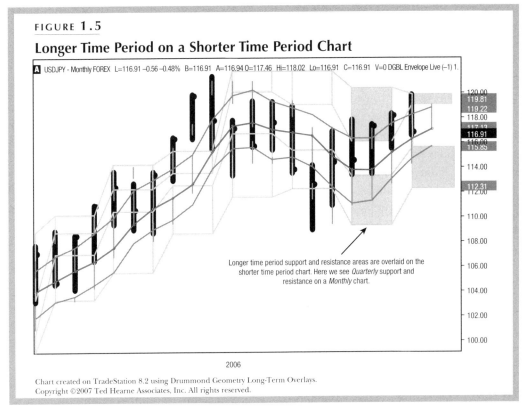

FIGURE 1.5

Longer Time Period on a Shorter Time Period Chart

Longer time period support and resistance areas are overlaid on the shorter time period chart. Here we see *Quarterly* support and resistance on a *Monthly* chart.

Chart created on TradeStation 8.2 using Drummond Geometry Long-Term Overlays.

with about three times the confidence that would otherwise be warranted for this trading situation. That's a huge advantage.

Figure 1.5 shows the same USDJPY Forex monthly chart that is featured in the first four figures, in which each bar represents one month of market activity. But a new element has been added, namely the support and resistance areas from the *quarterly* USDJPY chart. These areas are represented by the thin white lines behind the price bars. To make the last two quarters' support and resistance areas more visible, I have made them gray blocks. Note how useful this can be. Not only do we see where the projected monthly support and resistance are, we also see the projected quarterly resistance overlaying the monthly chart. With this information, we can see that for the last bar of this chart, which represents the month of October 2006, the high formed above the month's nearby resistance but exactly at the top of the quarterly resistance. A Drummond Geometry trader looking at this chart at the beginning of October would have a strong indication that selling at that point would be a very good idea.

Applying Drummond Geometry to a Long-Term Forex Trade

I suggest that charts from all time periods have similar patterns that occur and reoccur, and all time frames are related. In other words, a market top on an hourly chart will of necessity be reflected by a market top on the five-minute chart of the same symbol. Traders generally recognize that it can be useful to look at hourly charts and daily charts of a market, although the techniques of coordinating the time frames may not be widely understood. But it is a rare trader indeed who understands that the patterns in long-term charts such as monthly, quarterly, yearly, two-and-a-half-year, and five-year charts are all similar and can be profitably included in the trader's analysis.

If I were to show you a long-time-frame chart but without the time designations on the horizontal axis or the price designations on the vertical axis, there would be nothing to indicate whether you were looking at a fifteen-minute chart, an hourly or a daily chart, or a weekly or monthly chart. By now you can guess where I'm going with this: it could also be a quarterly chart, in which each bar represents the market activity in one quarter; or a yearly chart, in which each bar represents one year's market activity; or an even longer-term chart, in which each bar represents two and a half years' activity, or five years', or ten. On each of these charts, we can see trends, congestion, types of trading, dot pushes, terminations, and so forth. And on each chart the support and resistance levels can be projected into the future.

Why is this useful? A moment's reflection will make that clear. If we can project resistance and support on a yearly basis, then we have an advantage in predicting and monitoring market turns in those areas. If, for example, we can determine the market's yearly high or low in a major Forex market, then we can potentially take advantage of long-term moves with immense profits built into them. In the currency markets, with the eye-popping 400-to-1 leverage available even to small traders, very large profits are available.

Let's take a look at some charts and analyze these yearly charts and their shorter time frame components—for it is on the shorter time frames that we will first see the evidence of the yearly low or yearly high setting up and terminating energy in support and resistance.

In the tool chest of Drummond Geometry, there are concepts that can be used to structure many different kinds of trades. I will detail one entry signal here as an example, so that we can follow a sample trade on the long-term charts coming up. In **Figure 1.6**, we see a daily chart that shows what we call an "exhaust" and the entry signal that follows it. An exhaust is a market move of very high energy that breaks through nearby support or resistance and then reverses, much like a column of water in a fountain that has been pushed up and then tumbles back on itself when the energy that pushed it up can no longer hold up the weight of the water. For a trader, the challenge is to identify that exact moment when the push that sends price in one direction or the other has exhausted itself and the retracement has begun. Drummond Geometry offers the technical tools to identify this phenomenon. In Figure 1.6, we see this pattern: First the market breaks the nearby support level and the bar closes in that area. Then, in the following bar, the nearby support area holds and does not break. This pattern is an "exhaust buy" signal, and we will see many examples of this signal in the following chart analysis.

In **Figure 1.7**, we see three price charts of the USDJPY, which show how Drummond Geometry sets up time frame correlation. The support and resistance areas from the longer time frame chart are overlaid on the chart of the next shorter time frame. The left-hand chart is a two-year bar chart, in which each bar represents two years of activity. The large arrow shows how the nearby resistance for that bar is overlaid onto the chart to the right, which is a one-year

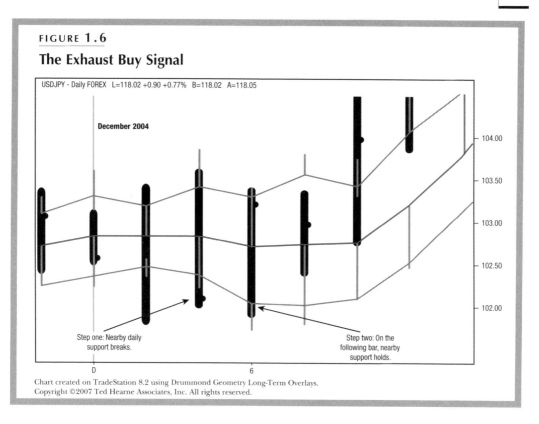

FIGURE **1.6**

The Exhaust Buy Signal

USDJPY - Daily FOREX   L=118.02 +0.90 +0.77%   B=118.02   A=118.05

December 2004

104.00

103.50

103.00

102.50

102.00

Step one: Nearby daily
support breaks.

Step two: On the
following bar, nearby
support holds.

D

6

Chart created on TradeStation 8.2 using Drummond Geometry Long-Term Overlays.
Copyright ©2007 Ted Hearne Associates, Inc. All rights reserved.

bar chart. On the one-year chart, the two-year resistance is plotted as light gray bars positioned behind the one-year price bars. Similarly, the nearby resistance and support areas from the yearly chart are overlaid onto the quarterly chart on the right-hand side of this figure. At this point, it becomes clear how this correlation of time periods can be graphically represented. I have also shown on this yearly chart an exhaust buy signal, which occurred in the USDJPY at the very beginning of 2005. Although the time frame is radically different—one year bars in Figure 1.7 versus the daily bars of Figure 1.6—the technical pattern of the exhaust trade is identical.

In addition to the buy signal in Figure 1.7, I have marked two target areas for this long-term trade. How do I establish these areas? According to Drummond Geometry theory, the market will move from resistance to support, and when it reaches support, it will move back to resistance, and that pattern will occur in all time frames. Resistance and support will either be weak and break through to a secondary level of resistance or support, or they will hold and be strong, kicking prices back in the opposite direction.

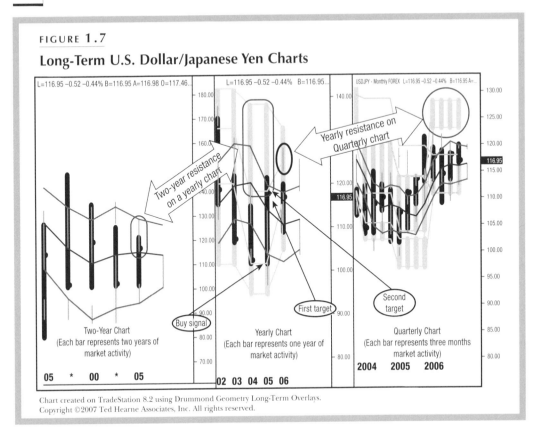

FIGURE 1.7

Long-Term U.S. Dollar/Japanese Yen Charts

Chart created on TradeStation 8.2 using Drummond Geometry Long-Term Overlays.
Copyright ©2007 Ted Hearne Associates, Inc. All rights reserved.

If we have a yearly low, then what is the target for this currency? Where can we expect it to go on a yearly basis? The yearly target, like targets in other time frames in Drummond Geometry, depends on where the market is when it starts.

If the price starts from:
- far above the envelope, then the first target is the envelope top
- at the envelope top, then the target is the other side of the envelope, depending on what happens to the PLdot
- inside the envelope, then the target is the other side of the envelope or lower

In the case of the yearly chart in Figure 1.7, because the close of the price bar for 2004 was near the envelope bottom as projected for 2005, the target for 2005 will be the PLdot, and if that breaks and the market continues to the upside, then the secondary target would be the opposite side of the envelope system. Note

FIGURE **1.8**

Trading the 2005 Yearly Bar

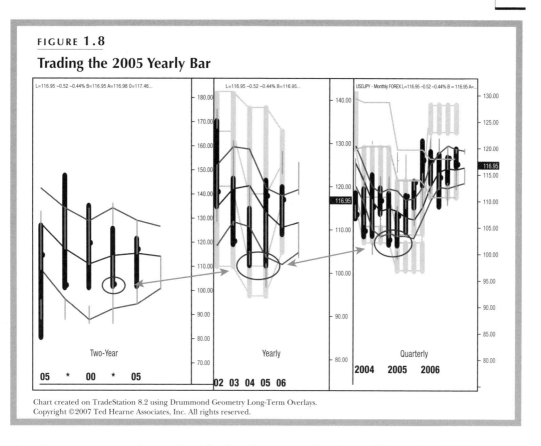

Chart created on TradeStation 8.2 using Drummond Geometry Long-Term Overlays.
Copyright ©2007 Ted Hearne Associates, Inc. All rights reserved.

that these targets are determined far in advance, at the close of December 2004, and projected out for 2005.

If we can say that it's likely that price, once it goes inside a channel, will go to the PLdot line or the opposite side of the channel, then we have a target for the year. And when the market gets to that target, then we reassess and make a judgment about the market's next goal.

Suppose that at the end of 2004, we were watching the U.S. dollar/Japanese yen exchange rate and were applying Drummond Geometry analysis to the market. What would we have been seeing? **Figure 1.8** (two-year, yearly, and quarterly charts) and **Figure 1.9** (monthly and weekly charts) lay out the basic dynamics, and **Figure 1.10** shows the exact entry points on a daily chart. From two-year bar charts all the way to daily charts—that's quite a span. But each contributes to the total picture and sets up a compelling case for a major market turn to the upside starting in December 2004 and January 2005.

(These last charts contain a lot of information and are a bit difficult to render

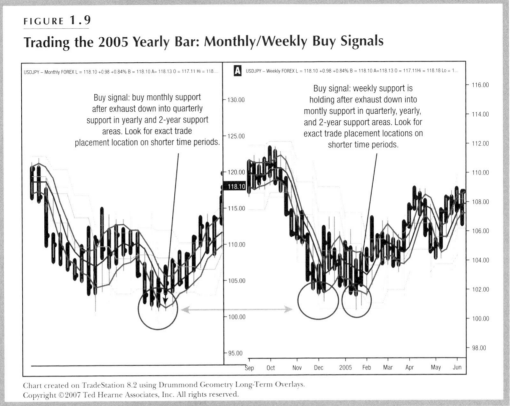

FIGURE 1.9

Trading the 2005 Yearly Bar: Monthly/Weekly Buy Signals

Chart created on TradeStation 8.2 using Drummond Geometry Long-Term Overlays.

in the black-and-white format necessary for print reproduction; on the computer screen, however, the use of color makes them easy and quick to read.)

Here is a breakdown of what we would have seen by applying this analysis:

On the two-year chart. The market was in congestion (successive price bars were closing on opposite sides of the PLdot), and the PLdot was moving sideways across the page. We were in the middle of two-year nearby support.

On the one-year chart. The market was in a trend rundown, with the next anticipated type of trading being congestion entrance to the upside. We were a long way below the yearly envelope bottom, and so we were looking for a move back up at least to the envelope bottom, and probably to the yearly PLdot, and possibly to the yearly envelope top. We were in yearly support and in two-year support, with a significant bias for a move to the upside. In January 2005, we would be watching to see if nearby yearly support would hold and become strong, and thus flag a yearly exhaust entry.

On the quarterly chart. We were in yearly support, and in quarterly further-

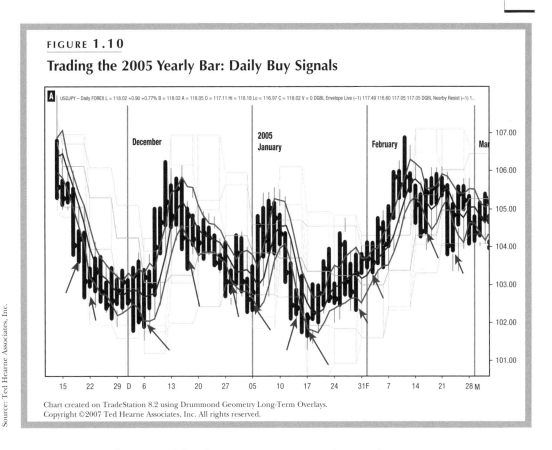

FIGURE **1.10**

Trading the 2005 Yearly Bar: Daily Buy Signals

Chart created on TradeStation 8.2 using Drummond Geometry Long-Term Overlays.
Copyright ©2007 Ted Hearne Associates, Inc. All rights reserved.

out support, and a potential exhaust pattern was setting up for a strong return to the quarterly PLdot. In the first quarter of 2005, we would have been monitoring the move away from quarterly nearby support to validate the exhaust buy signal.

On the monthly chart. On the left-hand side of Figure 1.9, we see exhaust entry signals as the market's downtrend stalls in monthly, quarterly, yearly, and two-year support. Monthly nearby support is holding and is showing to be strong.

On the weekly chart. On the right-hand side of Figure 1.9, we are again seeing multiple exhaust buy signals as the market tests support, bounces off, comes back for a retest, and then starts off to the upside with more conviction. The Drummond Geometry trader can take action on these exhaust buy signals with some confidence because he can see that we are in two-year, yearly, quarterly, monthly, and now weekly support, and all with definite upside targets.

On the daily chart. Taking all of this information into consideration, we come to the daily chart (Figure 1.10) and again see multiple exhaust buy signals as the dollar/yen exchange rate tests the major bottom that's being put in. If the trader has a long-term perspective, he could build a large position, buying on the dips. The multiple daily exhausts into multiple longer time period support during December 2004 and January 2005 provide the opportunity.

Of what value is the long-term chart analysis? In 2005, the dollar/yen exchange rate ran from approximately 101.67 to 121.39. That's a huge move in these markets, and Drummond Geometry had a set of indicators that helped the trader get in near the very start of this move. What's more, the methodology provides tools that help establish reasonable targets and monitor the position. The trader knows at all times what the market has to do if this trade is going to work out.

Monitoring

How do we know if our predictions and analysis are correct? The possibility of being wrong is always present because we're human, and so we need to have some means of monitoring the market activity to tell us if our predictions are on target and accurate or not.

The element of monitoring is essential to Drummond Geometry trading. To monitor effectively, we need to recognize the quality of market flow and to understand what the market looks like when it's moving successfully toward a goal, and what it looks like when that progress has slowed or changed. Flow can be defined in a number of ways. The simplest way is to note how the market is dealing with resistance and support on a shorter time frame. If resistance is holding and support giving way on the shorter time period, then the flow is down. If the reverse is true, the market is headed up. The methodology also includes more sophisticated definitions of flow using range, position of close relative to the high and low, progress through the envelope system, and advance/decline measures. But the bottom line is how the shorter time period handles resistance and support; if the weekly and monthly consistently break resistance and hold nearby support, then the quarterly and yearly bars are headed up, and the quarterly and yearly upside targets should be kept in sight.

The world is a complicated place. Huge geopolitical forces shape the global currency markets. Exchange-rate charts are the graphic reflection of massive changes as the fortunes of countries and peoples rise and fall. When major shifts occur—changes in interest rate policies, wars, shifts in national priorities, or changes in regimes—the relative values of the currencies of different countries can be on the move in a major trend for a significant period of time. Although it's not possible for the individual trader to know or understand all possible fundamental information, it *is* possible to make reasonable predictions about the extremes of yearly price action, to monitor those assumptions, and to trade them successfully, picking off the yearly highs and lows and thus preserving capital or building wealth, depending on your goals.

Trading is a difficult business. It requires both on-target perceptions and mental strength. First you have to see the opportunity. Then you have to take the opportunity. You have to stick with your decisions through thick and thin as you monitor the trade, knowing exactly what *has* to happen if you are wrong and what has to happen if you are right.

Trading the Forex with an eye on long-term Drummond Geometry charts can help the trader keep the market in context and withstand the many wide countertrend oscillations that will shake out the trader who is not equipped with the long-term perspective that yearly and quarterly charts provide. Seeing the yearly bar develop lets the trader watch the background, not just focus on the foreground. To be better than the rest in trading, as in so many fields, we have to do something different from the rest. In trading the global currency markets, one tool that can make a real difference is a careful analysis of the big picture, using the multiple time period analysis of Drummond Geometry.

CHAPTER 2

Trend Spotting With TD Combo

TOM DeMARK

Most traders are trend followers. They accept the widespread belief that the trend is a trader's friend. Many years of exhaustive research and trading experience have convinced us that this notion is flawed. For the sake of completeness, we have added a corollary to this premise—the trend is your friend, unless the trend is about to end.

Human nature is such that we are inclined to extrapolate current events into the future. Some expectations have outcomes that are immutable and universally applicable: The sun rises in the morning and sets in the evening. Cut your hand with a knife and you will bleed. Fall from an elevated level and gravity will pull you down. There are no exceptions. Other expectations may be disappointed: Flip a light switch and a dark room becomes bright—but what happens if the electricity is not in service?

Similarly, in terms of trading markets, as long as buying pressure is greater than selling pressure, a market's trend is up, and, conversely, as long as selling pressure is greater than buying pressure, a market's trend is down. To expect that buying pressure will continue to exceed selling pressure and extend an uptrend indefinitely or that selling pressure will continue to exceed buying pressure and extend a downtrend indefinitely is foolhardy. No market trend continues forever, just as no tree grows to the sky. Market dynamics are not dictated by the forces that govern human nature. Most traders are content to trade comfortably and with a trend, but what happens when buying and selling pressure move into equilibrium or when buying pressure overcomes selling pressure or when selling pressure overcomes buying pressure? During these transition periods of buying and selling pressure, market fundamentals, news, and expectations usually remain intact. However, under this veneer, the supply/demand dynamics are in fact being redefined. Maintaining a trading edge by anticipating these internal market changes is imperative to ensuring a trader's good mental and financial health.

Opposing the Marketplace

Contrary to the widely accepted notion that markets bottom due to smart, informed buyers having inside information and therefore accumulating positions prior to a rally, our research has shown that markets reverse a downtrend because of a lack of selling, and by default price moves sideways or higher. Similarly, a market top is not produced by savvy sellers learning of negative news prior to a decline and then coordinating their efforts and forcing price down. Rather, price peaks are made when the number of buyers diminishes and eventually disappears, and by default price moves sideways and then down. At these junctures, unless the pool of buyers or sellers increases, the lack of intensity creates a trend change. To extend or regenerate a trend, it is necessary for an entirely new pool of buyers in an uptrend and sellers in a downtrend to emerge. In other words, the fundamentals that dictate and define long-term price movements must be sufficiently attractive to entice a new group of adherents willing to commit funds to their beliefs. Trading the markets is not a game of lip service. Regardless of how vocal you may be in professing your market forecast or how convincing your arguments, the litmus test and the determinant of price movement is money.

It is human nature to seek approval for one's actions. This is ingrained in most. To contradict the majority is socially unacceptable. You risk being ostracized if you fail to conform to the rules and the values of society. Unfortunately, such behavior does not necessarily serve you well when trading the markets.

Having been involved exclusively with large financial institutions for more than thirty-five years, we know it's impossible for them to commit significant amounts of funds after a trend has been established. The competition is too intense and too many price concessions have to be made. Consequently, we had to be prepared to anticipate trend changes. In other words, we had to oppose the psychology of the marketplace and be prepared to buy weakness and sell strength. It was often difficult given the overall sentiment. But it was the only way to make large-scale commitments and to do so at propitious price levels. Trading discipline and objectivity were essential to this counterintuitive approach. TD Sequential was the first trading method developed to accomplish this goal. TD Combo is a related approach with more requirements and greater precision.

Markets advance and decline in a natural price rhythm that is often definable. Although the market does not always conform to this price pattern prescription, even when it deviates, the price pattern is still valuable because it forces a trader to buy into price weakness and to sell into price strength.

Determining Market Direction

Before committing to a trade, you must define the market environment. Is the market vulnerable to an advance or to a decline, or is it locked into a trading range? Much research and analysis have shown that a simple basic mathematical exercise, which we call TD Setup, will provide a clue to whether the market is likely to rally or decline. By comparing the market's close on the current price bar with the close four price bars earlier and then recording a series of similar consecutive price-comparison closes, one can draw highly probable conclusions regarding future price behavior. Specifically, by recording nine consecutive closes lower than the close four price bars earlier, a buy setup is formed; and by recording nine consecutive closes higher than the close four price bars earlier, a sell setup is formed. Often, the completion of these TD Setup series is associated with minor areas of price exhaustion—particularly when the TD Setups are properly price "perfected." Specifically, for a TD Buy Setup to be perfected and qualified for a short-term rally, either the low of buy setup price bar eight or the low of buy setup price bar nine must be lower than both lows of buy price bars six and seven. If neither price bar eight's nor price bar nine's low meets this requirement, then you must await the first subsequent low that fulfills this requirement before the price "perfection" is met. **Figure 2.1** illustrates just such a deferral. Note in **Figure 2.1** that once a low was recorded that exceeded the lows of TD

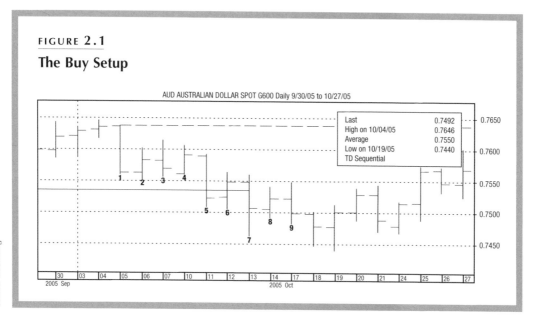

FIGURE **2.1**

The Buy Setup

AUD AUSTRALIAN DOLLAR SPOT G600 Daily 9/30/05 to 10/27/05

Last	0.7492
High on 10/04/05	0.7646
Average	0.7550
Low on 10/19/05	0.7440
TD Sequential	

Source: Bloomberg

Buy Setup price bars six and seven, the market experienced an advance of a few trading days.

Conversely, in **Figure 2.2**, once a high was recorded that exceeded the highs of TD Sell Setup price bars six and seven, the market experienced a decline of a few trading days. Granted, TD Setup price perfections are often preludes to speculative trades of an indeterminable duration; nevertheless, their value may be to forewarn of a likely interruption of an ongoing trend.

Once the minimum requirement of nine consecutive closes lower than the close four price bars earlier is recorded, the TD Buy Setup is complete. Similarly, once the minimum requirement of nine consecutive closes higher than the close four price bars earlier is recorded, the TD Sell Setup is complete. These setups serve to provide the trader with the market's likely trading environment. Most often they are preambles to countdown series that, once completed, identify zones of price-trend exhaustion. TD Combo is designed to select only those price bars of relevance and to ignore those that fail to adhere to rigid selection criteria regarding price relationships. Specifically, in addition to the setup phase, a subsequent and more onerous process is followed.

The Buy or Sell Countdown

Once a TD Buy Setup of nine consecutive closes lower than the close four price

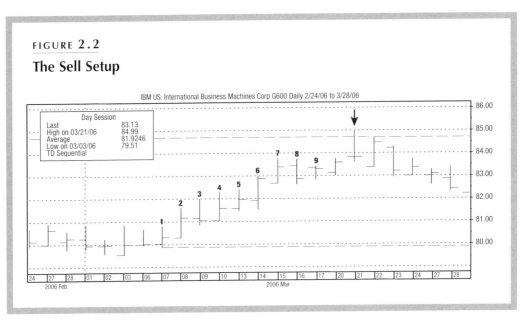

FIGURE 2.2

The Sell Setup

IBM US: International Business Machines Corp G600 Daily 2/24/06 to 3/28/06

Day Session	
Last	83.13
High on 03/21/06	84.99
Average	81.9246
Low on 03/03/06	79.51
TD Sequential	

Source: Bloomberg

bars earlier is recorded, the buy countdown process begins by referring back to the first price bar of the buy setup and making the following comparisons:

1.   The close of that price bar must be lower than or equal to the price bar's low two price bars earlier.

2.   The close of that price bar must be lower than the prior price bar's close.

3.   The close of that price bar must be lower than the close of the prior countdown price bar's close (note that the first price bar in the countdown series has no prior price bar close).

4.   The low of that price bar must be lower than the prior price bar's low.

Because countdown consists of a total of thirteen price bars that conform to the aforementioned prerequisites, or slight variations of them, one can readily see that the conditions necessary for countdown completion are strict and exacting. The same requirements, in reverse, apply to sell countdown.

Once a TD Sell Setup of nine consecutive closes higher than the close four price bars earlier is recorded, the sell countdown process begins by referring back to the first price bar of the sell setup and making the following comparisons:

1.   The close of that price bar must be higher than or equal to the price bar's high two price bars earlier.

2.   The close of that price bar must be higher than the prior price bar's close.

3.   The close of that price bar must be higher than the close of the prior countdown price bar's close (note that the first price bar in the countdown series has no prior price bar close).

4 .   The high of that price bar must be higher than the prior price bar's high.

Figure 2.3, the Philadelphia Gold and Silver Index (XAU), illustrates examples of both TD Combo low-risk bottoms and tops. Beginning December 21, 2005, and continuing the next eight consecutive trading days, the minimum TD Sell Setup requirement of consecutive price comparisons of closes higher than the close four price bars earlier was fulfilled. The numbers for the sell setup appear above each price bar, and the series stops at nine because that is the minimum number of consecutive price comparisons to complete a sell setup. Upon completion of the sell setup, countdown commences. Unlike with TD Sequential, the countdown process of TD Combo refers back to the first price

Source: Bloomberg

FIGURE **2.3**

TD Combo Low-Risk Bottoms and Tops

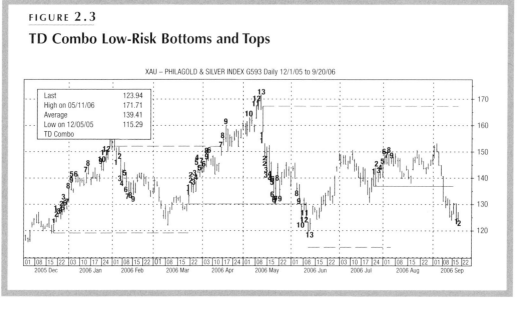

XAU – PHILAGOLD & SILVER INDEX G593 Daily 12/1/05 to 9/20/06

bar of the sell setup. The four prerequisites described earlier are then applied to each successive price bar.

Figure 2.4 provides a closer look at the same chart. Note that the close of day one of the sell setup failed to fulfill qualifier No. 1. It was not higher than or equal to the high two price bars earlier. Consequently, sell countdown is deferred until possibly the next trading day. The close of sell setup day two is higher than or equal to the high two days earlier. Also, the close is above the previous day's close, and the high is above the prior price bar's high. The requirement of a close above the prior countdown close is not applicable because there was no prior countdown close. Sell setup days three and four do not qualify as countdown days because both have down closes and qualifier No. 2 requires that the close be higher than the prior price bar's close. Sell setup days five and six meet all the sell countdown qualifications. Sell setup day seven does not qualify because its close is lower than the prior price bar's close. Sell setup price bars eight and nine do meet the requirements of sell countdown. At the time of completion of sell setup, there are already five sell countdown days. For the sake of comparison, note that TD Sequential would only now begin its countdown process, but at the same time, the countdown requirements for TD Sequential are less restrictive—in fact, TD Combo has four times the number of rules that TD Sequential has. Moving the process forward, two days after the sell setup is completed, the sell countdown series increases to six, and the next four trading

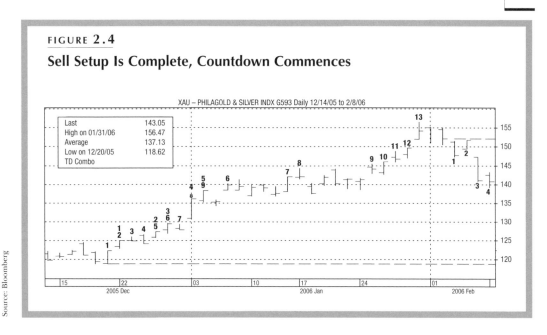

Source: Bloomberg

FIGURE **2.4**

Sell Setup Is Complete, Countdown Commences

days do not meet all the requirements. January 13 and 14 do meet the requirements, and the countdown proceeds to seven and eight. After a five-trading-day
interruption, the countdown quickly records five consecutive trading days that
meet all the countdown rules, and on countdown day thirteen the rally high is
recorded and price declines.

Price Exhaustion and Reversal

TD Combo is designed to anticipate areas of price exhaustion. It is the exception rather than the rule that TD Combo countdown day thirteen will coincide
with the precise price exhaustion peak or trough price bar, but often it will
occur within a couple of price bars of peak or trough, and it will alert a trader
to a market's vulnerability to a price reversal. Once countdown completion has
been recorded, at a minimum, one can expect price to undergo a trading range
before it is able to resume its trend. However, if there is no meaningful price
response after twelve price bars have lapsed, the likelihood of a price reversal
upon TD Combo countdown completion diminishes. Consequently, in these
instances, often the market is undergoing an interruption in the prevailing
trend. In either case, TD Combo inserts a level of discipline into a trader's methodology. As is evident in Figure 2.3, the peak price day and volatile trading day
of the entire sell setup and countdown period coincided with completion of sell
countdown and the expectation of price exhaustion and a price decline. Very

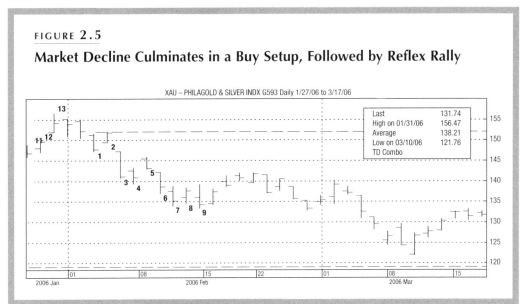

FIGURE 2.5

Market Decline Culminates in a Buy Setup, Followed by Reflex Rally

XAU – PHILAGOLD & SILVER INDX G593 Daily 1/27/06 to 3/17/06

Last	131.74
High on 01/31/06	156.47
Average	138.21
Low on 03/10/06	121.76
TD Combo	

Source: Bloomberg

optimistic news regarding precious metals was more than likely associated with this trading, and that information served to entice traders into the market and exhaust the near-term upside.

The subsequent market decline did culminate in the formation of a buy setup and, as you can see in **Figure 2.5**, because price perfection was fulfilled on February 15, the same day as the completion of the buy setup, there was a reflex rally of four trading days. Then the decline resumed as did the countdown process. As is often the case, the countdown series did not quite reach thirteen completions, rather only ten price bars fulfilled the countdown criteria. Once the March low was made, price rallied and the TD Combo sell setup series commenced, reaching the minimum requirement for completion. The countdown process was then activated, making comparisons starting with the first day of sell setup on March 24 (see **Figure 2.6**). Days one and two of sell setup were countdown days one and two, as well, because their respective closes were higher than both the highs two days earlier and each prior day's close. Additionally, each day's high was above the previous day's high, and each close was above the previous countdown day's close. Just as the prior sell countdown series recorded its thirteenth completion on its high day of January 31, so too this time, on May 11, the upside stopped precisely on the peak price day. However, note that the close of countdown price bar thirteen was neither above the high two price bars earlier, a higher close than the prior day's close, nor above the prior countdown

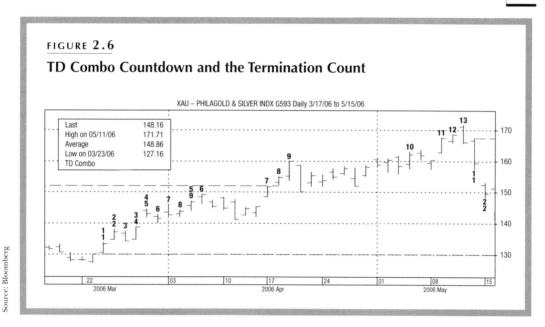

FIGURE **2.6**

TD Combo Countdown and the Termination Count

close. Why did a thirteen appear above this price bar? Because TD Combo countdown has an alternative for the thirteenth price bar, which is referred to as the termination count. Specifically, countdown thirteen can be recorded with the closing price relationships as are the other price bars from countdowns one through twelve, but an alternative option exists for the open to serve as a proxy for the closing price. As you can see, by replacing the closing with the opening of the price bar, the countdown series meets the requirement for completion thirteen.

Once the peak is recorded, price declines and records the minimum requirement for a buy setup—nine consecutive closes lower than the close four days earlier. The subsequent buy setup series was unusually steep (see Figure 2.3). As a result, a high number of price bars met the requirements for buy countdown. Buy setup days one through seven were TD Combo countdown price bars as well. Each requirement is identical to those applied to TD Combo sell countdown but in reverse. In other words, the close of each was lower than the low seen two price bars earlier and also lower than the prior price bar's close, and each countdown close was successively lower than the previous countdown day's close. Finally, each low was lower than the prior price bar's low. This comparison was applied to the subsequent countdown series, but notice that after countdown ten was recorded and specifically countdowns eleven and twelve, the previous rules were not adhered to. TD Combo version No. 2 is more liberal than version No. 1 and allows for the rules of countdown price bars eleven, twelve, and thirteen to be more liberally qualified. Specifically, the closes of countdowns eleven, twelve, and thirteen must be successively lower than one another to fulfill completion. Once again, but in reverse, see that price exhaustion thirteen was successful in identifying when a trend is about to exhaust itself and result in a price reversal.

In the previous examples, TD Combo thirteen sell and buy countdown completions coincided exactly with each trend's price exhaustion. Obviously, this is not what one should expect. The accuracy of TD Combo is just not this high, and to believe that this methodology will produce such precision in other instances is a presumptuous and serious mistake because you will be sorely disappointed. Consider such events to be exceptions to the rule and yourself fortunate just to have TD Combo successfully identify price zones where price might exhaust itself.

Just as the buy setup in February did, the sell setup in May, the buy setup in June, and the sell setup in August all identified likely short-term price reversals. All setups were "perfected," that is, the buy setups were accompanied by a low for price bar eight or price bar nine that was lower than the price lows for bars six and seven, and the sell setups were accompanied by a high for price bar eight or price bar nine that was higher than the highs for price bars six and seven. Although in each instance the price reversals were short term and the buy setup lows and the sell setup highs subsequently were exceeded, the trading opportunities existed. We do not recommend concentrating on setups, because the countdown completions are more likely to coincide with more significant price exhaustions and turning points. But price setups do provide context for trend followers, who can use them to add to positions subsequent to these reactions, or for traders who want to operate against the prevailing trends.

Aggressive Settings for TD Combo and TD Sequential

Figure 2.3 demonstrates how effective price-exhaustion techniques can be in identifying market tops and bottoms. The bane of trend followers has always been lack of liquidity, price gaps, and slippage. By anticipating price-exhaustion zones, one is both prepared and able to sell into market strength and buy into market weakness, which provides a trader a distinct timing advantage. It is difficult psychologically to act against the prevailing trend, but at the same time it is more rewarding because there is no lack of supply when the market is declining,

TD Sequential and TD Combo are capable of identifying areas of likely price-trend exhaustion, when they are silent and give no indication of likely price reversal, it behooves a trader to apply the aggressive versions of both to gain an enhanced trading edge, because their more liberal requirements make them more sensitive.

Both TD Aggressive Sequential™ and TD Aggressive Combo™ possess the same core parameters as their respective parents, TD Sequential and TD Combo. However, their countdown requirements are less restrictive and consequently identify price-exhaustion opportunities more frequently. Specifically, instead of relying on TD Sequential's strict comparison of a close versus the high two price bars earlier to identify upside price exhaustion and, conversely, a close versus the low two price bars earlier to identify downside price exhaustion, the aggressive version merely compares highs to identify a likely top and lows to do likewise at a prospective bottom. **Figure 2.7** shows the Philadelphia Gold and Silver Index (XAU) from August 1, 2005, through May 30, 2006, and illustrates the advantage of applying TD Aggressive Sequential vis-à-vis standard TD Sequential—the frequency of price-exhaustion occurrences increases as do potential trading opportunities at extreme price tops and bottoms.

Although the setup series are identical for both TD Sequential and TD Aggressive Sequential, the countdown comparison requirements are different. As

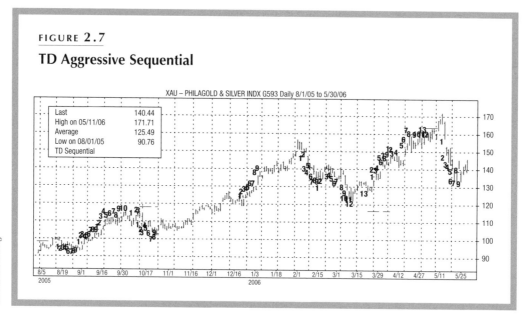

FIGURE **2.7**

TD Aggressive Sequential

XAU – PHILAGOLD & SILVER INDX G593 Daily 8/1/05 to 5/30/06

Last	140.44
High on 05/11/06	171.71
Average	125.49
Low on 08/01/05	90.76
TD Sequential	

Source: Bloomberg

a result, the countdown completions are different for each. This would become readily apparent were you to compare the location of the thirteens on the TD Aggressive Sequential chart with those for TD Sequential over the same period. Note that TD Aggressive Sequential recorded a single thirteen top—in October 2005—and a single thirteen bottom—in March 2006—and that TD Sequential failed to record a thirteen price-exhaustion indication during the entire period. That's because the more liberal construction of TD Aggressive Sequential allows for speedier countdowns, and the completion of its countdown almost always precedes the completion of conventional TD Sequential countdown. Obviously, times when both versions of TD Sequential speak simultaneously have greater import than when one occurs without the other. Nevertheless, expect to see the aggressive version if the conventional TD Sequential is there. In fact, count on seeing the aggressive version at or near the extreme price-exhaustion level, although the basic version is more likely to occur when the extreme exhaustion levels are tested.

What to Do Next

Sufficiently often, markets have responded to both perfected setups as well as completed countdowns to justify their use. As we discussed and demonstrated earlier, markets usually react immediately to perfected setups. The extent of the response depends on whether that setup has exceeded the extreme level of the opposite setup—the TD Setup Trend (TDST) level in the other direction. **Figure 2.8** is yet another chart of XAU showing declines in August and October 2005 that held above the TDST lines associated with the sell setups begun in May and September 2005. When the buy setups fail to penetrate the sell setup TDST levels such as in these two instances, the declines are usually pullbacks within the context of an uptrend. As these two examples illustrate, the market often supplies insight as to when to expect the setup to be succeeded by a resumption of the prior move and a price reversal and when to expect the trend to continue.

When a countdown thirteen has been recorded, some markets respond immediately, whereas others meander in a trading range only to resume the prior trend. How does one distinguish between the two expectations? Typically, if there is no appreciable response to a thirteen within twelve price bars, the likelihood of a failure increases. However, if there is a close above the close four price bars earlier and additional price-range follow-through occurs with next the price bar, the chance of a trend enhances considerably.

FIGURE **2.8**

TD Setup Trend (TDST) Lines

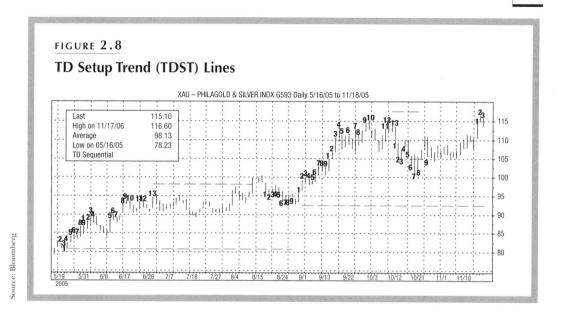

XAU – PHILAGOLD & SILVER INDX G593 Daily 5/16/05 to 11/18/05

Last	115.10
High on 11/17/06	116.60
Average	98.13
Low on 05/16/05	78.23
TD Sequential	

Source: Bloomberg

Many will question the ability of TD Combo to identify levels of price exhaustion and consider it voodoo analysis to try to do so; that is their prerogative. This reaction is not unexpected. However, we believe that to dismiss such a timing device is a mistake they make at their own peril. This approach is intended to provide fundamentalists and technicians alike with a timing device and, if nothing else, an element of trading discipline. Granted, the indicator is by no means a substitute for sound fundamental analysis and trading experience, but it certainly is a viable adjunct to a trading regimen. Its beauty is its versatility and application globally to all markets and time periods. Once fundamental screens have identified attractive trading opportunities and conventional technical analysis has confirmed them, installing TD Combo as an overlay serves to fine-tune trading activity and ideally should enhance trading results. If TD Sequential or other DeMark Indicators, particularly short-term indicators, are introduced, you should be able to improve timing trading opportunities even further.

CHAPTER 3

Charting With Candles and Clouds

NICOLE ELLIOTT

Ten years ago when I joined a Japanese bank as an experienced technical analyst, I arrived armed with my bar charts, now conveniently drawn by computers and displayed on computer screens. The traders there asked me why I did not use candle charts, a tool they considered much more effective. An English dealer kindly lent me his copy of Steve Nison's *Beyond Candlesticks* (Wiley & Sons, 1994). I read it surreptitiously, at home, and discovered what the more enlightened British, European, and U.S. chartists had already seen. Bars and candles are actually one and the same; what varies slightly is the display format. Candles are clear, easy, and above all fast. This is precisely what makes them so superior.

Their advantages are clear: speed, speed, speed. I look at between 200 and 400 charts per day, so speed is of the essence. Candles inform faster than bar charts, and they also provide more detail and use more of the available information.

Candle Basics

First, a candle has a skinny bit: high to low points as in a bar; and a fat bit (the real body): the difference between the opening price and the closing price. In official markets it is easy to know exactly at what price an instrument started trading. In over-the-counter markets it is a lot more difficult, as it is with markets that trade twenty-four hours a day. I tend to use the Wellington (New Zealand)/Tokyo opening prices and the New York/Chicago closes. If the opening is above the close, the candle is colored in—black if you are using a pencil, any of fourteen different colors if you are using the Bloomberg terminal's GPC charts. I like to use the "house colors" (which for us is dark blue) as do many other professionals because it links the research and the institution. If the closing price is above the open, the real body is left white—based on white graph paper.

Second, as the hours, days, and weeks progress, the candles change shape. In the morning on the first of the month, the week, or at the top of the hour it can be very difficult to imagine how the candle might look thirty days later. What may look extremely bullish at the start of the time frame can, of course, fizzle out into something inconclusive or even become a reversal candle.

For example, prices kick off in the morning at X (a horizontal line). They then rally 2 percent, and the candle now has a large white body and is looking pretty bullish. The market then collapses in the afternoon by 2.5 percent, so you now have a long thin bit above a squat black candle. That produces quite a different picture, a very bearish one. The point is to look at the candles at the end of the time period. This is why, in ascending order, daily, weekly, monthly, and quarterly closes above or below key chart levels are important. Imagine getting gung-ho with some share you tipped, earning brownie points as it breaks to a new all-time high. Then, by the end of the month the stock's value retreats to just below the point at which you bought it. The candle would look like the one with bearish implications, which is known as an *evening star* or *reverse hammer* (picture a mallet). Think again about this company's shares. If you had recommended it to colleagues, friends, and family, how would you feel? Gutted probably, or at least disappointed. And would you buy more? Probably not, as your instinct would suggest sitting it out for a while to see if things improve.

There is one downside to candlesticks: their larger size. Each candle is fatter than a bar; therefore they use more space on a page and, more important, more width on a computer screen. This means you see less of the hourly, daily, weekly, or monthly data and therefore lose some of the footprints and meanderings of prior moves. With markets you follow closely, this is not too much of a problem as you have the road map in your head. With instruments you look at only occasionally, it can be trickier.

Reversal candles are another substantial type of market indicator. Important reversal candles have lovely

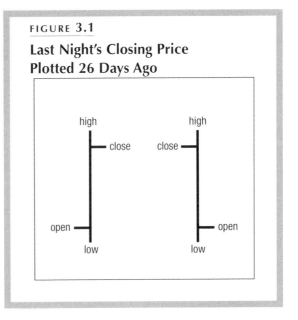

FIGURE 3.1

Last Night's Closing Price Plotted 26 Days Ago

names, including *shooting star, bearish engulfing, three black crows, abandoned baby*, and my favorite, *hanging man*. The rest are mere foot soldiers. Look at the shapes carefully and try to imagine what happened on that day or week, how price action evolved over the period, the implications for buyers and sellers and how they might be thinking at the time. As well as these single, double, or triple candle reversal formations, note that the Japanese also use traditional patterns as we do in the West: rounded bottom, double tops and triangles, head-and-shoulders, and rectangles.

Cloud charting is the second Japanese technique I have incorporated into my method. Ichimoku Kinko Hyo—the correct name for cloud charting—was invented by a Japanese journalist, Goichi Hosoda (1926–1983), who wrote under the pseudonym Ichimoku Sanjin. (The Chinese characters that make up his name translate roughly as "at one glance...of a man standing on a mountain.") On the Bloomberg terminal, cloud charts are called General Overview Charts (type in an instrument code and then GOC), which gives a much better feel for what these charts can do. The method was revived by Hidenobu Sasaki (1950–) who updated it in the very successful book *Ichimoku Kinko Studies* (Toshi Raider Publishing, 1996). For the mathematically minded, or for those who would like to set this up on a PC, the formula for the different lines is detailed in **Figure 3.2**. For those like me with a pathological fear of algebra, whose eyes glaze as soon as they see a Greek letter, we shall work through step-by-step in plain English how these charts are set up and how they work. (Also, remember that the Bloomberg terminal will draw all the lines for you.)

What follows are the five steps necessary to set up these charts.

1. Plot daily candlesticks of your chosen instrument. Because the Tokyo stock exchange closes for lunch, some traders plot morning and afternoon sessions separately. Although traditional theory says only daily candles can be used, many bend the rules and use hourly and weekly candles. One reason to try and follow the conventions is that if you don't you may be the only trader whose averages have crossed (and you will be wondering why all the others have not leapt into action). In fact, if you are too clever and tinker excessively, you may be very precise, but you will miss the crowd psychology.

2. Look at the shapes of the candles first to see if there are any reversal formations. These are easier to spot before you start drawing in all the other lines.

3. Next, add nine-day and twenty-six-day averages. These averages are based on mean price (high minus low divided by two), not closing price.

FIGURE 3.2 **Formula for Ichimoku Kinko Hyo**

$$\text{Tenkan-sen}_i = \frac{(\text{highest}_i(\text{High},k) + \text{lowest}_i(\text{Low},k))}{2}$$

$$\text{Kijun-sen}_i = \frac{(\text{highest}_i(\text{High},l) + \text{lowest}_i(\text{Low},l))}{2}$$

$$\text{Senkou Span A}_i = \frac{(\text{KijunSen}_{i-l+1}(\text{High,Low},l) + \text{TenkanSen}_{i-l+1}(\text{High,Low},k))}{2}$$

$$\text{Senkou Span A}_i = \frac{(\text{highest}_{i-l+1}(\text{High},m) + \text{lowest}_{i-l+1}(\text{Low},m))}{2}$$

$$\text{Chikou Span}_i = \text{Close}_{i+n-1}$$

Where:

$\text{highest}_i(\text{High},l) = \max(\text{high}_i,\text{high}_{i-1},\ldots,\text{high}_{i-l})$

$\text{lowest}_i(\text{Low},l) = \min(\text{low}_i,\text{low}_{i-1},\ldots,\text{low}_{i-l})$

$\max(a,b,\ldots,z) = $ maximum of $a,b,\ldots,$and z

$\min(a,b,\ldots,z) = $ minimum of $a,b,\ldots,$and z

$\text{high}_i = $ highest value over the *ith* interval

$\text{low}_i = $ lowest value over the *ith* interval

$\text{close}_i = $ close value of the *ith* interval

Parameters

Tenkan-sen period	k	1-400	(default 9)
Kijun-sen period	l	1-400	(default 26)
Senkou Span B period	m	1-400	(default 52)
Chikou Span period	n	1-400	(default 26)

The default settings are the values that Goichi Hosoda (a.k.a. Ichimoku Sanjin) determined to be the best for the Nikkei Index. Other instruments may work better with different values.

Through extensive manual back-testing, Ichimoku Sanjin decided that these two time frames worked best. It may have something to do with the fact that in his day everyone worked a five-and-a-half-day week and each month contained twenty-six working days. Many have suggested changing the number of days in the averages, perhaps to ten and twenty. I would, if most other people had, but as they haven't, I won't. Again, you are trying to tune in to the mind-set of other investors. There is no point being ahead of my time; I want to know when the thundering herd will react.

The averages are employed as in conventional Western methods. The shorter one (known as the *Conversion Line*) whips around the longer one (called the *Base Line*). When the nine-day average drops below the Base Line, it is time to convert from a long position to a short one. On the way up, the opposite action is called for so the trader always has an open position in the market. (Obviously this strategy only applies to situations in which one can go short.) The crucial insight about all moving averages is that they work well in trending markets but are hopeless for sideways moves. The tricky bit is deciding whether and when the market has switched from one mode to another, and for how long might it last. Sometimes the individual candles can help with this—say a *doji* (a candle in which the opening price and the closing price were the same, forming a crossbar figure) appears at the edge of a current horizontal move; this suggests that the range will hold even if the averages have crossed. More often than not I would wait for confirmation with a weekly or monthly close outside the previous congestion zone to conclude that there is indeed a new trend.

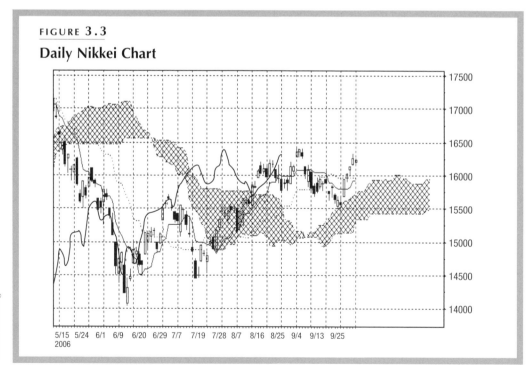

FIGURE **3.3**

Daily Nikkei Chart

Source: Bloomberg

FIGURE **3.4**

Daily Japanese Government Bond Chart

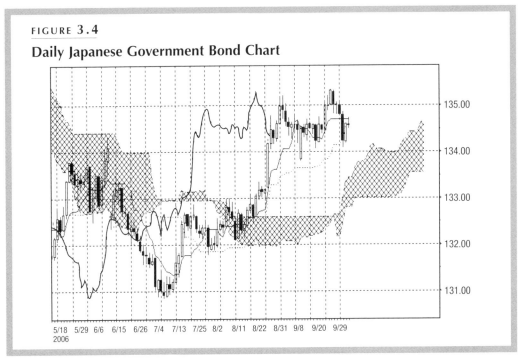

4.   After plotting the candles, move on to the clouds. Clouds are defined by an upper edge and a lower one, both called *Span*, which, as in English, means length of time. *Leading Span 1*, also known as *Senkou Span A*, is the sum of today's values of the moving averages divided by two, plotted twenty-six days ahead of the last complete candle. *Leading Span 2*, or *Senkou Span B*, is the highest price of the last fifty-two days, minus the lowest price of that period, divided by two and again plotted twenty-six days ahead of the last complete day's trading. The space between these two is shaded, or cross-hatched as in the figures in this chapter, but may be rendered in any color or combination of colors your heart desires. Even though the upper edge and the lower edge have similar names, they are constructed very differently. Like the Conversion Line and the Base Line, Leading Span 1 and Leading Span 2 work together. Span 1 is faster, providing the arias, whereas the slower Span 2 provides the underlying beat. When these two march in the same direction, the market is clearly trending: bullish when Span 1 is above Span 2 or bearish when Span 2 is above Span 1.

5.   The final line to plot is the *Lagging Span*, called *Chikou Span* in Japanese. In the figures in this chapter, the Lagging Span is the thickest, darkest line. It is last night's closing price, not the current price, plotted twenty-six days ago.

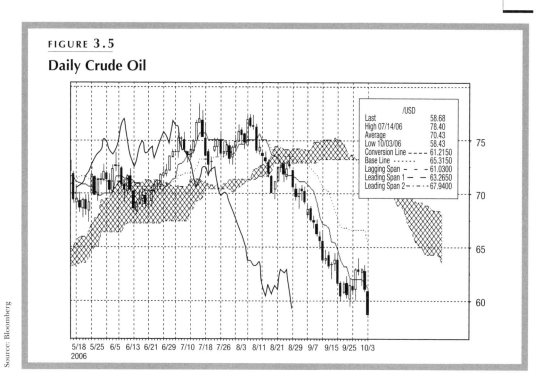

FIGURE 3.5

Daily Crude Oil

Source: Bloomberg

Lagging Span is a line chart that has been displaced back in time, hence the name. Some computers have trouble with this one and plot the current price twenty-five days ago. If this is the case, the line will bob up and down during the day as the current price changes. This is irritating, but not an enormous problem. However, the reason for using the closing price is sound. As I pointed out earlier, today's price action can take all sorts of shapes during the day. The goal is to work with what it eventually ended up looking like. Learn to be patient.

These lines identify support, resistance, and the trend. Ichimoku Kinko Hyo is a system designed for trending markets and is not useful for anything that is crawling across the page. Because it relies on daily candlestick charts, day traders and very active market-makers won't find it too valuable. On the other end of the spectrum, it is a little too short term for pension funds looking to invest for very long time horizons. I have found that this last problem can be overcome by using weekly candles, and that these often work exceeding well. Monthly charts are not much good because Leading Span B uses data of up to fifty-two prior time periods. Fifty-two months is more than four years, meaning that the slower span hardly changes (and therefore the cloud does not move much) and may be a million miles from current prices. My Japanese colleagues bend the rules of this system by working with hourly and five-minute charts. They have been trying it with weekly ones for a long time. Feel free to fiddle and experiment.

To recap quickly, the six most useful elements are:
- the candles themselves, individually and in groups and patterns
- two moving averages, nine-day (Conversion Line) and twenty-six-day (Base Line) simple ones
- two Leading Spans, which make up the cloud itself
- one Lagging Span

Working With the Elements

The candles, as mentioned, are used in exactly the same way as bar charts. First look for clusters of support and resistance, patterns, congestion zones, and trendlines. Then look for reversal candles, which usually appear either singly (easy to spot because they are often the biggest) or in clusters of twos and threes. Gaps in the price action, especially if associated with a reversal candle, are also important, rather like Western "island reversals."

Use the moving averages in the usual way. Take a long position when the nine-day one is higher than the longer average; switch to a short position when the nine-day drops below the twenty-six-day average. The Base Line is a sort of drumbeat, keeping the pace, while the Conversion Line forces you to act, shifting between long and short positions. This is not necessarily noise, but worth keeping in mind when deciding whether the Conversion Line's moves are significant. This method of trading keeps you in the market 100 percent of the time, not necessarily a good idea (vast losses pile up in sideways markets) and perhaps not even an achievable one—for example, if you cannot borrow shares that you have sold short. The averages themselves are used as support and resistance levels for today's price action. In a bull trend the averages move northeast more slowly than the candles. If there was a small downward correction, the nine-day average would be the first support level, the twenty-six-day average the next. The value of the instrument might drop below the nine-day one and hold somewhere between there and the lower average. At that point, scrutinize the candles themselves for signs of a reversal. At this stage the averages should not cross. If they do, at least cut the position. And never forget: moving averages work well only in trending markets.

The edges of the cloud also act as support and resistance, both for trending and sideways markets. In an ideal bull market, Leading Span 1 will lie below the nine-day and twenty-six-day averages and above the Leading Span 2. These support you all the way up and everything is plain sailing. The opposite happens in a perfect bear market: all the lines feel top-heavy and grind the market down. This is a series of four lines which should limit any corrective move. Picture them as two pairs. In the first pair, the longer moving average is more important than the short one. In the second pair, Span 2 is of critical importance, whereas Span 1 may or may not stem the move. I think of this as an advance force versus rearguard action. If prices move through leading Span 2, then any position should be cut and probably reversed. If this one goes, watch out! As always, at support and resistance levels watch for reversal-type candles which will hint that the level will hold. These often break through Span 2 intraday and then close back inside the cloud, forming a good reversal pattern.

The most interesting thing about the clouds is that they are plotted twenty-six days ahead of today's prices. They therefore indicate where support and resistance levels will lie over the coming month. The thicker the cloud, the more likely it will contain price action. If it is thin, and if the lines cross from bull to bear, then the odds increase that the trend will change. So looking forward, the cloud gives you some idea whether to consider reversing tactics. In this situation, price action will be nonexistent. If coupled with a reversal candle at this point, whether it confirms that the trend will hold or hints that it will change, extra attention to detail and willingness to go with the move is warranted. The distance between the current price and the cloud is not considered important. It does not indicate whether the trend is overstretched, as the relative strength index (RSI) or other oscillators that try and measure market excesses would do. However, if the price had say shot up suddenly and far faster than usual, meaning the clouds were an awful long way down, and an evening star or a hanging man candle formed, then it may be worth taking profits as the corrective decline might not stop until a very long way down.

I tend to give infinitely more weight to the clouds than I give the averages. Am I correct in doing so? To be honest I still use conventional Western techniques—classic Dow Theory is how I would describe my methods. Therefore, patterns are the most important, followed by trendlines and retracements, averages, and a couple of oscillators. Volume and open interest can also contribute if available. As to averages, I have done extensive back-testing (with a computer) and know that no single set of averages works consistently well over time. The nine-day and twenty-six-day moving averages of Ichimoku are not superior to the traditional Western ten-day and twenty-day combination.

Over the last ten years I have added Ichimoku clouds because they have completely new elements—including their position today and their position at the end of a month. Their thickness or lack thereof indicates whether prices will break through and when a topping or bottoming formation may occur. Let's say, for example, a congestion pattern has been apparent for some time. Is it a double top? If the cloud thins, it is indeed quite possible that the market is reaching an interim high. As with conventional methods, only a decisive break below the lower edge of the pattern and a break below the lower edge of the cloud can confirm this. If, on the other hand, the cloud gets thicker, then chances are that price action is consolidating in a "rectangle" and not a major top.

The Lagging Span, or Chikou Span, which is last night's closing price plotted twenty-six days ago, is a bit of a dark horse. It is also difficult to review the chart and decide whether it worked. This line is yet another in the series that indicates where today's support and resistance levels lie.

If this thick black line is above the candles of twenty-six days ago, in a bull market, then the real body of the candles should ensure that today's closing price will be above the twenty-six-day-old low point. It is a bit tricky and conceptually very different from Western analysis. Playing with time lines, shifting things forward and back again, is certainly not the usual Western approach. This is precisely why the method adds something to the body of knowledge. At the very least it is a lot more than a repetition of traditional methods or a simple tweaking of conventional technical analysis. Interpreting this line is a bit like surfing a wave—anticipating both the arrival of a good one and when it might collapse, allowing for a graceful exit rather than crash and bang.

On the way down, the indicators are exactly the opposite of what they were on the way up. In a bear market, if the Lagging Span is below the candles of twenty-six days ago (ideally a cluster of tightly grouped ones), the real bodies will act as resistance. Often the Lagging Span weaves itself slowly through a pattern of candles, a rectangle for example. Then, when it breaks out of the congestion zone, it soars or plummets dramatically. In other words, once the Lagging Span has been set free, today's market gathers momentum and manages a big move. The clouds of twenty-six days ago also act as support and resistance for this black line, which often grinds prices lower if it is trapped below a fat cloud. When the cloud thins, the chances of the Lagging Span's breaking out increase significantly. I realize this is a difficult concept to grasp. The twenty-six-day lag time is particularly mysterious. Why should what happened then affect here and now? Nonetheless, experience has convinced me that all these lines do work well together, reinforcing trends and underlining where the key levels lie. It pays to bide your time, respect the lines and patterns, and rid yourself of too many preconceptions.

I look at the Lagging Span (Chikou Span) very closely because it is not available in a conventional tool kit. (This one is a lot easier to spot when working in color.) Some feel that using a displaced price (twenty-six days ago) to understand today's market is far-fetched. It is a little like being a time traveler: now, tomorrow, yesterday, back-and-forward juggling with a total fifty-two-day period. It's a bit like watching a seesaw, wondering which way it will tip next. I find this a truly fascinating idea that probably warrants further investigation. Ichimoku Kinko Hyo's key concept is that price and time are inextricably linked. Just as with today's candles, the elements that provide support and resistance act in the same way with this Lagging Span. So, nine-day and twenty-six-day averages, then the two edges of the cloud, and finally the candle of twenty-six days ago also provide support for Chikou Span (not all day long, but for the closing price of today, the only data plotted). This is especially strong support if the elements cluster together. Interestingly, if the market was moving into a congestion zone twenty-six days ago, then probably today's, tomorrow's, and the next week's worth of price action will be range-bound, halting, and difficult. This is because the old candles (especially their real bodies) limit current price action as the Lagging Span snakes its way through them. I don't actually know how or why this works. This is what the theory says and, having used the method extensively, I can say that it really does work quite often. Additionally, this is a theory that Mr. Hosoda back-tested extensively before sharing it with the world.

Could this be a self-fulfilling theory? Do so many people use this method that they actually create it by their actions? The evidence is against this. First, comparatively speaking, only a few of the world's technical analysts use Ichimoku Kinko Hyo. However, in Japan, the situation is reversed. So many Japanese dealers constantly refer to screens with this type of chart that I would be negligent if I were to ignore the clouds in these sectors and markets.

Since January 2004, as demonstrated in **Figure 3.6**, the U.S. dollar/pound currency pair has been moving sideways in a very broad band between 1.7000 and 1.9200 (most of the time). From April 2006 to date it has been trending higher, with a lengthy consolidation period from mid-May to late July.

Here's how the different Ichimoku Kinko tools work in this chart.

Moving average crossovers have captured the significant moves throughout

FIGURE **3.6**

Daily $/GBP

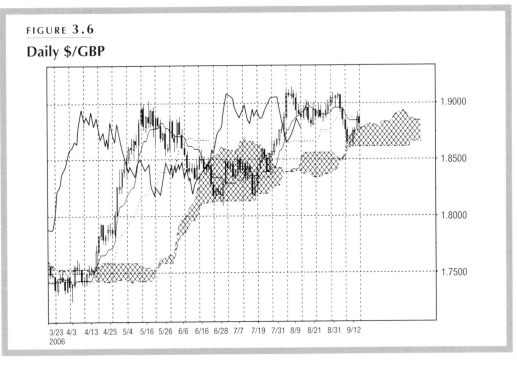

Source: Bloomberg

but are mixed at the moment. The Base Line is often flat.

The cloud, which was incredibly thin until early April, nevertheless manages to keep the cable (a nickname for the exchange rate between the U.S. dollar and British pound) below it. Note the hammer candle on April 3. A clear break and daily close above the top of the cloud on April 17 kicks off a strong rally with the nine-day average limiting the lows of the candles on the way up.

The moving averages cross over on June 7, and prices slide suddenly to their lowest levels in a month. The top of the cloud supports the candles in mid-June, but they then drop to the lower edge of what is by then a fat cloud with an almost horizontal Leading Span 2. For the next month (until July 26) the cable snakes its way sideways limited both on the upside and on the downside by the Leading Spans. Midway through this period the averages turn bullish, and both of these then limit daily lows until September 5, by which time the Leading Spans cross.

September's dip to 1.8600 was again stopped by the bottom of the cloud, and the last prices on the chart are just above the top of it. The cloud gets fatter, again with a horizontal lower edge, and this may allow the pound to creep higher even if the moving averages continue to flip around each other.

The Lagging Span, not surprisingly, was not very helpful when prices were

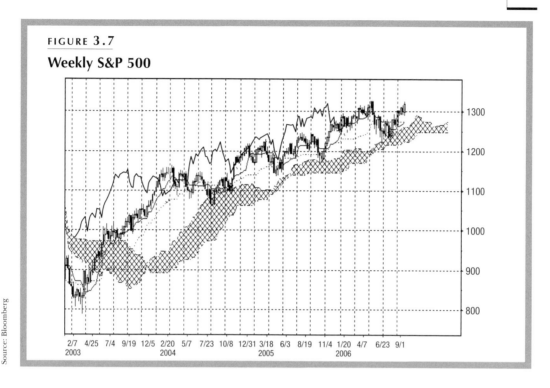

FIGURE 3.7

Weekly S&P 500

Source: Bloomberg

moving broadly sideways. Note however that on June 12 the cloud pushed this black line decidedly higher, acting as support for prices on July 17. Also look at August 7, where the twenty-six-day average pushes the Lagging Span up again. At the time of writing (mid-September 2006), the Lagging Span is under the candles of twenty-six days ago, suggesting we may snake slowly sideways under these for another two weeks.

The outlook, according to this chart: Generally we expect the cable to move very slowly higher over the next month, possibly more quickly if the averages turn clearly bullish.

Support levels:

1.8770 (top of the cloud but note this moves higher until mid-October)

1.8660 (twenty-six-day average twenty-six days ago for the Lagging Span)

1.8600 (the bottom of the cloud)

Figure 3.7 charts the S&P 500. Since March 2003, the trend has been decidedly bullish, with lengthy periods of consolidation along the way. A moving average crossover trading strategy would have kept you invested most of the time, except for a fairly long spell from June to October 2004. The averages also switched briefly to a short position between April and July 2005 and in June 2006.

The clouds have worked admirably, the index clinging to the top edge of these on most pullbacks. Since February 2005 the cloud has been a lot thinner than in previous years, but even so has provided support. Note that the Leading Spans have never crossed over.

The Lagging Span has held above the twenty-six-week moving average throughout, bouncing strongly from it in February 2004, April 2005, and January 2006.

Looking ahead to September 2006, the nine-week average crossed over the twenty-six-week one, so perhaps the S&P 500 will start to climb higher again, helped along by the top of the cloud which is also rising slightly. However, prices might initially drop to or into the cloud, meaning that the averages will turn down again. The reality is that these two might whip around each other for quite some time, which suggests that the moving average crossover system should go on the back burner for now. The Lagging Span is just above the top of the candles themselves, and so may provide support for current prices. To conclude, there will be very gently rising prices, but watch out in January 2007 as the cloud becomes thin.

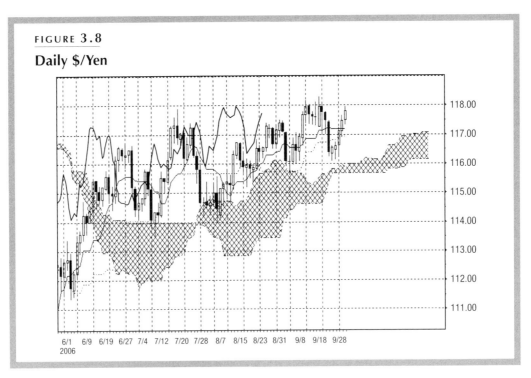

FIGURE **3.8**

Daily $/Yen

Source: Bloomberg

Compared to most so-called trending systems, Ichimoku Kinko Hyo can work very well in a congestion zone (with minor adaptations). As **Figure 3.8** shows, the $/Yen has been in a bull market. In September 2006, it started moving sideways. The upper edge of the cloud is the first support (after the nine-day and twenty-six-day averages), and the lower edge of the cloud is the key support. Leading Span 1 (the upper edge of the cloud) will hold dips most, but not all, of the time. Prices will dip into the shaded area and then rally ahead of Leading Span 2. The market will often then creep erratically within the cloud, moving slowly between its two edges. I included this fairly recent chart here so you can judge the usefulness of these techniques for yourself. Had I included only historical charts, I would have given the impression that the system always works. I hope you will discover how well the system works as events unfold.

Taking a larger perspective on the markets, I've found that while it may be useful to have some sort of road map and some idea of how far along you have come, it's smart to be flexible. Do not get obsessed with terrorist threats, economic slowdown, and house-price bubbles. Look also at information and chart patterns that contradict your view, not just the ones that support it. Also try to find as many parts of the puzzle that fit together as you can, but think more carefully about the ones that do not. Look at similar and related instruments to see if the moves confirm each other. So if the cable looks as though it is going up, then $/Yen should be on its way down. If copper is at a record high, then other base metals should be on the expensive side. Do not try to force a piece of the puzzle in, but try to look at it from a different perspective. Being a bit of a contrarian myself, I enjoy questioning conventional wisdom and often trade against prevailing views. This often works well, as too much has been priced into the market way ahead of the expected date.

—m—

I WILL CONCLUDE with some advice.

Charts are all about reading psychology and smelling raw emotion. Do not forget this.

Do not think that you can move into or out of any financial instrument without causing ripples (or tidal waves at times). Everything you think, do, and feel makes the market. After all, any market is the sum total of our actions, hopes, and fears.

Some markets, like foreign exchange, are huge. Changing money for your holiday will have practically zero effect. But consider that there are hundreds of thousands of these small transactions going on every day and the cumulative amounts do matter. In tiny markets—tightly owned shares in a small company, for example—the impact is far greater and more immediate. Say private equity company X has decided to amass a significant stake in Y at fifty pence—the chart will have a horizontal at 50 because the bid is there. And if the bid is upped to sixty pence, the lows will immediately be limited at this point.

Look at charts, imagine what people are thinking. Remember: They are voting with their pockets.

The name *technical analysis* sounds very scientific and rational. It isn't. Nor are the markets we endeavor to follow. Like classic cars and golf club memberships, there is a lot more to the value at which these change hands than purely financial considerations.

The more confident you grow with any new technique, the more likely you are to tinker with it. Confidence begets creativity. Think of Renaissance painters and Greek philosophers. When working within very tight constraints, the truly gifted can and will come up with something stunning and original. My Japanese colleagues astonishingly use hourly candles, particularly with things like $/Yen and the Nikkei 225. Try these and see what you think. I have had fifty-fifty results with this so far, not nearly close to my usual standards. Often it can be worth sticking with the crowd.

When dealing with financial markets, self-knowledge and a sense of perspective are the most difficult things to master, as is knowing when to pounce and when to stand back and be patient. With technical analysis, you'll come to distinguish between unnecessary "noise" and indications the market is about to move.

As you can see, this chapter is a mix of new (to us Westerners) technical analysis and down-home advice. Which is the most important? The basics, of course. But I have added Ichimoku Kinko Hyo to my armory, and I hope you will too.

CHAPTER 4

Reading Candlestick Charts

YOSUKE SHIMIZU

There are many different kinds of stock charts in use, but candlesticks are probably the most common form in Japan. The name *candlesticks* comes from the practice of representing price movements with white and black sticks that look like candles, particularly the form with a white box on the bottom and a thin line extending upward.

This style of charting is considered to have its roots in the Edo-period rice markets of Dojima (near modern-day Osaka). Historians estimate that they took their present form in the latter half of the Meiji period (late 1800s). Originally, they were just sticks drawn in red or black.

What Are Candlesticks?

Let's start by looking at how candlesticks are drawn. **Figure 4.1** is a list of fictitious intraday stock price movements.

FIGURE 4.1

INTRADAY STOCK PRICE MOVEMENTS							
1	10,160	11	10,170	21	10,200
2	10,150	12	10,170	22	10,200
3	10,160	13	10,180	23	10,190
4	10,160	14	10,180	24	10,190
5	10,160	15	10,180	25	10,180
6	10,170	16	10,190	26	10,190
7	10,170	17	10,190	27	10,190
8	10,170	18	10,170	28	10,200
9	10,180	19	10,170	29	10,200
10	10,180	20	10,190	30	10,180

If prices move in order from 1 to 30, they produce a line graph like the one marked No. 1 in **Figure 4.2**, which we can express as a candlestick, as shown by No. 2.

If the movement were like the chart in **Figure 4.3**, the candlestick would be

FIGURE **4.2**

Price Movement for a White Candlestick

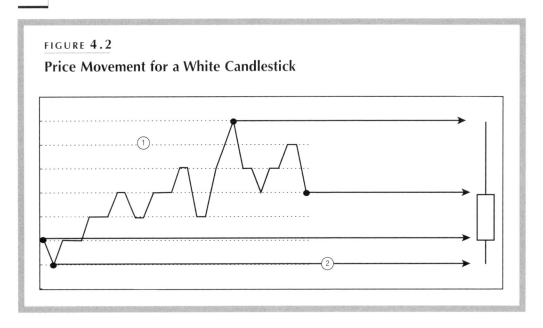

colored black. A black candlestick indicates that the opening price was higher than the closing price. In other words, prices spent the day more or less sliding downward. This is called a black candlestick. The same charting technique can be applied to yearly price movements as well.

FIGURE **4.3**

Price Movement for a Black Candlestick

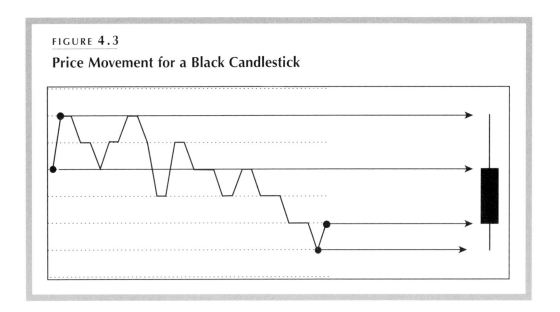

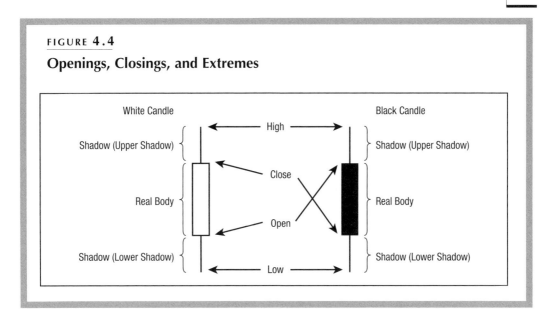

FIGURE 4.4

Openings, Closings, and Extremes

The difference between a white candlestick and a black candlestick is whether the opening price (the first price of the session) was higher than the closing price (the last price of the session). As **Figure 4.4** shows, if the closing price is lower than the opening price, a black candlestick is used; if it is higher, a white candlestick. The lines extending out from the black or white bodies are called *shadows* and represent the price extremes (highest and lowest prices) during the day.

In a daily chart, a single black or white candle expresses price movements for a single day; in a weekly chart, a single candle expresses price movements for an entire week; in a monthly chart, for an entire month. Charts can be drawn in almost any increment. Some traders even use one-minute and five-minute charts.

Regardless of the time frame, the form of the candlestick and its combination with other candlesticks can be used to identify the market's direction and its relative strength or weakness. That is the main purpose of candlestick charts.

How to Read Candlesticks

Candlesticks express stock price movements over a set period of time (ordinarily either one day or one week). Each stick will have a different shape and color (black equals a downtrend; white equals an uptrend), and each means something different. For example, if there is a long white box, one might surmise that the same price trend will continue and prices will rise even higher the next day.

FIGURE 4.5

Types of Candlesticks

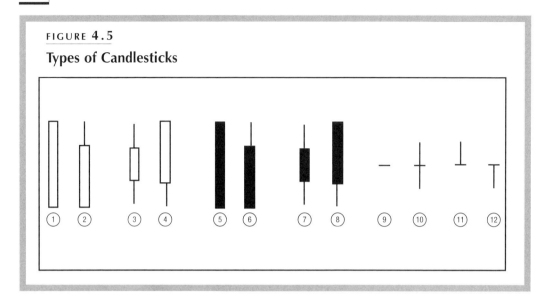

If a stock experiences selling after it opens, later rises higher, but closes the day at the same price as the opening price (the very first price of the day), one might conclude that the market is having difficulty deciding on a direction.

In other words, each candlestick has a meaning and tells a story. There are twelve basic types of candlesticks (see **Figure 4.5**). Let's look closer at their meanings and what their combinations have to say about market direction.

The twelve types of candlesticks break down into three basic categories.

- *White candlesticks.* The closing price was higher than the opening price (Nos. 1–4 in Figure 4.5).
- *Black candlesticks.* The opening price was higher than the closing price (Nos. 5–8 in Figure 4.5).
- *Doji.* The opening price and the closing price were the same, forming a cross-bar figure (Nos. 9–12 in Figure 4.5).

Within these categories, there are many different shapes. For example, a large white box with no shadows, called a *marubozu* (shaved) candlestick (No. 1 in Figure 4.5), indicates that the closing price was far higher than the opening price.

Candlesticks also can differ in the length of their shadows, whether they have shadows or not, and in the size of the real body itself. Each candlestick offers a hint about what is likely to happen next.

Ordinarily, a white candlestick indicates that prices may be higher the next day and is therefore bullish, whereas a black candlestick is bearish and indicates that

FIGURE 4.6

Bearish and Bullish Signals

	Name	Shape	Meaning
Bullish candlesticks	White Marubozu		Extremely bullish
	White Opening Marubozu		Bullish indication
	White Closing Marubozu		Bullish indication
Bearish candlesticks	Black Marubozu		Extremely bearish
	Black Closing Marubozu		Bearish indication
	Black Opening Marubozu		Bearish indication

prices may fall (see **Figure 4.6**). Other shapes indicate reversal points. Examples include *doji* and *spinning tops*, that is, very narrow real bodies, indicating a narrow range between the opening and closing prices (see **Figure 4.7**). However, you have to be careful. Candlestick meanings are contextual. The meanings of candlestick shapes differ depending on whether they appear near the top of the range or the bottom. Meanings will also differ if several candlesticks are clustered together. In other words, a specific group of candlesticks can indicate either an extremely bullish market or an extremely bearish one.

FIGURE 4.7

Reversals

	Name	Shape	Meaning
Reversal candlesticks	Spinning Top (black)		Indicates indecision and lack of direction (prices moving in a narrow range, but somewhat bearish)
	Spinning Top (white)		Indicates indecision and lack of direction (prices moving in a narrow range, but somewhat bullish)
	Dragonfly		Indicates reversal
	Gravestone		Indicates a break in the action. Could be a reversal or a lack of direction.
	Takuri		Indicates a reversal. If it breaks upward, sell; if downwards, buy.

Reversal Patterns

It is possible to use candlestick analysis to discover market turning points—the tops and the bottoms. One approach is to look for distinctive, easily seen patterns that mark a top or bottom. The other is to examine whether tops and bottoms have predictable patterns. In practice, it's difficult to make judgments from a single pattern. A single pattern may have two, opposite, meanings, depending on whether it comes after the market has made a substantial rise or a substantial fall (in fact, the meaning is the same in that the pattern indicates a market reversal, but it means the opposite in the sense of going up or going down). The key, therefore, is to examine not only the shape but also the timing of the pattern.

Takuri and Hanging Man Shapes

Takuri and *hanging man* shapes, with a small real body (the rectangular portion) and an extremely long lower shadow, are often seen at the bottom of the market. Some examples are found in **Figure 4.8**. They can be quickly spotted in real charts. The point to watch is the lower shadow. The relative size of the real body is not that important, nor is the color—white or black—or the presence of a short upper shadow. As long as the lower shadow is noticeably long, it fits the pattern.

Takuri. Strictly speaking, takuri refers to a black candlestick that opens low

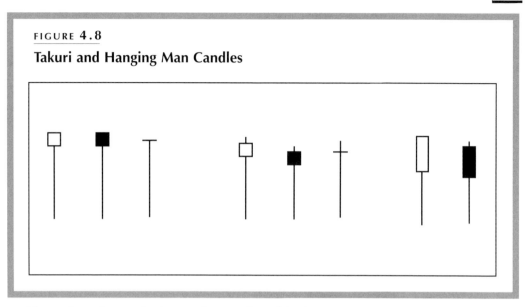

FIGURE **4.8**

Takuri and Hanging Man Candles

and has a long lower shadow and a small real body, but it can also be a white candlestick and can have a bit of an upper shadow or a large real body, as long as the lower shadow is substantially longer than the real body. Takuri also covers doji shapes like the *dragonfly* and the *hammer,* in which the open and close are the same, as long as the lower shadow is of sufficient length. Takuri shapes are usually seen after the market has experienced a substantial drop, and they represent an opportune buying signal, especially if they are accompanied by high volume (see **Figure 4.**9).

A white takuri accompanied by volume (far greater trading volume than the previous day's) very likely marks a bottom. The reason for that is quite simple. Consider the psychology of investors when a takuri is formed. If the market has been in a prolonged decline, investors begin to wonder why it hasn't stopped and when it eventually will. The psychology flips back and forth between "Hurry up and stop already!" and "Could the market go down any farther?"

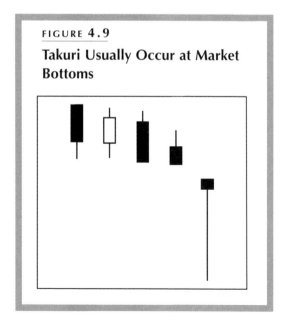

FIGURE **4.9**

Takuri Usually Occur at Market Bottoms

In a situation like this, if the market opens with more selling than usual, it means that investors have become desperate and think that the stock will drop even farther. More people decide to dump their shares (cut their losses and run), so the price declines. Other investors see this and jump aboard the selling bandwagon. Once the desperation selling and dumping are over, however, few shares are left for sale, and even a small amount of buying will push the price back up. By the end of the session, the closing price is at or very near the open. In other words, a takuri means that all the sellers have sold and there is no more selling to come. The bears have seen their supply lines cut, which makes the bulls stronger, and that is why this shape often means that the market has bottomed out.

Hanging Man. The hanging man has the same shape as an ordinary takuri, but it's a white candlestick that occurs at the top and is often the precursor of a steep decline (see **Figure 4.10**). The name comes from the market wisdom that you'll end up hanging yourself if you buy on this shape. Here too, it does not really matter whether the shape's real body is black or white or whether it's a doji or still a takuri.

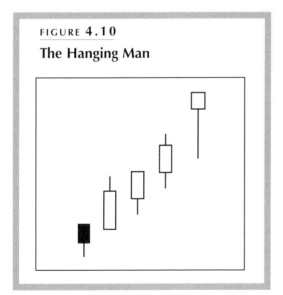

FIGURE **4.10**

The Hanging Man

The hanging man does not appear often and so should be watched carefully when it does. You're far less likely to see a hanging man appear at the top than you are a takuri at the bottom or an inverted takuri at the peak. Nor does the hanging man generally appear by itself.

Once again, investor psychology explains why this shape indicates a peak. Unlike the takuri, in this case the shape would appear at first glance to be bullish. The bears have been in charge and pushed the price down, but the bulls were able to push it back up during the day, and they appear to be quite strong. But if the bulls were really that strong, they would have taken the sharp drop at the open, pushed back up, and kept going quite a bit farther. It's a question of "Is that all you can do?" If that is as far as the bulls can go, then they are weak and about to be hung.

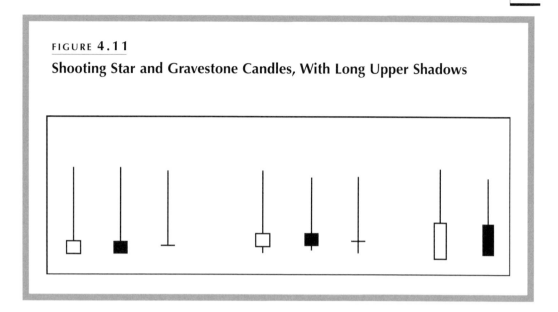

FIGURE **4.11**

Shooting Star and Gravestone Candles, With Long Upper Shadows

Shooting Star and Gravestone Shapes

Like the long lower shadow shapes, there are also shapes with long upper shadows, which are illustrated in **Figure 4.11**. And like those with long lower shadows, long upper shadow shapes indicate a top when they appear in a rising market and a bottom when they appear in a falling market. Similarly, it's not that important whether the real body is white or black, or whether the shape is a doji, or whether there is a slight lower shadow. A long upper shadow is considered either a *shooting star* or a *gravestone.*

Shooting Star. When a shape with a small real body (expressing the spread between the open and close) and a long upper shadow appears after a significant rise, it's called a shooting star and indicates a top. In other words, until the previous session, the rising trend was moving along nicely and prices were being bid up, but the bulls' supply lines have now collapsed. Traders looking to buy have bought pretty much all they want and there are no more buyers left, so the market has peaked.

Gravestone. Strictly speaking, a gravestone (**Figure 4.12**) is a doji with a long upper shadow, and when it appears near a bottom or after a sharp decline, it usually indicates that the market has bottomed out. As with the shooting star, the gravestone can be interpreted more loosely to be any shape with a long upper shadow that appears near a bottom.

The gravestone is interpreted the same way as a hanging man is near the top.

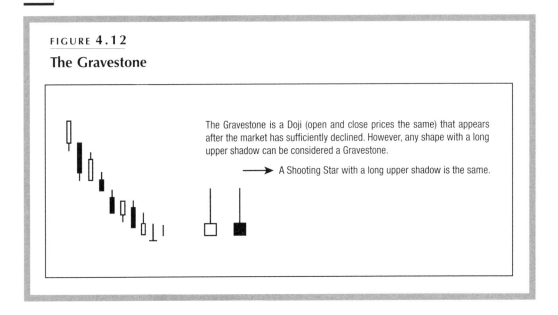

FIGURE 4.12

The Gravestone

The Gravestone is a Doji (open and close prices the same) that appears after the market has sufficiently declined. However, any shape with a long upper shadow can be considered a Gravestone.

→ A Shooting Star with a long upper shadow is the same.

The bears have sold the stock back down but have been unable to break very far through the low, which indicates that a bottom has been reached.

The Logic Behind the Shooting Star and Gravestone

In contrast to takuri and hanging man, these patterns have long upper shadows and small or no real bodies (doji). If the real body is small, it is a shooting star because the long upper shadow looks like a comet's tail; if it's a doji, the shape is called a gravestone because the long upper shadow looks like a gravestone extending upward from the ground. Both indicate reversal points. Generally, a shooting star near the top indicates that the price has peaked, while a gravestone near the bottom indicates that it has bottomed out. However, in practice, the distinction is not that important. What is important is the price movement in the next session, the same as for a spinning top or *harami*.

If a shooting star appears near the top of an uptrend and the next day produces a large black candlestick, it is a *shooting star on the eve of three rivers*—and a decisive top signal; if it is followed by an *engulfing pattern (tsutsumi)*, it is also a top reversal signal because the stock is being "carried for the last time." Similarly, after a downtrend, a gravestone followed by a three rivers pattern would be a decisive bottom signal, whereas an engulfing pattern means that the stock is being "picked straight up."

Both upper shadows and lower shadows can indicate tops or bottoms. It's more common for a long lower shadow to appear after a downtrend than an uptrend, and likewise a long upper shadow is more common after an uptrend than a downtrend. In other words, a takuri is more common than a hanging man, and a shooting star is more common than a gravestone.

Another classic pattern near the top of a trend is the *dark cloud cover (kabuse)*. This pattern often is seen when the market is in an uptrend and thought to be continuing upward, but when it appears near the top, it should be interpreted as a warning sign. The inversion of a dark cloud cover is the *piercing pattern (kirikomi)*, which appears near the bottom and indicates the market is bottoming out. Although they differ in their bullish and bearish indications, these patterns have exactly the same psychology at work in their production.

Dark Cloud Cover

In this pattern, a comparatively large white candlestick is followed by a black candlestick that opens higher than the white candlestick's close (higher than the top of its real body and resembling a dark cloud on top of the white candlestick). If a large black candlestick is formed near the top and extends below the median price for the previous day, it usually indicates a reversal. However, if the next day's price exceeds the black candlestick's high, the dark cloud cover has broken and the uptrend commonly accelerates. (**Figure 4.13**)

There are other variations on dark cloud cover, depending on the degree of coverage. Some examples include *atekubi, sashikomi,* and *irikubi,* but they can be

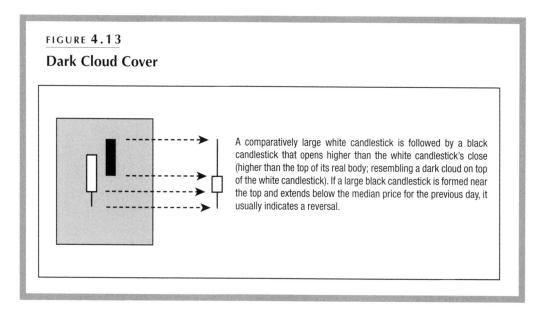

FIGURE 4.13

Dark Cloud Cover

A comparatively large white candlestick is followed by a black candlestick that opens higher than the white candlestick's close (higher than the top of its real body; resembling a dark cloud on top of the white candlestick). If a large black candlestick is formed near the top and extends below the median price for the previous day, it usually indicates a reversal.

considered to have the same basic meaning.

A fairly convincing argument can be made about the formation of dark cloud cover and the reason the psychological state among market participants leading to it results in the formation of a top. Here's what happens: The market is in an uptrend, and a fairly large white candlestick is formed. If the session closes at or near the high, most people believe that there will be more gains the next day because this stock still has a long way to go. If it does indeed open higher the next day, it would not be uncommon to think that the bulls will crowd in because their anticipation has been confirmed. In some cases, there is a *window* or *gap* (see Figure 4.22) that is opened and the price continues to soar. But what if that doesn't happen? The stock has gapped significantly higher, but at (or near) the high, it begins to slide. More investors decide that this must be the end, and the decline accelerates. If the market is indeed still bullish, the decline should stop at the previous day's high or close, but if it breaks through the previous day's close and still does not stop, more selling piles on. At the end of the day, the stock closes far below the previous day's close and investors ask themselves, "What were yesterday's gains all about anyway?" A top has formed. If, on the third day, the stock opens even lower, then the worst has been confirmed and more shares are dumped, as if to corroborate the peak.

If these two days of movement were compressed into one, it would produce an upper shadow or a lower shadow—the same shape as a shooting star or hanging man. This is yet another and very convincing reason why dark cloud cover is a pattern that indicates a top.

The Piercing Pattern

In this pattern, the first day has a large black candlestick followed on the second day by a large white candlestick, extending above the middle of the black candlestick. Often the pattern indicates that the selling is over; a long downtrend has come to an end and an upward reversal has begun.

This pattern is exactly the opposite of dark cloud cover. The price has been sliding downward, and there is a large black candlestick causing most people to think that the stock has even farther to drop. If, in the midst of this market sentiment, the stock opens significantly lower, most people might think that it's heading farther down and become bearish. However, if the opening is actually at (or near) the bottom and the price starts to rebound, investors who sold short begin to buy back their positions, and bargain hunters decide that they had better jump in quickly, amplifying the rebound so that the stock closes significantly

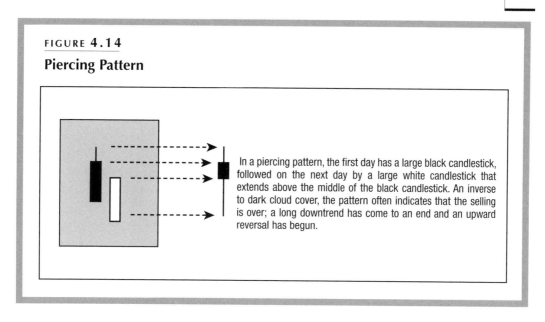

FIGURE **4.14**

Piercing Pattern

In a piercing pattern, the first day has a large black candlestick, followed on the next day by a large white candlestick that extends above the middle of the black candlestick. An inverse to dark cloud cover, the pattern often indicates that the selling is over; a long downtrend has come to an end and an upward reversal has begun.

higher than it did the previous day and participants perceive it to have bottomed out.

It may be easier to understand this if the two days' movement is compressed into one. A large decline followed by a higher close will produce a long lower shadow, and this shape—appearing at or near the bottom—is the same as a takuri and usually marks the bottom of the trend. (**Figure 4.14**)

In a piercing pattern, the first day has a large black candlestick, followed on the next day by a large white candlestick that extends above the middle of the black candlestick. An inverse to dark cloud cover, the pattern often indicates that the selling is over; a long downtrend has come to an end and an upward reversal has begun.

The Engulfing Pattern

This pattern is sometimes referred to as *tsutsumi* or *daki* (hug). A candlestick with a small real body is engulfed by a larger candlestick, resembling a mother hugging her child. In other words, the first day is white and the second day is also white, and the second day has opened below the first day's open and closed above the first day's close. Regardless of whether white or black candlesticks are involved, the key characteristic of the engulfing pattern is that the real body of the second day is larger on both the top and bottom than the real body of the first. Were the two days' movement compressed into one, it would form a long

FIGURE **4.15**

The Engulfing Pattern

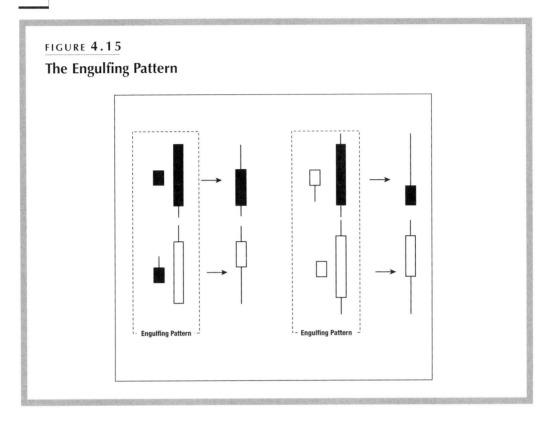

upper shadow or lower shadow, which makes it easy to understand why it is a top or bottom reversal.

If, at or near the top, a large black candlestick engulfs the previous day's smaller candlestick, it's not surprising that this would mark the peak, but a large black candlestick near the bottom of a downtrend, which would seem to indicate further declines, often marks the bottoming-out point. Similarly, a large engulfing white candlestick at or near the bottom of a downtrend is easily taken as an indication that prices have bottomed out, but it is surprisingly common for this same engulfing white candlestick to mark the top in an uptrend (see **Figure 4.15**).

Harami

In the harami pattern, a large candlestick of either color is followed by a smaller candlestick, resulting in a shape that resembles a pregnant woman (which is the meaning of harami). Harami is another reversal pattern; the child is seen as separating from the mother (see **Figure 4.16**). When this pattern appears at or near the top of an uptrend and consists of a large white candlestick followed by a small white candlestick (white/

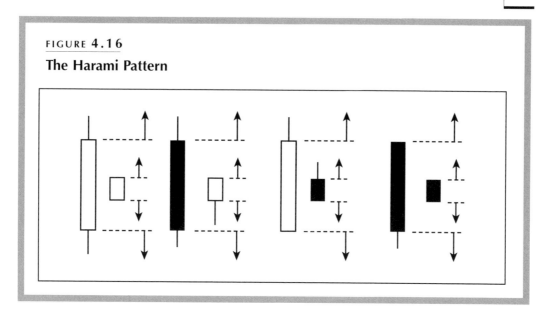

FIGURE 4.16

The Harami Pattern

white harami), it is common for the trend to break downward, marking a peak. Conversely, when this pattern appears at or near the bottom of a downtrend and consists of a large black candlestick followed by a small black candlestick (black/ black harami), it is common for the trend to break upward, marking a trough.

Harami pattern is the opposite of an engulfing pattern. Price movements are entirely within the range of the previous day. The question is not really whether they are white candlesticks or black candlesticks. The decision to sell or buy depends on where the pattern is seen (near the top or near the bottom). The first day's candlestick is considered the mother; the second day's is the child she carries. A reversal in the trend is very common when the child is a doji. Market wisdom says to follow the break with a harami. If either the previous day's high or low is exceeded, the trend usually continues in that direction.

Whether the shadows are included in the large candlestick is disputed. Some argue that the shadows should not be included in either the mother or the child; others believe that for the mother (the large candlestick), the shadows should be included, whereas for the child (the smaller candlestick), they should not be included.

Figure 4.17 shows the kind of price movements likely to produce a harami pattern, which is the same as the triangle, or pennant pattern in other forms of technical analysis. The top is flat and the bottoms keep moving higher, or the bottom is flat and the tops keep moving lower, or the bottoms rise and the tops

FIGURE **4.17**

The Harami Triangle or Pennant

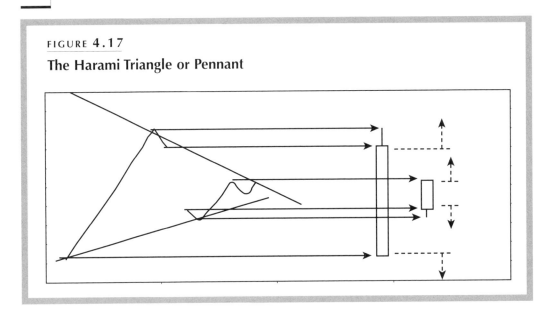

fall at the same time within a limited range of movement. In the triangle pattern like that in Figure 4.17, the break comes when the price breaks through either the upper resistance line or lower resistance line.

Therefore, if a harami appears in an uptrend and breaks downward the next day, the price tends to keep falling and a bear market ensues. On the other hand, if it opens higher, it's highly likely that further gains will follow. By contrast, a harami in a downtrend followed by a lower open the next day indicates that the market is still far from bottoming out (except in cases in which there is a sharp rise after the open), whereas a higher open the next day makes it likely that the bottom has been reached.

White/white harami and black/black harami. Market wisdom says to follow the break with a harami pattern, but if the market has already had a good rise (and is at or near the top), a large white candlestick followed by a small white candlestick in a harami pattern tends to indicate a peak (in other words, the harami tends to break downward). On the other hand, if there has already been a significant drop (prices are at or near the bottom) and a large black candlestick is followed by a small black candlestick in a harami pattern, it's highly likely that a major bottom has been reached. Nonetheless, market wisdom says to follow the break. If you have a long position when there is a white/white harami, it may be wise to sell—at least temporarily. If the price breaks upward, you can buy back your shares; if it breaks downward, you can sell short. Likewise, if you

FIGURE **4.18**

White/White Harami; Black/Black Harami

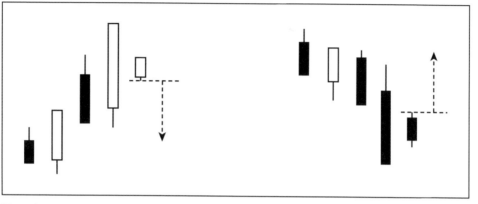

Harami presumably has its source in an indecision pattern like a spinning top, with a small real body and small shadows. When there is a break in an indecisive market, investors suddenly have direction and they all tend to move the same way.

have a short position and there is a black/black harami, it's probably wise to buy back the position and wait for the break. If the pattern breaks downward, you sell short again; upward, you go long (see **Figure 4.18**).

The Tweezers Top

Sometimes referred to in English as a double top, the *tweezers top* forms when the first day's high and the second day's high are the same, resembling a pair of tweezers (see **Figure 4.19**). The highs do not need to come on consecutive days. The pattern can form over a period of several days or even several weeks. With the exception of a *narabi aka* (a continuation pattern of two white candlesticks at the top, which is discussed later in the chapter), tweezers usually indicate that a peak has been reached, and the important point to watch is whether the previous peak can be exceeded. Ordinarily, it is not just the close but the intraday high (corresponding to the shadow) that must be taken into account. It is also not necessary that prices be exactly the same. If they are roughly the same, it is still a tweezers pattern.

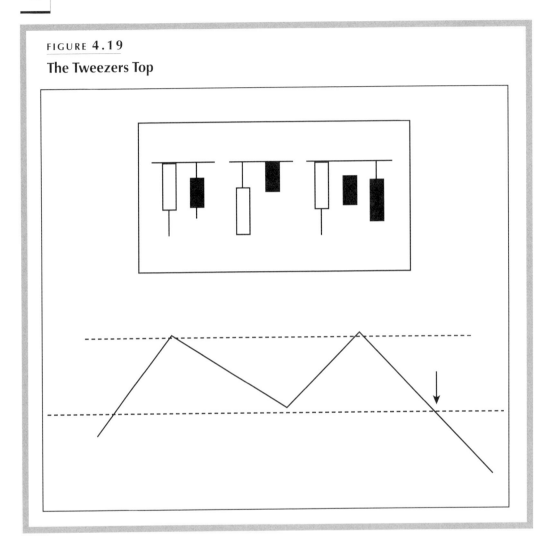

FIGURE **4.19**

The Tweezers Top

The Tweezers Bottom

This pattern is the inverse of the tweezers top. In English it is sometimes referred to as a double bottom. The first day's low and the second day's low are the same, resembling a pair of tweezers. The lows do not need to come on consecutive days. The pattern can form over a period of several days or even several weeks. The important point is that the previous low was not exceeded, which indicates that the bottom is solid (see **Figure 4.20**).

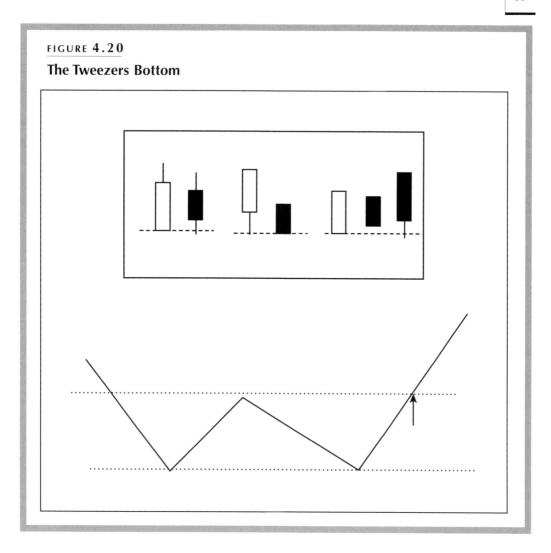

FIGURE **4.20**

The Tweezers Bottom

The Window

In the window, or gap, pattern, there is no overlap between the first day's and the second day's candlesticks. The gap between the two is referred to as a window (see **Figure 4.21**). If a trend is setting new prices or breaking out of a holding pattern (moving significantly in either direction after a period of narrow moves), market wisdom says to follow the break. It's generally easier for the price to move in the direction of the window. In the case of holding patterns, the window is often closed (trading is active at the gap), and it is common for prices to return to their original levels.

FIGURE **4.21**

The Window

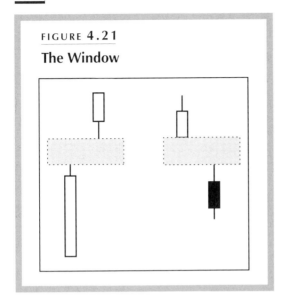

The Reversal to the Window

If a market is in an uptrend and produces a rising window (gap), the next minor reversal will often return prices to the gap, effectively closing the window (see **Figure 4.22**). Once the window is closed, it is common for the trend to reverse upward; if it fails to do so, it is common for the price to return to where it originally was (called *going home*). Likewise, a downtrend that has a falling window will also often see the window closed on the next minor reversal, providing an extremely effective opportunity for additional buying or selling.

FIGURE **4.22**

The Reversal to the Window

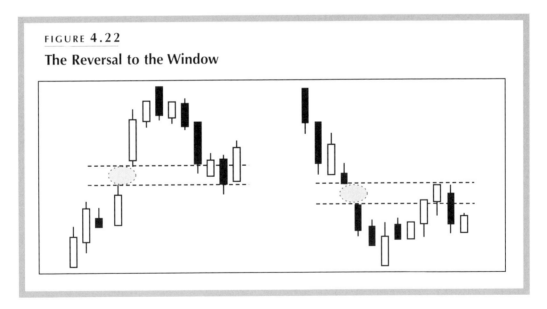

Indecision Patterns

The Star, Cross, and Spinning Top

The star, cross, and spinning top are considered indicators of indecision and potential reversal. However, one should not simplistically conclude that the market has peaked when one of these shapes appears near the top or that it has bottomed out when one of the shapes appears near the bottom. The important points are how the shape appears and how prices move afterward. In other words, the shapes say that the market is indecisive and has not yet determined whether it wants to go higher or lower. It will follow the next direction for which there is significant momentum. A large black candle after an indecision shape or an open that is significantly lower will often be followed by further declines, whereas an open that is significantly higher is often followed by further advances.

Example 1 in **Figure 4.24** shows a case in which there is indecision at the top of the range, indicating resistance to going any farther. This is very likely to be the peak. Example 2 resembles an *evening star on three rivers* occurring in conjunction with a pattern indicating the top. There was a relatively large white candlestick, followed by an indecision shape (star, cross, spinning top). If on the third day there is a relatively large black candlestick that opens lower than day two's close, it's called evening star on three rivers, or *evening cross*, and considered an indication of a peak. However, if this pattern occurs after a relatively large white candlestick and the next day opens higher and produces another white candlestick, it's common for the gains to accelerate, so the star cannot blindly be taken as an indicator of the peak.

Example 3 shows the inverse of Example 1. The market is holding at or near the bottom, and this figure indicates that downward resistance has solidified and

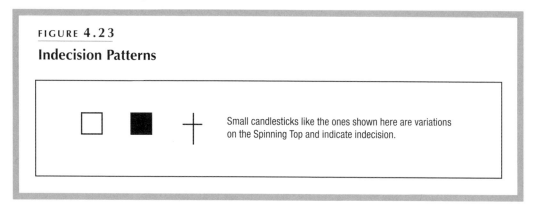

FIGURE **4.23**

Indecision Patterns

Small candlesticks like the ones shown here are variations on the Spinning Top and indicate indecision.

FIGURE **4.24**

The Star, Cross, and Spinning Top

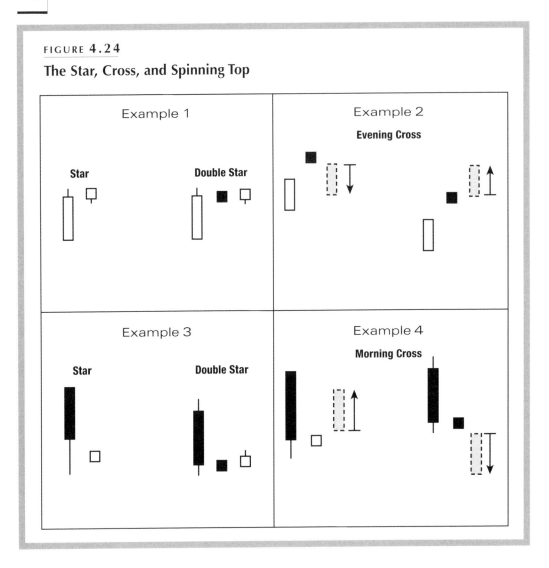

prices are likely to bottom out. Example 4 is the inverse of Example 2. If this pattern occurs after a fairly large black candlestick, it would appear that prices are bottoming out. If the final day opens higher than the previous day's close and produces a relatively large white candlestick, it is a *morning star on three rivers*, or *morning cross*, and indicates a bottom. However, if the next day's open is lower than the previous day's low and a fairly large black candlestick is produced, it's common for selling to accelerate. In other words, there may be an opposite buy or sell signal, depending on the next day's opening.

Special Patterns Worth Noting

So far we have looked at patterns and shapes that indicate peaks, troughs, and indecision. Other special, more complex patterns provide the same indications.

The Belt Hold

A belt hold is a white candlestick that opens at the low or a black candlestick that opens at the high (see **Figure 4.25**). A white belt hold can also be called a *white opening marubozu* and is a bullish pattern indicating further rises; a black belt hold can be called a *black opening marubozu* and is a bearish shape indicating further declines.

In either case, the candlestick must be relatively long. A bearish belt hold appearing near the top of a range indicates a decisive selling opportunity; a bullish belt hold near the bottom of the range indicates an excellent buying opportunity. Belt holds are considered to be extremely important patterns. The proverb says, "Belt holds are Sakata's lifeline," in reference to the birthplace of legendary trader Munehisa Homma.

Side-by-Side White Lines (Narabi Aka)

Aka means red, and the name narabi aka goes back to the premodern convention of drawing bullish candlesticks in red and bearish ones in black. The market gaps higher to produce two very similar white candlesticks (see **Figure 4.26**). When this pattern is seen during an uptrend, it indicates a

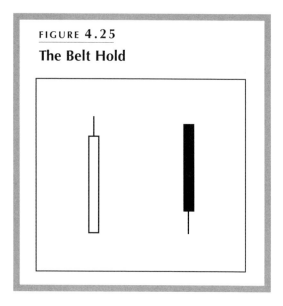

FIGURE 4.25

The Belt Hold

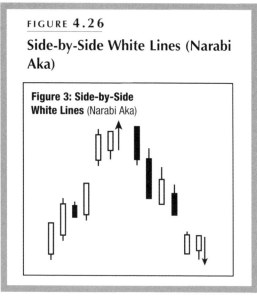

FIGURE 4.26

Side-by-Side White Lines (Narabi Aka)

Figure 3: Side-by-Side White Lines (Narabi Aka)

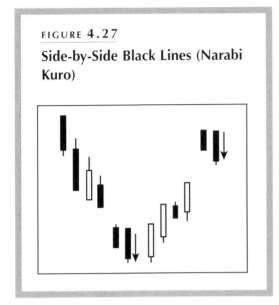

FIGURE 4.27

Side-by-Side Black Lines (Narabi Kuro)

break upward and bullish sentiment, providing an opportunity for further buying; in a downtrend, it indicates a break downward and a great opportunity to sell.

Side-by-Side Black Lines (Narabi Kuro)

The inverse of side-by-side white lines, side-by-side black lines, occurs after a gap (**Figure 4.27**). If the pattern occurs in an uptrend, it means that the bears are strong and there will be a reversal downward; in a downtrend, it means that selling will accelerate. Unlike side-by-side white lines, side-by-side black lines always indicate bearishness.

Some chartists distinguish side-by-side black lines occurring in a downtrend from those occurring elsewhere, but the indication is the same.

Osaekomi

The *osaekomi* pattern is similar to *three black crows* or dark cloud cover, but it is dis-

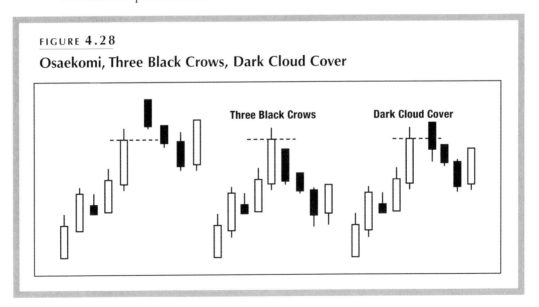

FIGURE 4.28

Osaekomi, Three Black Crows, Dark Cloud Cover

Three Black Crows

Dark Cloud Cover

tinguished by a gap between the first black candlestick and the previous candle (see **Figure 4.28)**. If, during an uptrend there are three consecutive black candlesticks (or sometimes four, or even two) followed by a white candlestick that exceeds the previous day's high, market wisdom says that there will be a break upward the next day. This is a buying opportunity. The key with the osaekomi pattern is the gap before the first black candle; in the three black crows pattern, the first black candlestick starts below the white candlestick; in the dark cloud cover pattern, the first black candlestick begins above the white candlestick. Either way it is a sell signal. The three patterns are compared in Figure 4.28.

FIGURE **4.29**

Dark Cloud Cover, Upward Break

Dark Cloud Cover, With Upward Break

Market wisdom says that a dark cloud cover occurring at the top of the range may push prices down, but if the market can break out of it, there will be a

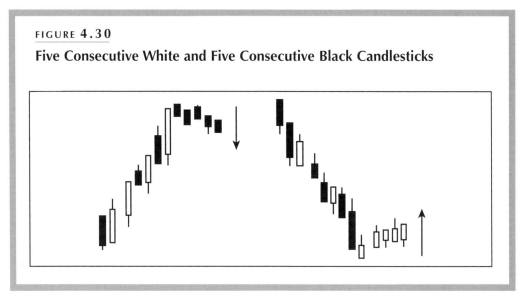

FIGURE **4.30**

Five Consecutive White and Five Consecutive Black Candlesticks

reversal upward. Therefore, even if there is dark cloud cover in a rising market, if prices can return and set a new high (generally within five moves), the proper course of action is to buy (see **Figure 4.29**).

Five Consecutive White and Five Consecutive Black Candlesticks

There are times when a series of short white candlesticks is produced after the market has experienced a significant decline (see **Figure 4.30**). Convention says that five of these candlesticks confirm the bottom and are a buying signal. The converse is also true. A series of five consecutive short black candlesticks near the top of the range is considered to confirm the top and be a selling signal.

Sakata's Five Tactics

We've examined the shapes of individual candlesticks and combinations of two or more. Sakata-style tactics take these patterns and turn them into techniques. They were developed by Sakata's celebrated trader Munehisa Homma, who made his fortune in the Edo-period rice market. (One song from the time goes, "I may never be a Homma, but maybe I can be a lord.")

There are five basic stratagems in Sakata-style tactics: *three mountains, three rivers, three gaps, three soldiers,* and *three methods.* There are many variations on each. We will look at some of the more common ones.

Three Mountains, Inverse Three Mountains

Three mountains (*three Buddhas*) indicates a major peak. The market has peaked and fallen three times, and the second peak was particularly high. This corresponds to the triple top or head-and-shoulders pattern used in Western charting that's also considered to be an indication of the top. The "neckline" is formed by connecting the low points of the three valleys. The three mountains pattern is completed after the third mountain is formed and the price breaks downward from the neckline. This is sometimes called three Buddhas because of the resemblance to Buddhist statuary—Syakamuni is often flanked by two bodhisattvas. Traders will sometimes refer to this as the three Buddha top. This is considered a classic topping pattern, especially if volume declines over time (as the chart moves to the right) (see **Figure 4.31**).

Inverse Three Mountain Bottom

In the inverse of three mountains, or inverse three Buddhas, the mountains

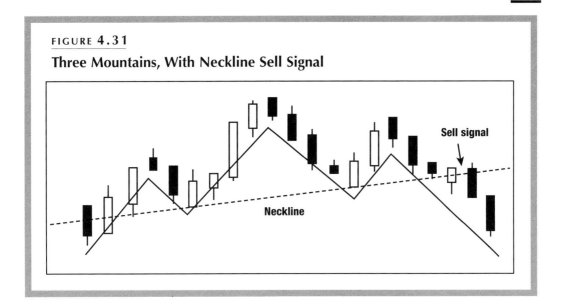

FIGURE 4.31

Three Mountains, With Neckline Sell Signal

appear upside down. Like three mountains, the inverse three mountains pattern is completed only after the price breaks through the neckline. Once it does so, it can be considered a buy signal. After a buy signal has been given, the neckline is the target for any reversals (see **Figure 4.32**).

Three Rivers

Three rivers indicates a small white or black candlestick called star, or indecision line, or doji (called a cross), between large white and black candlesticks. This is generally considered to be an indication of reversal. If the market has had a significant rise and then produces a large white candlestick, followed by a gap upward the next day to produce a star of white or black (or cross), and then on the third day gaps downward to produce a large black candlestick, it is called a morning star (cross, shooting star) on three rivers and is a selling decision line. On the opposite side, a large black candlestick followed by a gap downward to an indecision pattern in the form of a small white or black candlestick, or cross, with a large gap upward to form a white candlestick on the third day indicates that the market has bottomed out and is a buying signal. This is considered a classic pattern, indicating either the peak or trough.

It's easy to understand why the three rivers is taken to signify a top or bottom if one considers the process of its formation. The market has experienced a strong rise and produced a large white candlestick, but the next day it struggles

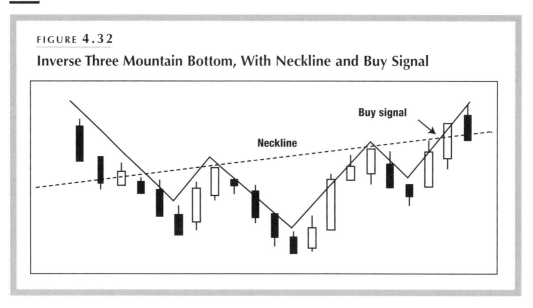

FIGURE **4.32**

Inverse Three Mountain Bottom, With Neckline and Buy Signal

to make further gains or actually loses a little ground. It is indecisive, and this indecision followed by a large black candlestick on the third day shows that the market has decided to turn down. The downward momentum is confirmed, further downward pressure is exerted, and prices drop sharply. In other words, the interpretation is basically the same as following the break for a harami pattern (see **Figure 4.33**).

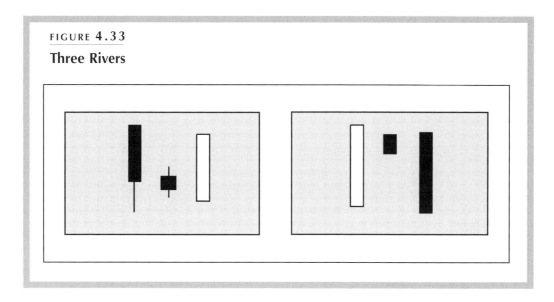

FIGURE **4.33**

Three Rivers

Evening Star/Evening Cross

An evening star on three rivers is a strong signal indicating a reversal downward when it occurs in the process of an uptrend. When the market is stalled or trading in a narrow range, the proverb says to "look for abandoned children." There may be times when the window is closed on the star (pricing at the gap where the price has jumped higher), but this pattern coming in an area of new highs is a precursor to a fall (see **Figure 4.34**).

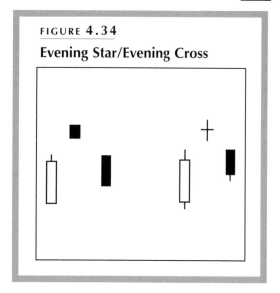

FIGURE **4.34**

Evening Star/Evening Cross

Morning Star/Morning Cross

The morning star, or morning cross, is the inverse of the evening star, or evening cross. If the star candlestick represents a new low, it's highly likely that a bottom has been reached. However, a star, or cross, does not necessarily indicate a bottom. Confirmation of a bottom comes only with the completion of the three rivers pattern (see **Figure 4.35**).

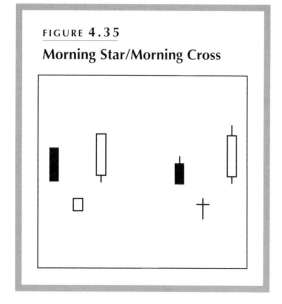

FIGURE **4.35**

Morning Star/Morning Cross

Three Soldiers

Three soldiers occurs when there are three white or black candlesticks all moving in the same direction. Three white soldiers is a pattern of three white candlesticks that do not open higher but consistently close higher. It's considered a precursor to a major uptrend. The inverse, in which three consecutive black candlesticks produce declining highs, is called three black soldiers (also three black crows) and predicts a significant decline. The Japanese have traditionally considered the crow to be an unlucky bird, and the black of the candlesticks, corresponding to the black of the crows, is considered bad luck for the markets, the beginning of a decline.

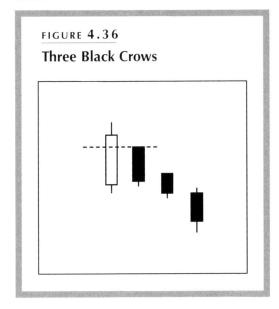

FIGURE **4.36**

Three Black Crows

On the other hand, three white soldiers appearing in an uptrend signals
resistance to higher prices. If the white
candlesticks become progressively smaller, the soldiers are "at a dead end" and
the market is likely to peak.

Three Black Crows

Three black crows is a classic indication
that a bear market has begun. This pattern occurs in an uptrend when there are
three consecutive and contiguous (no
gaps) black candlesticks. It's considered
to signal the start of a prolonged bear
market, but must occur at a relatively
high point for the pattern to hold. Note
also that if the first black candlestick gaps
upward, it is an osaekomi pattern and a
buy signal (see **Figure 4.36**).

Three White Soldiers

This pattern is the inverse of three black
crows, or three black soldiers. It commonly occurs when prices have been sliding
downward and the market is searching
for a bottom. The three consecutive white
candlesticks are relatively small, but indicate that the market is on better footing
and has bottomed out. The bottom is confirmed only if prices do not fall below the
first white candlestick (see **Figure 4.37**).

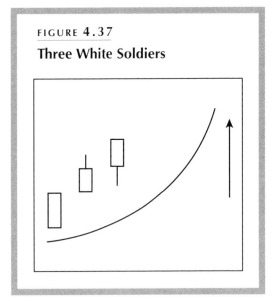

FIGURE **4.37**

Three White Soldiers

Three Gaps

As the name implies, three gaps is a series of three consecutive gaps. Market
wisdom says that in an uptrend you should "sell into three jumps up," whereas in
a downtrend, you should "buy on three poundings" because this often signals a
major trough. Pounding refers to a selling climax after the third gap downward,

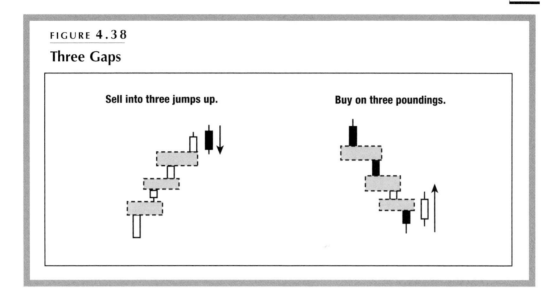

FIGURE 4.38

Three Gaps

Sell into three jumps up.

Buy on three poundings.

because the bears have sold all they have to sell.

When there is no overlap between the first day's and the second day's candlesticks, the gap between the two is referred to as a *window.* If a trend is breaking out of a holding pattern (moving significantly in either direction after a period of narrow moves), market wisdom says to follow the break. It's generally easier for the market to move in the direction of the break. The holding pattern will often close the window (actively trade at the gap), and it is common for prices to return to their original levels. This is considered a turning point in the market. The occurrence of three of these turning point gaps in a row is considered extremely significant (see **Figure 4.38**).

Three Methods

The legends of Munehisa Homma (and there are many) say that he had a third method he emphasized in addition to selling and buying: resting. If the market is trading in a narrow range, frequent buying and selling is unlikely to increase earnings. The more often you trade, the higher your costs (in the form of trading commissions) and the more likely you will take a loss. It's important at these times to rest—and knowing when to time your rests is just as important as knowing when to time your buying and selling.

The three methods pattern shown in **Figure 4.39** is the candlestick combination that tells you to rest. Three methods is also referred to as *three rules* and refers to the three choices of selling, buying, or resting.

FIGURE **4.39**

Three Methods

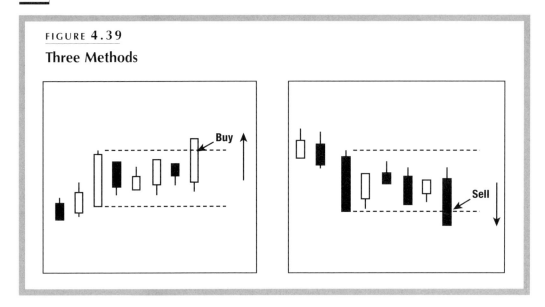

In the top pattern of Figure 4.39, an uptrend has produced a large white candlestick followed by harami patterns (either white or black). There is then the large white marubozu that exceeds the previous high to form a classic breakout from a holding pattern. The small harami patterns indicate a break in the action. The bottom of the large white candlestick has become a support line and the top a resistance line. Having broken through the resistance line, the pattern appears very bullish, but the important thing according to the three methods is to forgo either buying or selling until the price breaks out. The same is true of the inverse pattern. The bottom pattern in Figure 4.39 occurs in a downtrend and appears to be bearish, but you refrain from trading until the downward break.

—⁀⁀⁀—

OVER A CENTURY has passed since candlesticks took their present form. The fact that traders still use techniques that were pioneered in the Dojima rice markets is a testament to their value in illustrating the dynamic movements of price. While many technical indicators have been developed to measure trends, gauge momentum, and identify price targets, candlesticks serve as the foundation to which other techniques are applied. With a solid understanding of candle patterns, you will find that you are able to use conventional indicators with more precision and confidence. From Munehisa Homma's handmade candle charts to the sophisticated charting software we now enjoy, candlesticks continue to jump off the screen and let traders truly feel the rhythm of the markets.

CHAPTER 5

Price and Time

CONSTANCE BROWN

Price projection accuracy is possible when the concept of confluence is clearly understood. Confluence is a precise target zone derived from multiple price projections utilizing the natural expansion and contraction of price movement found in all markets and time horizons. The results form a mathematical grid that allows precise entry and exit strategies prior to any trade, with measurable risk-reward ratios. The concept of price confluence is then developed further to study confluence targets on the diagonal and vertical axes to determine time projections as developed by W.D. Gann. Gann accurately timed the start, magnitude, and duration of the crash of 1929.

Oil will be key to global equity indexes into the year 2012. These global equity indexes are being set up right now, allowing us to use the current market data in November 2006 to consider the implications before us.

Fibonacci Price Targets

To determine support or resistance price levels, many favor the use of Fibonacci retracements. But this method of subdividing a range is not used to its full potential. Basic applications simply define a market swing and subdivide the range between a selected price high and a price low into the ratios 0.618, 0.50, and 0.382. Unfortunately, this method overlooks the fact that markets have a natural expansion and contraction cycle. To traders, this means their Fibonacci targets will work in markets producing equality swings only; however, they will fail when the market is expanding or contracting relative to the range first selected.

When a contraction cycle influences a rally or a decline, the Fibonacci targets derived from a major price high and low will be exceeded. In a contracting cycle, traders are stopped out by entering the market too early, only to see the market reverse and take off without them. In an expansion cycle, the trader's entry level is never achieved. The market reverses, forcing a chase that increases the capital risk and compels the trader to establish a smaller position as the opportunity

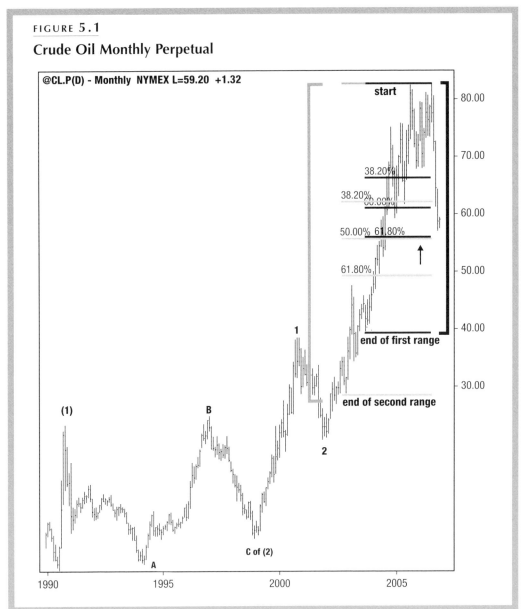

FIGURE 5.1

Crude Oil Monthly Perpetual

@CL.P(D) - Monthly NYMEX L=59.20 +1.32

slips away. For this reason many abandon the use of Fibonacci ratios; they feel they work only some of the time. In essence, they are right. But Fibonacci retracements are not the problem; it's their application that needs to be changed.

Figure 5.1 displays the current monthly continuous futures contract for crude oil. The monthly chart shows the recent market decline into November of 2006 and raises the first question: how far will this decline carry the market? Although sharp, this is a correction only if the scenario into 2012 is correct. This is the important pullback for the long-term horizon; therefore, we need precise targets to monitor. This can be done using multiple Fibonacci retracements.

When defining support for a correction in a rallying market, *always start at the top and only then select a low.* The first point selected should be zero. The first calculation within the range below zero should be a value of 38.2 percent, followed by 50 percent and 61.8 percent. The price low selected at the bottom of the range is 100 percent. Bloomberg does these calculations correctly, but TradeStation defines the first point selected as 100 and reverses the order. Recognizing a 38.2 percent and 61.8 percent ratio will fall on the same price levels within the range, it becomes understandable why different quote vendors have different opinions about how this should be programmed. However, most vendors force the user to remain generic and take away the user's ability to use the geometric proportions that develop within the market's data swings. Study the charts in this chapter and compare the steps to your vendor's tools, and it will become clear whether the vendor is backward. TradeStation does correct its logic in the Fibonacci expansion tool. CQG will draw its Fibonacci levels backward, away from the newest data in your chart. Setting the default to extend the lines across the entire screen will fix this.

You may find some vendors have a default value of 75 percent. Turn this off, as well as any other range offered as a default. Just use the primary three listed. It doesn't matter whether you add, subtract, multiply, or divide a Fibonacci value, because it will always produce another Fibonacci ratio. Therefore, we will calculate the other ratios by using multiple ranges. You'll see how this becomes important in Figure 5.4.

In Figure 5.1, the same price high is used for two different Fibonacci retracement calculations from different ranges. The lows selected are internal pivot points within the larger swing. Each is selected for a reason. Look for reversals that develop directional signals such as key reversals, gaps, and secondary retracements that begin strong swings within the larger trend. These internal milestones are markers, revealing the price levels the market is using to build future price swings. There are discernable mathematical relationships between one key market pivot and another that tie the pivots together within all time horizons.

The important price levels can be identified by starting at the "top" and then examining each pivot price low as a possible new range. In Figure 5.1, bold lines clarify the start, end, and resulting subdivisions within the range. The 61.8 ratio bisects $56. It is highlighted with an arrow. With just one Fibonacci grid in place, it's impossible to know whether the levels within the subdivided range are major or minor support.

Starting from the same high, a second low is selected, just under $30. The resulting subdivided range produces a 50 percent retracement near $56, which overlaps the 61.8 percent retracement from subdividing the first range. These different Fibonacci ratios that overlap form a *confluence target*, which is major support.

If this chart were inverted to represent a market in a downtrend, producing a sharp upward retracement, the calculations for resistance would always be started at the bottom, and then price highs would be selected. Starting retracements in this manner allows the internal swings to be examined. If you start in reverse, you are always forced to go straight to the market extreme top or major bottom, and the internal dynamics of the data would never be considered.

Price Projection Using Geometric Proportion

The monthly chart for crude oil futures in **Figure 5.2** includes a third range to the price low at the bottom of wave 2. The confluence zones that form define major support for this current decline at $56, $50, and $44. However, an important change was made in Figure 5.2. All the Fibonacci ranges start from a price high that truncates the spikes into the double top. That's done to clearly illustrate that the same starting point is always used for each range selected, but the price high itself is not always the best place to start. Sometimes it makes sense to truncate spikes when the majority of closing periods fail to record a close within the range of the spike. To simplify the chart, add a horizontal line at the confluence zones to mark major support targets. The targets in Figure 5.2 are near $56, $50, and $44. In practice, it is important to be aware of the width of the confluence zone and not just a single value within the target range.

A 14-period relative strength index (RSI) indicator was added to the bottom of Figure 5.2. An oscillator can confirm the key pivots. In this chart the 14-period RSI has two moving averages. The averages are calculated from the RSI, not from price. Moving averages serve as support and resistance levels for the indicator. Points P and Q mark two momentum extreme lows. Notice the character of these momentum lows. Both form a W pattern before the market successfully engages in a strong advance. Past character is nearly always repeated in the time frame being studied. So we know two things from reading points P and Q: First, this

FIGURE 5.2

Crude Oil Monthly Perpetual

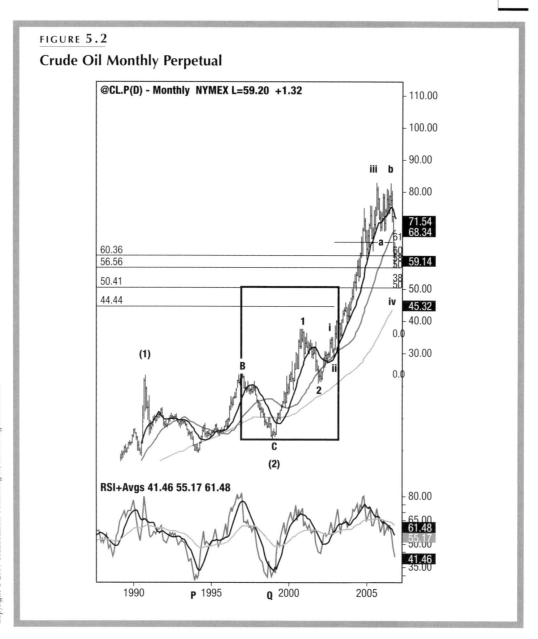

market likes to produce a complex W, so we need not take the reversal seriously until it does. Second, the market does not have such a pattern in place now. It can further be said this market may be oversold, but it has not defined a final bottom. Because the market is at $56, the confluence zone under the market

FIGURE 5.3

Crude Oil Monthly Perpetual

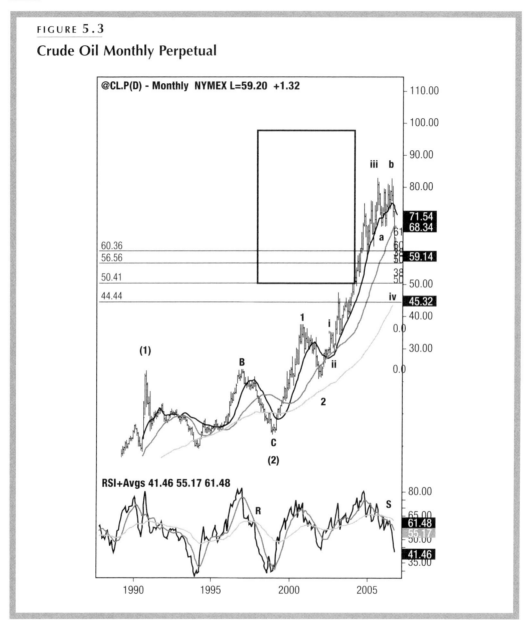

becomes the more likely target at $50. An extension would allow a move to $44, but just under this zone becomes the precise area at which the market should not trade if the opinion is correct that this market will make a full retracement back to the highs. Knowing where the market should not go gives us a clearly defined risk-reward ratio. It also clearly defines a level at which the implications for global rates and equities could change. For this reason, the decline is setting up the long-term picture in financial markets.

The confluence zone defining a price target at $50 is of particular interest. If you find the Elliott Wave Principle a challenge, this approach will be invaluable to you. Notice the swing low marked C, or the bottom of wave C of (2). A box is now drawn from this pivot low up to the confluence zone near $50.

In **Figure 5.3**, the box is moved without changing its height to project an equality move up from $50. The box defines a future market swing projection based on geometric proportion. There are other geometric proportions that require close study. As an example, the $50 level also marks the halfway or midpoint between a range from the high, marked iii, and the low, marked wave 2. This independent observation about a geometric proportion does not depend on a wave count, but it helps us train the eye to look for balance and proportion within the chart. The box high produces a price target near $97. Such a move would have serious consequences for the strong rallies developing since the 2002 or 2003 price lows in global equities.

In Figure 5.3, the RSI has two formations marked at points R and S. Point R is subtle. It is the RSI "kiss" just under the crossover point where the short average crosses down through the longer-period average of RSI. This exact junction should always be monitored because markets often produce strong moves from this internal momentum signal. At point S, the market forms a choppy top but breaks down because the RSI fails under the averages again. Do not look for divergences alone in RSI, because there is a wealth of information in the details.

Using RSI to Define Trend

In all time horizons, study the range traveled in the RSI. Notice in Figures 5.2 and 5.3 the RSI momentum highs challenge the 80 level. In November of 2006, the current market data was moving RSI toward 40. Bull markets track well above the RSI 65 level, whereas bear market rallies will top within the 60 to 65 range for RSI. Corrections in bull markets often stay above 40, but the declines in bear markets will break down below the 40 level. These range guidelines apply to all time horizons within a 14-period RSI. It is critical for the analyst to let the market show where these levels of respect form. As an example, one market may use 42 as support and develop a history at this level. Another market or time horizon may use 39. Allow a couple points for the market to tell you more precisely how it wants to operate by reading the chart from right to left closely. More information can be found in my book *Technical Analysis for the Trading Professional* (McGraw-Hill, 1999); illustrations are included to help detect transitions from bull to bear markets and vice versa within RSI.

In **Figure 5.4**, the box created in Figure 5.2 projects an equality swing from $50, showing a price target at $97.72. If we subdivide the box itself by the Fibonacci retracement tool, we discover the current highs fall on the 61.8 percent ratio. The fact that the market is respecting the internal Fibonacci ratios within our box bolsters greatly the confidence that it will respect our target at $97.72. It also confirms that we correctly used $50 as the midpoint of the rally. Although this is a target, it does not imply that oil will take a straight path.

The daily futures data for crude oil are shown in **Figure 5.5**. Using the same method demonstrated in the monthly data to project a rally target, we can define a midpoint for the decline developing in the daily data to project a possible bottom. If you use Elliott Wave analysis, pick the top of a fourth wave within wave iii down. If you are not familiar with Elliott Wave jargon, look for the middle swing that's the strongest. Then draw a horizontal line across the screen that bisects this strong swing into two fairly equal proportions above and below the data range.

This particular chart uses a small previous fourth wave within the decline, because that level is further challenged in a subsequent wave 4 bounce. Back-to-back fourth waves are always critical milestones. Repeat the steps to draw a box from the start of the swing to the horizontal line, marking a midpoint within the decline. Draw a second box of the same size and move it so that the top of the box is at the midpoint line to produce an equality price swing down. The target is again $50. This is the same target as the one derived from the monthly data taken from entirely different pivot levels. Most assuredly, the $50 area is extremely important. Further subdivide the box by Fibonacci ratios. We find the current lows are on a 61.8 percent relationship of the box height at $56. This is a repeating price level that shows we have a confidence in the price grid this market is defining as support. (Box width has no meaning and should not be used for time projections.) The reason these repeating levels form, at exact prices from different internal data, is due to harmonic intervals forming within the market swings.

The RSI in Figure 5.5 provides additional value. Momentum indicators that have been normalized, forcing them between a range of zero and one hundred, contribute their own message about support and resistance. Study the indicator's performance from right to left within the chart. In this chart, a horizontal band

FIGURE 5.4

Crude Oil Monthly Perpetual

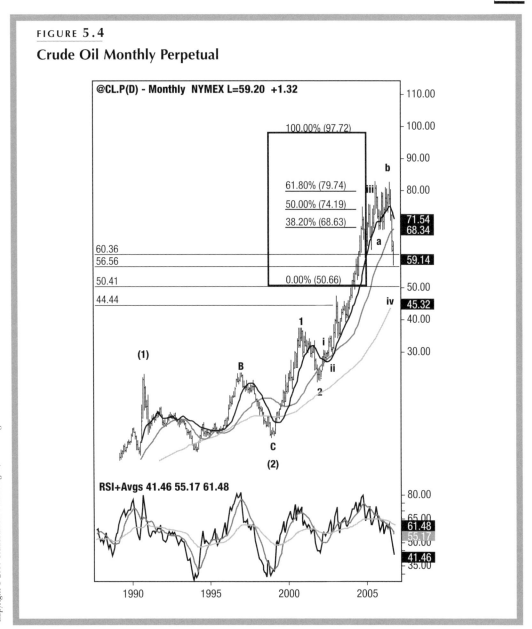

has been drawn around the RSI 45 level. The last swing up in the indicator near 45 produced the price high marked wave iv up. RSI tested the same area in August 2006, when the market defined wave ii up. Often RSI movement exhibiting similar amplitude displacements will help to confirm that a wave count is still in the

FIGURE 5.5

Crude Oil Daily

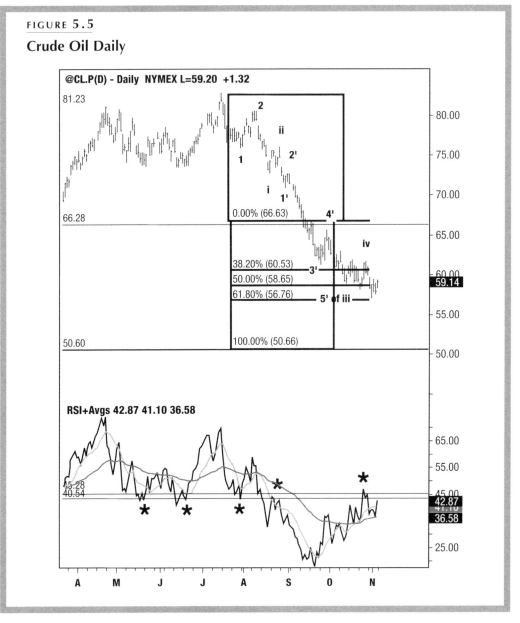

same degree. (Waves ii and iv produced similar momentum swings to the same 45 level in Figure 5.5.) The asterisks show RSI used the 45 level to define support in May, June, and July 2006. The breakdown and subsequent test and failure under this band was very significant in August. When the resistance zone in RSI was

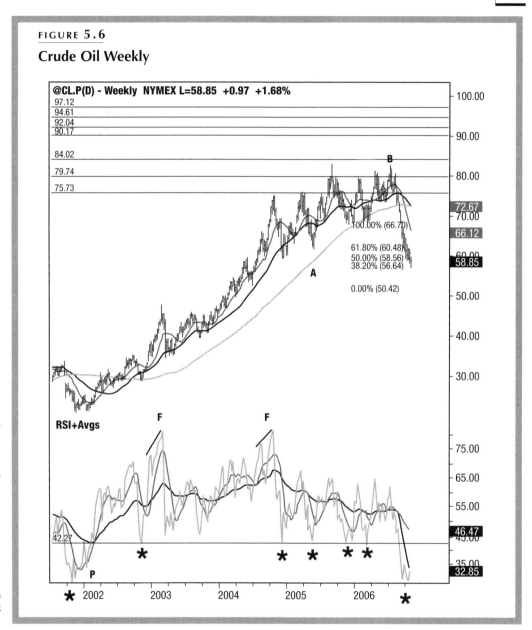

FIGURE 5.6

Crude Oil Weekly

challenged and failed in October, this offered a warning that an extension in the decline could form, allowing the target at $56.76 to be realized. When RSI exceeds this band at 45 in the daily chart, we will have confirmation that wave 3 down in the corrective decline is complete. Wave 4 up will not exceed the midpoint at

$66.63 if oil is going to fall further toward $50 in the intermediate picture.

All three charts—monthly, weekly, and daily—should be given consideration before forming a strong opinion about a market. The intraday periods of greatest interest will compare time ratios of one to four. Weigh the evidence in each time horizon independently and then consider any conflicts or similarities across all the charts. Within each time horizon, the 14-period RSI can give critical information about the position of the market now relative to key milestones of the past for the similar time horizon under review. In **Figure 5.6**, showing the weekly futures data for crude oil, the decline into November 2006 has formed an RSI displacement equal to the extremes that developed in 2001. The character in 2001 shows a W formation that was not the final bottom. A bounce developed that was followed by a decline to pivot P. This was the start of the major rally.

The opinion we considered from the daily chart that a bounce up should then lead to a new low toward $50 is an ideal scenario that fits the RSI position we see at point P in the weekly chart. The weekly chart is an incomplete decline, adding weight to the earlier scenarios of the daily chart work.

The asterisks under the 40 zone in RSI reinforce the RSI range guideline that bull markets often hold this area in pullbacks. Notice that the market then produced rallies that failed to let RSI exceed 65. That is the warning to take notice that a bull market is shifting into a bear market.

It is important to know when RSI makes a new extreme displacement. In Figure 5.6, the RSI held the support level near 45 from 2002 through early 2006. *Old horizontal support levels will be retested in the RSI.* Knowing this helps paint a picture that a swing up with another sharp break could be the setup that allows RSI to diverge by holding the old support zone near 45.

Using the Composite Index to Detect RSI Divergence Failures

In Figure 5.6, the two Fs over the RSI momentum extremes highlight one of the weaknesses of RSI. The indicator is prone to fail to develop divergence to the price data at key market reversals. The cause of this failure is in the normalization of the indicator formula. A solution is to couple an indicator with the RSI that has not been normalized. The Composite Index is a formula I developed to identify divergence failures within the RSI. The formula is protected by copyright

The Composite Index

The TradeStation Format

Create two functions in EasyLanguage first. The first is a 9-period momentum study of RSI. This can be written as

RSIDelta = MOMENTUM(RSI(CLOSE,14),9)

Then a smoothed short period RSI is created,

RSIsma = AVERAGE(RSI(CLOSE,3),3)

The indicator can then be created:

INDICATOR: COMPOSITE INDEX

Plot1(RSIdelta+RSIsma,"Plot1");

Plot2(average((plot1),13),"Plot2");

Plot3(average((plot1),33),"Plot3");

The MetaStock Format

A = RSI(14)-Ref(RSI(14),-9)+Mov(RSI(3),3,S);

Plot1 = Mov(A,13,S);

Plot2 = Mov(A,33,S);

A;Plot1;Plot2;

The history behind the development of this formula was recounted in "The Derivative Oscillator," which appeared in the Winter 1993–Spring 1994 issue of the Market Technicians Association's *Journal of Technical Analysis*. Copies of the article can be obtained at my company's Web site: Aerodynamic Investments Inc, www.aeroinvest.com.

by the Library of Congress, but the time has come to release the formula because it has unique properties that traders value. The formula warns when RSI is failing to detect market reversals so that the trader is not caught by the change in trend. It has been used in all financial markets and time horizons for more than twelve years.

The Composite Index was developed to solve the divergence failure problem in the RSI, but its ability to provide specific horizontal levels of support within the indicator adds to its value. The Composite Index takes the normalized for-

FIGURE 5.7

Crude Oil Weekly

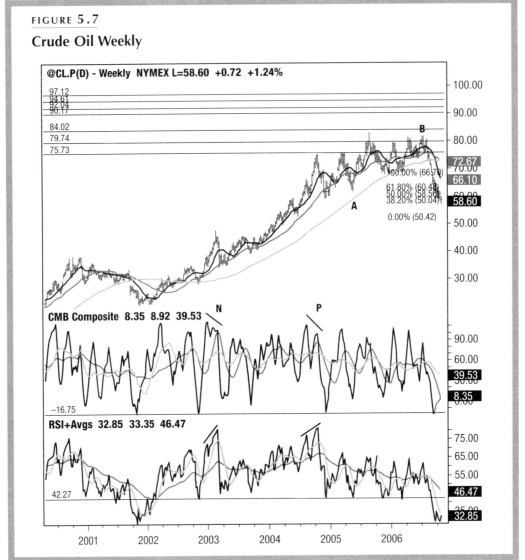

mula of RSI and removes the normalization range restrictions. In **Figure 5.7**, the divergence to RSI in the Composite Index is seen at points N and P. The formula for the Composite Index uses an embedded momentum calculation with a short-term RSI smoothed. The concept of embedding a momentum study can be used within MACD (moving average convergence/divergence), but stochastics should not use this concept in fast formulas. If slow %D is used, this concept can be applied, but extensive testing is recommended, as this is not how I used the formula to gain confidence under fire in all financial markets in a real-time environment.

Detrending

Another way to experiment with divergences between normalized formulas and unrestricted indicators is to detrend simple spreads between moving averages. This method is not as effective as the Composite Index for detecting RSI divergence failures, but the spread between averages has properties that should not be overlooked.

In Figure 5.7, the horizontal lines over the market are Fibonacci confluence levels derived from multiple Fibonacci expansion swings. Selection of a swing from price low to high defines the range used to create proportional swings of 61.8 percent, 100 percent, and 161.8 percent. These are then projected from a subsequent low that immediately follows the range selected. Multiple projections derived from different ranges, but projected from the same pivot low, developed price resistance zones at $84, $90, $92, $94.50, and $97.12. The latter confirmed the geometric calculation we developed in Figure 5.3. It is important to notice the spread between these zones. The $84 level would be an ideal spot for oil to fail in a consolidation that needs a complex pattern to develop. But in excess of $84, oil would run quickly toward $90, because there are few lines of resistance to interfere. It becomes clear that we need to monitor momentum indicators at these key targets to decipher the actual path oil will take as it works toward $97.

In **Figure 5.8** the monthly chart is displayed on the far left, with the weekly and daily data compared in the middle and far right. The oscillator extreme is the difference between two averages plotted as an oscillator. When the averages cross, the oscillator crosses through the zero horizontal line. Therefore, the spread differential between the averages is plotted as a displacement from zero, which is another example of detrending. The three time horizons are always compared together. The monthly chart displays an extreme negative displacement. The daily chart shows it is neither overbought nor oversold. The weekly chart might be suggesting that one will see a new price low after a price rebound. The reasoning behind this opinion is that a new momentum extreme developed at Y and we should expect the old extreme, at X, to be retested in the future. The Composite Index is a much better measure of this type of retesting pattern into old lines of horizontal support or resistance. Such a retest often produces a new price low.

FIGURE 5.8

Crude Oil Monthly, Weekly, Daily

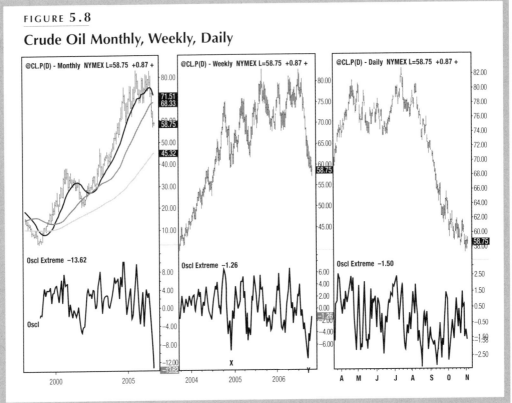

Everything we monitor as analysts should contribute to our inner barometer or intuitive gut feeling. It's like having two inner poles: One pole weighs bullish evidence; the other, our negative pole, measures the mounting evidence to sell. As evidence builds on one side, conflicts can develop to offset the results. When there's a conflict, we stand aside. This balance becomes the art of technical analysis. All that we do should contribute to our sense of probability based on the historical outcome of our technical tools. Therefore, methods that provide valuable information and use different techniques can enhance our accuracy.

Figure 5.9 shows a one-month chart for the 3-month Eurodollar (bar chart) and an inverted one-month view of Brent crude oil (line chart). The inverse correlation shows periods when the 3-month Eurodollar would lead the oil market or provide significant divergence to raise questions about the relationship between these two markets. As in 2003, when a highly correlated or inversely correlated market is leading, it's a good opportunity to examine the leading market to gain a jump on the market of real interest such as oil. If we could determine

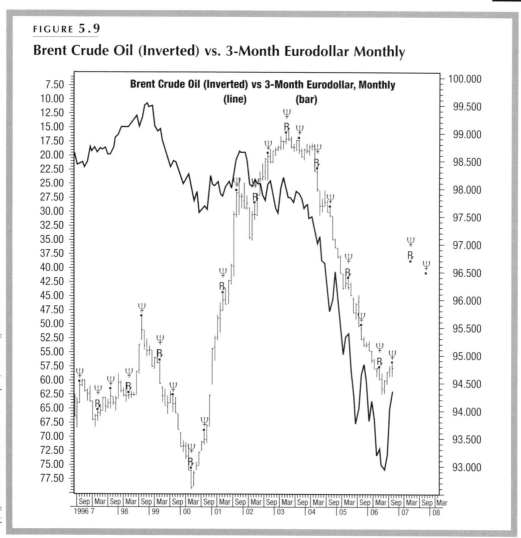

FIGURE 5.9

Brent Crude Oil (Inverted) vs. 3-Month Eurodollar Monthly

the calendar window when a market turn may develop in the leading market, it would offer an even greater advantage.

W.D. Gann

Defining the dates for high-risk market reversals can be done. However, the methods are far more sophisticated than the conventional cycle analysis commonly in practice today. Markets expand and contract along both price and time axes. Most people use fixed-period cycles in which a constant interval is sought to connect market price lows. This is a method that depends on finding a correlation after the fact with hope it will repeat in the future. This method can never reveal the underlying cause of the cycle, and fixed-interval cycles cannot contend with expansion and contraction phases within the market's natural progression.

In Figure 5.9, a time study has been added to this intermarket chart to introduce the cycle analysis of W.D. Gann into the discussion. The analytic work of W.D. Gann (William Delbert Gann, 1878–1955) is widely misrepresented, causing much confusion for students of cycle analysis. The man himself wrote in a veiled language all his own, making his work even more difficult to understand. But he had compelling reasons for writing in such a manner.

The interest in understanding W.D. Gann's methods are growing as technical analysis gains acceptance around the world. In the 1920s, Gann reportedly made $56 million trading stocks and commodities. He wrote several astonishing public forecasts. His most well known is the report for 1929 which detailed the timing, duration, and magnitude of the Crash of 1929. Although his ability to forecast the crash is impressive, it is exceeded by his further advice to his clients to aggressively buy stocks at the lows of the Great Depression in 1932.

One of the most useful original Gann charts to study is his May Soybeans chart. It is a hand-drawn chart (posted in the Chart Gallery on my Web site at www.aeroinvest.com) demonstrating Gann's use of confluence along horizontal, vertical, and diagonal axes. Confluence further forms from multiple methods along the diagonal, which is rarely applied or discussed correctly in today's books concerning W.D. Gann. The start of the downtrend is not the price high, but the small secondary high that marks the start of the major decline. It is at this secondary retracement before a significant trend change develops that his methods converge, forming a confluence target in price, time, and geometry. Gann often stated that the actual start of a new trend is not at the conclusion of the prior campaign or trend. He viewed the first retracement that fails to make a new high or low as the start of the new trend and a safer entry for trading. This realization often occurs to more experienced traders. Patience and risk management are two reasons Gann was so successful.

Gann was the most sophisticated practitioner of confluence analysis. The Fibonacci target price zones we explored earlier cannot answer the question of when the target zone will be realized and which major target is the final pivot. Yet Gann was able to identify the price, duration of the trend, and timing for the start and end. This level of clarity is impressive.

The written forecasts prove Gann's methodology, but then the new student faces a major obstacle to learning his methods of market analysis. Most books on the market today contain the work of John L. Gann and not the methods of his father. Traders then mistakenly apply the son's methods with poor results and abandon their desire to learn more. Confidence was further eroded when John Gann claimed his father was a fraud and did not have the financial assets to substantiate the trading gains within the United States. These questions overshadowing W.D. Gann can all be explained.

A closer look reveals that John may have been a bitter man carrying a grudge to his grave. Gann divorced John's mother, Sadie, in 1937. When Gann married again in 1944, his third wife, Londi, was thirty years younger. John apparently never accepted the union. Add to this the fact that John L. Gann inherited no cash upon his father's passing—it passed to his surviving wife, Londi—and you have all the motive needed for why the father and son did not see eye to eye.

The most important question needing clarification is whether Gann's money trail can be tracked. It was common practice of high-net-worth individuals to take funds out of the United States to avoid income tax, which was staggering during the Depression. During this period of high taxation, Gann frequently flew to the Cayman Islands out of Miami. His lifestyle substantiated his trading success as he maintained his Wall Street office through the Great Depression and kept his employees on a time-share basis throughout this difficult period. He was also one of a handful of businessmen able to own two planes and retain a pilot during this historic economic contraction.

Gann's pilot, Elinor Smith, worked for him for more than twenty years. Their many flights included Gann's sojourns to the Cayman Islands. Elinor Smith's fascinating stories substantiate and clarify Gann's transfer of funds out of the United States. My interview with Elinor Smith is the most interesting I've ever conducted. She represents the history of aviation. She was the youngest professional pilot, with a pilot's license signed by none other than the father of aviation, Wilbur Wright. Gann and Elinor spent months preparing for her solo flight attempt to Rome from New York City. Clearly, Gann had hoped to find a route by air to Egypt to pursue his research (a connection that will be explained more clearly in a moment). Unfortunately, because of the exorbitant costs during the deepening depression, the plane was eventually sold, to Amelia Earhart no less. The lost opportunity to break Charles Lindburgh's record for the longest solo flight was Elinor's greatest disappointment, though at one time she held every aviation record within the continental area of the United States. Gann never forgot this and upon his passing, he gave Elinor a gift of tremendous value, the significance of which she admitted was hard to fully comprehend. Without even knowing it, she held the key to Gann's methods. Some day Smith's full story needs to be told, but her greatest contribution to the followers of W.D. Gann was the old black leather suitcase secured by two leather straps, which became a gift to me after the interview.

To understand the chart work of W.D. Gann, one must study the man. As his obituary states, Gann was a 32nd degree Freemason of the Scottish Rite Order. The suitcase Smith passed to me was filled with the source graphics taught by the Freemasons that Gann applied to his chart work. The teachings of the Freemasons are so pivotal to Gann's market analysis that he draws the insignia of the Freemasons on the cover of his book *The Tunnel Thru the Air* (Lambert-Gann Publishing, 1927). The diving airplanes turn into set squares. The insignia itself is on the bottom of the front cover at an exact 61.8 percent ratio from the left corner. Gann's pool of knowledge from the Freemasons was the source of his market analysis methodology, and the son would have no part of the years of study required to master the principles and concepts.

The Scottish Rite has a number of various side orders such as the Royal Arch, Rose-Croix, Rosicrucian Fellowship, and Knights Templar. The European orders guarded their secret teachings and Greater Mysteries with punishment of death should one openly reveal the content. The teachings can be traced back to the Egyptian priests who trained Pythagoras and Plato, from whom the philosophies of modern-day civilization emerged. Pythagoras is credited with the discovery, around 580 BC, of the golden mean ratio of 1.618 through sound harmonics.

As a 32nd degree mason, Gann's standing was only one degree less than the leader of multiple lodges, and he was bound by the ancient custom of secrecy. Therefore, in order to openly teach his market analysis, which draws on the Freemason teachings, he wrote in a veiled language and used his son's work to disguise his own. The student armed with this background can discern in his writings the valiant effort he made to reveal all he knew. Without this clarification, the market brilliance of W.D. Gann becomes lost in a tangled veil of mystery and confusion. It is ironic that the material within Gann's suitcase was passed into Smith's hands and then mine, because the order's teachings are denied to women.

Gann traveled to Egypt not only to study the historical prices of cotton, but also—and primarily—to further his understanding of the ancient quadrivium. The word is derived from the Latin roots *quad* (four) and *via* (ways, roads): a crossing of four roads of study. In medieval universities, the quadrivium consisted of the four subjects: arithmetic, astronomy, geometry, and music. These disciplines remain within the body of knowledge passed on by the Freemason orders. *Gann's market analysis incorporates all four disciplines.*

The subject of music within the quadrivium was originally the classical subject of harmonics, in particular the study of the proportions between the musical intervals of a monochord, which can be translated as the harmonic proportions within a range. In modern applications, the quadrivium may be considered the study of number and its relationship to physical space or time: arithmetic is pure number, geometry is number in space, music is number in time, and astronomy is number in space and time.

Time Analysis

Gann was a master of confluence cycle analysis. Few students of Gann realize the first edition of his book *How to Make Profits Trading in Commodities* (W.D. Gann & Son, Inc., 1941) describes different charts than does his revised 1951 edition (Lambert-Gann Publishing Company Inc.) in distribution today. There are so few copies of the 1941 edition that they are hand corrected. Gann's time analysis goes much further than mapping market turns. His method mapped the social, economic, and geopolitical cycles defining periods of prosperity and contraction. In the 1941 edition, he wrote a segment titled "Why Hitler Will Lose the War," about the coming war with Germany *before the United States entered WWII.*

Gann's 1951 release of *How to Make Profits in Commodities* not only removed the commentary with his opinions on the war but also changed some of the charts he used for his illustrations. Why? The charts he used in the second edition to replace those in the first proved that the same methods still applied in different examples a decade later. Furthermore, the advanced student will discover *the two books together* reveal his application of sacred geometry to mark inflection dates and that there are measurable harmonic relationships between significant market turns. Because markets respect the mathematics of harmonic frequency ratios, it explains why a market can develop a perfect signal in momentum indicators that becomes a failure. The signals that develop in charts outside these key confluence points must be ignored as they are out of phase or should be considered disharmonic signals of low probability. Seeking confirmation of signals across different charting periods and finding inflection points with target confluences in the same chart all serve to find the harmonic key the market is respecting whether the trader is aware of this concept of harmonic relationships or not. Sadly, because of the obscure manner in which Gann released his methodology, many of the books in print today fail to recognize these essential concepts that enhance many of today's technical studies.

Gann's methods warn that the years 2008 to 2012 will be difficult ones. There will also be an economic contraction that will be felt globally between 2019 and 2021. The cycle of bear markets is actually one of the easier time targets to uncover. But it takes discipline to master the methods to detect precise target dates at defined price levels. Gann was the master of the conceptual use of confluence zones. The use of multiple Fibonacci calculations provided an introduction to the formation of confluence targets. But Gann's use of confluence was far more sophisticated because his work viewed confluence as the intersection where horizontal, vertical, and diagonal projections converge. Horizontal is price, vertical is time, and diagonal is geometric space. In Figure 5.9, the 3-month Eurodollar displays one type of time cycle Gann used. It's called a retrograde cycle. The bullet over a price bar does not mean a projected swing high; it denotes a time target. To understand the cycle displayed in this chart, a description of retrograde is required.

Retrograde Motion

The illustration in **Figure 5.10** is a time-lapse photograph of Mars's motion across the sky, ending on July 26, 1997—a celestial sphere as seen from a fixed point on Earth. The constellations are drawn to offer a reference point. Such a discussion fits the quadrivium's study of astronomy, which is number in space and time. Keep in mind that this is not astrology, which has subjective interpretation. We are looking only at the factual scientific cycle and its repeatable occurrence. The National Astronomical Space Administration (NASA) Web site is a gold mine of scientific and historical reference data that Gann analysts can use.

Two observations concerning the planets were very difficult for astronomers of the Middle Ages to explain. The usual motion of planets as they "wandered" on the celestial sphere was eastward against the background stars. This is called "direct motion." However, it was observed that at times the planets moved westward for a period on the celestial sphere; this movement was termed "retrograde motion." The second observation that was difficult to explain in the Middle Ages was that planets were brighter at certain times than others.

A major reason for the difficulty of explaining these phenomena was the influence of the Greek philosopher Aristotle on medieval thought. His philoso-

FIGURE 5.10

Geocentric Path of Mars (East to West Direct Motion)

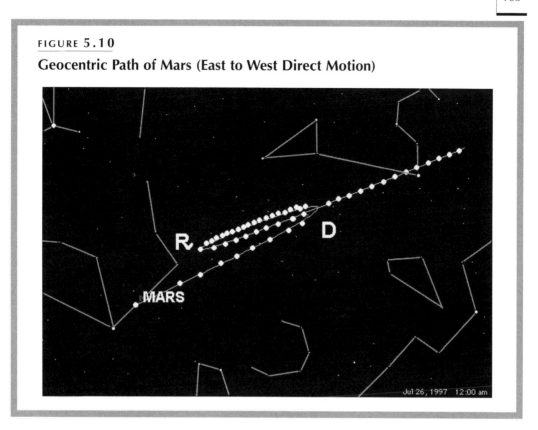

phy held that the heavens were more perfect than Earth and that objects in the heavens were unchanging. The representative image used to denote heaven and earth is the circle framed within the square. This is a Gann charting pattern that most equate with his famous squaring of price and time.

The Copernican system banished the idea that Earth was the center of the solar system, thereby giving an immediate and simple explanation for both the varying brightness of the planets and retrograde motion. The planets in such a system naturally vary in brightness because they are not always the same distance from Earth. The retrograde motion could be explained in terms of geometry—a planet with a smaller orbit moves faster and appears to overtake the slower planet. This is similar to two speeding trains heading in the same direction on parallel tracks. As the faster train catches and passes the slower train, there is a brief period of time where the slower train appears to be moving backward. It never actually does.

In Figure 5.10, the perceived path of Mars shifts from tracking east to west at the point marked ℞. This is the astronomical symbol marking Mars's entry into a period of retrograde motion. When the planet appears to track from east to west again as perceived from Earth, the point of change is marked "D" to indicate Mars has returned to direct motion.

In Figure 5.9, the planet glyph for Neptune is Ψ. When this symbol is notated on the chart, the planet is returning to direct motion. When Neptune enters a period of retrograde, the glyph convention is Ψ_R. The time bullets throughout the chart show a correlation to inflection points within the Eurodollar's history. These are not fixed interval cycles.

Gann's written astrological discussions always use the phrase "the study of natural cycles." This is but one simple example to offer a conceptual introduction to the study of natural cycles. Time, or the vertical line of resistance, was the most important trigger for Gann. But our discussion is not complete until confluence is detected in the vertical, horizontal, and diagonal. Before moving on, it's important to notice in Figure 5.10 that a natural cycle is not a fixed-period cycle. It should also be understood that each component within vertical, horizontal, and diagonal analyses has its own method of creating confluence target zones through the use of multiple projections. This in turn serves to increase the probability of each component.

In **Figure 5.11**, we see a different retrograde cycle plotted within a weekly Brent crude chart. This chart maps the retrograde cycle of Mercury. This chart has the dimensions of horizontal and diagonal analysis we need to explore next.

Running behind the chart's data are dotted horizontal lines. Focus on these lines as you compare the price data directly under or above solid black blocks throughout the chart. These horizontal lines are harmonic inflection points, all radiating from a single price pivot we will look at more closely in **Figure 5.12**. At this stage, just study the numerous highlighted pivot points to observe how this market is respecting the background grid in place. The grid does not show equal spacing between each line through the range of the chart. Another trait, which requires an astute eye for geometric proportion to detect, is a repeating pattern that forms with increased spacing at the higher price levels compared to the grid's spacing nearer the bottom of the chart. There is a logarithmic function to the grid. For now, accept that the market is showing some respect toward the horizontal grid. We will return to the discussion of these lines.

Figure 5.11 is partially shaded to help emphasize the diagonal lines through the chart. In the middle of the chart are two parallel lines forming a channel. The price high, near $80, demonstrates Gann's confluence in all three dimen-

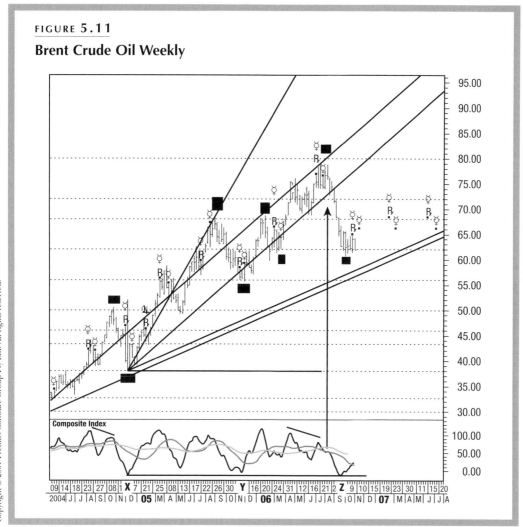

FIGURE **5.11**

Brent Crude Oil Weekly

black box is highlighting the price target on the horizontal dotted line. Diagonal is the geometric measure. The price high is testing the upper diagonal channel running through this chart. Furthermore, we have the Composite Index forming the kiss under the rollover of two moving averages following divergence that was discussed earlier for the RSI in Figure 5.3. Look at points X, Y, and Z, as well, in the Composite Index. The indicator gives permission to buy or add at the support zones tested by the market on the dotted lines. Momentum indicators work best when they are studies at specific price targets to offer permission to take action. In this chart, the price high demonstrates the point at which everything comes together at the same time and place, providing a high-confidence sell signal. Understanding how the diagonal lines were created is critical to the outcome because these lines are set at precise geometric angles.

Gann Angles

The weekly chart we just examined in Figure 5.11 was actually a close-up of the weekly Brent crude chart in Figure 5.12. At first glance, it looks extremely complex, but if you looked at a chart with multiple Fibonacci retracements without guidance, it too would trigger the same first impression as a Gann chart. Breaking down the components so that one knows what to focus on changes the entire complexion of these charts.

The diagonal lines are projected Gann angles. Many software vendors offer Gann angles, but they are only speed lines unless precise angles are used. If you take a price low for a stock trading under $25 and plot a line with a growth rate of $1 for one unit of time, or 1×1, you would draw a 45° angle within the chart. On a computer screen, it would not look like a 45° angle, because the number of pixels on the width of your screen versus the height is not equal. When you use a Gann angle tool without precise angles defined, you are only creating speed lines that can be used for acceleration analysis. It is not Gann analysis. The process becomes more difficult when you desire a precise 45° angle in a market like the Nikkei Stock Index—it is not realistic to use $1 versus one unit of time for the rise.

But there is a way to solve the problem. Figure 5.12 shows a series of boxes whose corners are connected, creating a cross within each box. Because there are fifty-two weeks in a year, the weekly chart is using the square of fifty-two. But if you look closely at the price scale, it is clear that one box does not cover a price range of $52. Multiples or *proportional divisions* can be used and the angles within the original square of fifty-two still retained if only a single box were displayed mapping fifty-two weeks along the horizontal, versus $52 against the vertical. Although one large box is not useful, four boxes and sixteen boxes still produce the same angled lines across the chart. When the internal corners are connected, the grid produces both positive and negative true geometric angles of 45°. Therefore, a simple solution is to draw the Gann boxes, establish a true 45° line, and then remove the boxes. The outside frame of each box is a fixed cycle. Gann would use the cycle formed by the Gann boxes in several ways, including further

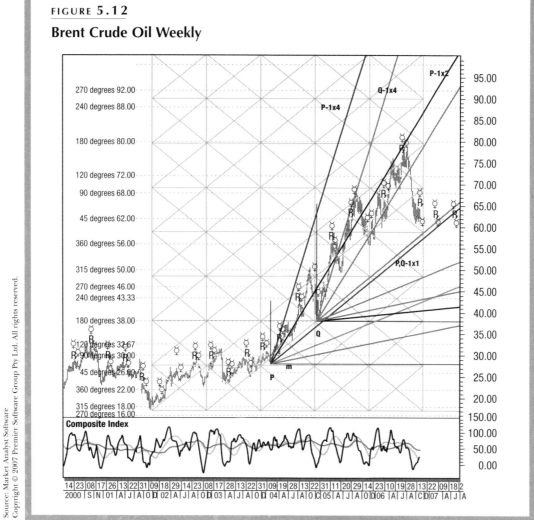

FIGURE 5.12

Brent Crude Oil Weekly

subdivision of the square by thirds or eighths. However, for this discussion we will not venture down that road.

The Gann angles of interest are the 1×1 (45°), 1×2 (63.75°), 1×4 (75°), and 1×8 (82.5°), and occasionally we need the 1×16 (86.25°). For declines, we again consider 1×1, then 2×1 (26.25°), 4×1 (15°), 8×1 (7.5°), and, on occasion, 16×1 (3.75°). Sometimes the 1×3 and 3×1 are used with angles of 71.25° and 18.75°, respectively. Gann discusses these angles as "moving-averages," which can cause confusion in modern context because computers allow us to chart true moving averages derived from price or indicators. In this discussion, referencing Gann angles will serve us better.

The starting placement of the Gann angles in Figure 5.12 will raise a question because they are not projected from blatant price lows. Gann teaches that a sharp decline, as an example, does not begin a new trend upward at the price low of the decline. The price low is the conclusion of the prior bear market campaign. The start of the new trend of greatest interest is the first secondary pullback. In Figure 5.12, Brent crude was nearly becoming a parabolic rise, so the Gann angles were projected from pivots marked P and Q. Why? Notice point Q is on a vertical and horizontal support in reference to the box. But it also has a Mercury retrograde target in the vertical axis for time. Had you created a Fibonacci confluence grid in the chart using the methods defined earlier, this area would have been major support.

We also have one other clue that this is a key price pivot. Scan the horizontal line near Q to the left. Under this level is a dotted line that becomes visible at the far left with the label "180 degrees at $38." The 180° notation is important because point Q is a confluence zone within the chart. Point P was selected after setting Q, because the radiating line marked P-1×4 tracked the price trend near *m* in the first swing up from point P. The Gann angle P-1×1 also supports the minor pivot at point *m*. The rise is identical from each pivot so a channel forms. The market high stopped directly under P-1×2, or under the channel capped with a bold black line. The actual line it fails at is radiating from a start at point P. Gann was right to say secondary pivots will prove to be of paramount importance later in the trend.

The channel the market is declining toward in the most recent data is formed by the 45° angles radiating from points P and Q. The 45° angles are always of great importance. Notice that the current market data has not reached the border of the nearest underlying box frame. Then notice that the outer wall of the box coincides with when Mercury returns to direct motion. This will give confluence in the vertical and horizontal, but not the diagonal, so it is of lesser importance than the confluence that formed into the data high near $80.

Finally, with respect to Figure 5.12, we made careful note to study the fine horizontal dotted lines the market was respecting in Figure 5.11. The same lines in soft gray are present in Figure 5.12 and have labels on the far-left frame of the chart. The most recent data up to November 2006 show the market is respecting the 45° support line at $62 for Brent crude. This is a harmonic series of price targets generating upward from a single price pivot. The calculations are derived

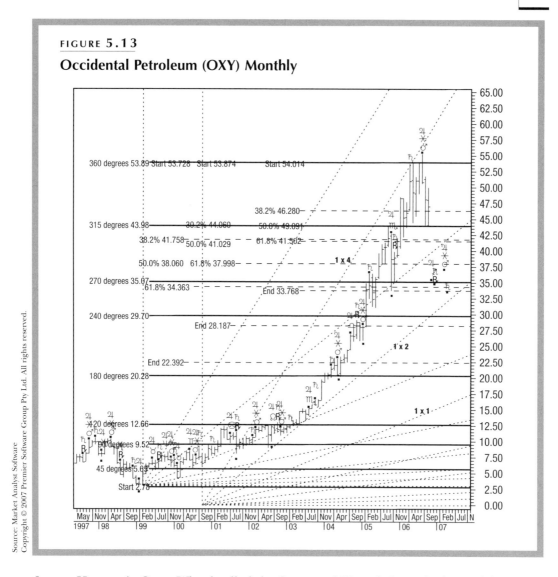

FIGURE 5.13

Occidental Petroleum (OXY) Monthly

from a Harmonic Gann Wheel called the Square of Nine. It is a calculator with very special properties.

Figure 5.13 displays a monthly chart of Occidental Petroleum (OXY). Cycles other than retrograde have been added because confluence is being sought. The Gann angles are again used, but this time one is projected from the zero line, which aligns with a secondary retracement above in the data series. This is a technique described in Gann's original stock market course and a good place for a new student to begin. We can see the 1×4 angle (75°) bisects a horizontal line near $54 at the high. Look to the far left of this line and you will see the label "360 degrees at $53.89." The angled degrees we want from the Gann Wheel calculator are 45°, 90°, 120°, 180°, 240°, 270°, 315°, and finally a full cycle at 360°. This is a harmonic series that contains some of the Fibonacci ratios we first studied. All harmonic scales contain Fibonacci ratios, but not all Gann projections are Fibonacci numbers.

The reason for this is fully explained in my presentation called Great Market Technicians of the 21st Century: Galileo, Fibonacci, and Beethoven. This is a multimedia presentation developed for the Silver Anniversary of the Market Technicians Association. (The visuals for this presentation can be found at www. aeroinvest.com in our chart gallery. The full presentation with audio and video was donated to the Market Technicians Association after 9/11 to help rebuild the library. It can be purchased from them at www.mta.org.) The taped lecture will not give you better market targets, but it will give a better understanding of why the Gann Wheel is a harmonic calculator and proves key market swings have harmonic relationships. The hard angles at 45°, 90°, 180°, 270°, and 360° from the wheel are important, but none more so than a full cycle at 360°, which will have a natural logarithm relationship to the first number used to create the series. In Figure 5.13, the market high shows in respect to the 360° projection. It then falls swiftly to the target line below it at 315°.

These charts demonstrate that the Gann Wheel can be plotted directly on the market data, making Gann analysis far less labor intensive than it once was by hand. (More information about the step-by-step methods to obtain price targets from a Gann Wheel is available without charge on my Web site at www .aeroinvest.com.)

We conclude where we began, because the decline in OXY to the Gann level marked 315° on the far left is also a Fibonacci confluence zone. A multiple overlap developed confluence with a 38.2 percent and 50 percent retracement forming at $43. The void of targets between $54 and $44 gave early warning about the character of the decline that would develop.

Clearly, the confluence zones we first developed using just Fibonacci ratios were the conceptual beginnings of something much greater. But the study of Gann is a journey down many rabbit holes of knowledge. Gann analysts will find a book written by Manly P. Hall, *The Secret Teachings of All Ages* (Philosophical Research Society, 1998), to be of great interest in their pursuit of some of the core teachings of Freemasons. We begin to see astounding results from our charts and beg to understand why this is so. Gann was applying the secret teachings from all ages that led to a greater wisdom. When the many fields of study within the quadrivium become clear within the analytic methods of W.D. Gann, the revelation becomes humbling, because we understand why Gann restated the words of Solomon: "Knowledge is of more value than gold."

CHAPTER 6

Unlocking Gann

DAVID E. BOWDEN

W.D. Gann made his reputation by making market calls long before the events took place. Some of these calls proved to be amazingly prescient. Some of them were wrong. To publish a market top, say, twelve months in advance and have your forecast proved correct is every bit as thrilling as winning a gold medal at the Olympics—and probably rarer, too. To know where the market is going presently is hard enough. Is it at a top? Is it a bottom, or is it in the middle of a run? These questions are difficult enough to answer about the next several weeks, never mind going twelve months out. Indeed, sometimes it's a big enough challenge just to have a solid opinion *after* an event without being asked to make projections that hinge on events that haven't happened yet. In 1989, for example, some twenty-six years after the fact, Gore Vidal was asked what he believed would have been the outcome had Khrushchev and not Kennedy been assassinated in 1963. After some thought, he replied, "With history one can never be certain, but I think I can safely say that Aristotle Onassis would not have married Mrs. Khrushchev."

In this chapter, I'll explain in detail how I constructed—a year in advance— my forecast for the Australian share market in 1989 and why I went to the trouble of getting it published. Beyond that, I'll share with you my experiences of being both right and wrong, and of how to make the most of both.

Choosing Your Path

In trading there are few paths to success and many to failure. In this book, individuals who have been involved in the markets for a considerable time share their secrets. Each goes about the business of studying the markets in a different way, but you'll find some common denominators among all of them.

Many professionals, in their own way, have used the rules laid down by W.D. Gann before he died in 1955. My own approach to the use of Gann's rules is essentially a combination of things I've put together over the last twenty years.

Some of these methods come from authors other than Gann, and some are rules that I've developed on my own. Everything I'm sharing with you here has worked for me, but none of it was apparent from the start. I only wish someone had taken the time to explain these things to me when I first started out.

I started trading late in 1985. My training consisted of trading for two weeks with an old pro whom I had known for many years. He was my mentor. After that, I was on my own and I've never had a real job since. During my introduction to trading, my tutor and I spoke about the works of W.D. Gann, but he had little faith in what Gann had to say. For some reason, there seems to be a well-above-average number of mathematical and grammatical mistakes in the lessons left by W.D. Gann. But I focused only on what was right, discarding what was wrong, and became a convert. The mistakes never bothered me much. They only made it more of a challenge and made me read the lessons very carefully. I thought that if I could make sense out of just one section of Gann's lessons, I would be ahead of the crowd and could move on from there.

Calculating a Range

The first thing I worked out was how to calculate a range by taking the lowest point that the market had traded from the highest point. That gave me a range. I realize that this can hardly be called a "breakthrough in technical analysis," but it was all new to me.

I bought all of the Gann books, and he seemed to be talking a great deal about ranges. I know that Gann did not have a monopoly in this area of technical analysis. Many authors based their theories on ranges and still do. It's called price action and reaction. Over time, my research showed me that these ranges were often repeated, exactly, in both time and price. So I started to believe that the time range (that is, the elapsed time between, say, a bottom and a top—often called a wave or a cycle) was every bit as relevant to my decision-making process as the price range. I began to realize that time was more important than price.

Time was also more consistent. Being more consistent, my research showed, made time more tradable. I also found that the time spans from bottom to bottom and top to top gave me cycles that repeated. That's the information you need to complete a forecast. If you're going to get your forecasts correct and use them to make trading decisions, you have to identify cycles that repeat. If and when they repeat, you'll be right. It's as simple as that.

Later, I was to see this confirmed in major trading books like *The Major Works of R.N. Elliott*, edited by Robert R. Prechter; *The Elliott Wave Principle* by Prechter and A.J. Frost; and in the work of Frank Tubbs and just about everyone else who had written about price action and reaction. But seldom did I see these masters treat time as an entity. In this, my inspiration came first from the works of W.D. Gann and what he had to say about ranges.

My next inspiration came from Gann's discussions of "natural time." Put simply, he divided the year into the four seasons and the price was divided into 360°. By simply doing some price action and reaction, I was able to learn the lessons as outlined by Gann. It's best to master the price lessons first, then move on to time. After you've completed the second part of the lesson and have gained an understanding of how these things work, you can combine both lessons and get a time and price forecast. To begin, you may draw a trend line or a moving average.

Market-Testing a Trading Plan

So far we've talked only about a theory, but you must acquire some data and back-test your theory on a market. This should result in your developing a trading plan. You'll have a percentage of winning and losing trades over a set period of time. That's called paper trading. Next comes the fun part: You must take your trading plan to the market, and the market will tell you how good you are. Sometimes, as Jesse Livermore so aptly put it, "When the market moves against you, it is like having an amputation without anaesthetic." Until you've market-tested your program, you've achieved nothing. Remember, everything looks good before it's tested. I see this in building race cars. In the shop, everything looks like a winner. Only out on the track do the defects come to light. In trading—as in racing, or a business agreement, or a marriage for that matter—it all looks good at the start.

In technical analysis, all players are like sailboats. When the starting gun is fired—in this case, the start is the opening bell—we're on our way. We may take a different tack, looking for that magic puff of the wind to take us from point A to point B in the shortest possible time. But it's not always the shortest course that works best. We're all heading in different directions to the same finish line.

There is no monopoly in market smarts. The best indicator is usually the checkbook, but this is not always the case. We enjoy the process of winning, but in most cases we learn more from losing. Perhaps that's because we ponder our losses more. Never fear change, but make sure you have a process to discriminate between changes that are for the better and those for the worse. Then follow up with an unremitting willingness to shoulder whatever responsibility is required.

You must have a passion for trading. You must love it, or you will never last. I have found that too many wins usually lead to a false sense of pride, and we all know that "pride cometh before a fall." You can either learn that lesson at the start or have the market teach it to you later on.

Over the years, I've found that many traders are fighting a fear of monetary doom, some sort of financial Armageddon. But if they do their research carefully enough, they can neutralize this fear. Many times I've been broke and just had to get back up off the floor. So it seems reasonable to me that I have lost this "fear of financial insecurity."

Fears notwithstanding, developing and proving a good trading plan is a must if you want to arrive at the port called "financial security." Initially, a large proportion of the capital you have on the table will be your own. If you have all your eggs in one basket, it pays to watch that basket carefully. I say this because I've done it. In my case, it was necessary. When you have a win, make sure you retain some of the profit. Don't keep doubling up against the house, because at some point the house is going to take the lot. Read whatever you can get on money management. You will be told to risk somewhere between 1 percent and 10 percent of your capital. The hard part is that you must take the greatest risks when you start out. It's a learning curve. Is it possible to put an old trader's head on a young trader's shoulders? I'm afraid not.

Your trading plan is your ticket for the trip. Not that a plan gives you any guarantee of financial security; the point is far more important than that: It's possible to completely lose that feeling of impending doom just by doing your homework. Your trading plan is your security. To paraphrase Ludwig Wittgenstein, "The world of the successful trader is quite different from that of the unsuccessful trader."

Technical analysis offers a smorgasbord of alternatives. The object is not to eat the lot. The idea is to select what you want. The methods used in technical analysis, such as those presented in this book, have been proven by each individual's success. There is no guarantee that any of them will work exactly the same way for you, but there is a high probability that you will find something of value in your journey as a trader. It's often said that past results are not always indicative of future performance, but in testing a trading plan, I would rather see it produce a profit than a loss. Past performance means something to me. I doubt I'm the only one who sees it that way.

Following Gann's Lead

I'm happy that I took my first cues from W.D. Gann. He started trading on August 15, 1902, and his methods have stood the test of time for more than a century. I have had to adapt some of his lessons to suit the current markets and, in some cases, I've had to modify some rules. Not only do we have new financial products that trade twenty-four hours a day, but also many of the markets he traded so successfully no longer even exist. It's not a matter of writing new rules; it's more a question of adapting and simplifying the old ones so that they're workable in the twenty-first century. The process is a bit like deciphering the da Vinci code, and, to me, W.D. Gann's methods are the holy grail of technical analysis. I think I am as qualified as the next bloke to make this statement.

From the start, Gann seemed to me to have the answers. Sometimes they were the wrong answers, but they were the only answers available at that time. So I did not start out with a grand plan; nor did I have a lot of money, which is an advantage. Heaven help those who start out trading futures with a lot of money—especially other people's. Since then, I've made every possible mistake: I've traded with borrowed money. I've often overtraded my account. I've traded against the trend, and I've traded while under so much pressure that all I could do was squeak.

I traded on my own from late in 1985 through February 1986. During that time, I made some money, which I promptly withdrew from the trading account, basically to live on. Of course, I should have left the profits there as a buffer for the hard times that would surely come, but I didn't. So when I took a hit, all that I had to show for my six months of work was a margin call. That nearly ended my trading career, but my broker pointed out that overall I had not actually made a loss on my trading. I had increased the number of contracts I was trading, while decreasing the capital.

As I pondered all of this, my trading account stayed in arrears. After a couple of weeks, I decided to put more money into the account and take one trade based on what I'd learned. I resolved that if I made money on that trade, I would go back to my research and try to become a successful trader. If I lost money, I would quit for good. Well, I made back more than I'd lost. So I returned to my research feeling like a winner. Of course, my victories weren't enough to keep me from having to collect unemployment benefits to eat.

I thought I could write a trading plan in about six weeks, but it took more than six months. I borrowed some money to open what I called a specimen account and gave myself three months to succeed. I had been fighting the tax courts for about four years. In the middle of my three months of test trading, the court ruled against me and I went bankrupt. I lost the house, the cars, the works. My family and I had to move to rental accommodation. So much for timing. Nobody believed that I could trade my way out of trouble, but at the end of the three-month trial period, I had turned the borrowed $30,000 into more than $100,000, and it was all systems go.

A Matter of Time

I succeeded by applying Gann's natural time secrets. When I was doing my work on the Australian Share Price Index (SPI) futures contract it had been trading for only two years, so I did not feel I had nearly enough history to prove anything. I decided to research the Australian All Ordinaries cash, which had been in existence in one form or another since 1875. I also broadened my research to include the May soybean contract, because that had been one of Gann's favorites, and plenty of data could be obtained on it. My plan was to decipher the soybean contract, then apply what I learned to the Australian markets. I was doing all this tracking manually and had been trading for fewer than twelve months. I had no one in Australia to whom I could go for advice. In the long run, that proved to be a good thing because I was forced to rely on my own work to survive. It was as simple as that. I believe it was Henry Kissinger who said, "The absence of alternatives clears the mind marvelously."

I started out researching the cycles of price and later came to realize that time also ran in cycles. There is a reason for everything. It all fits together. The rub is that we sometimes don't work out how until well after the event. These time frames can cover centuries, but I have found that cyclical patterns work on wars, they work on the weather, and they work amazingly well on the markets.

When I got a grip on price, I saw the current tops, bottoms, and ranges were only reflections of previous tops, bottoms, and ranges. It was like looking down a hall of mirrors, reflecting over and over again. That's how I would get my calls right. (Of course, there were times when I woke up to what was going on only well after the event.) I found that this approach worked equally well on both time and price. Sometimes, I found myself working with both. For example, say the market moved up or down 180 points; I might find there would be a major change in trend in 179 to 182 days from the start of that cycle. Sometimes, the market might move up exactly 180 points in 182 days and I would say time and price were square. I will give you some examples of how I came to grips with that phenomenon.

As luck would have it, I started trading on my own on the high of 1985, which occurred on October 24. The market then ran down 26 days, so that cycle low occurred on November 19. I was in the market all of those days and seemed to have more wins than losses. At that time, I was studying the two-year history of the Share Price Index contract, and I saw that a number of changes in trend occurred on either the 22nd or the 23rd of the month. The contract had started trading on February 16, 1983. I saw the low for 1986 come in on February 13, approximately on the contract's third birthday, and I wondered if that was just a coincidence. Gann had said that anniversaries, particularly the first day that a stock or a contract traded, were of major importance. With this information, I found I could be close to the market when it changed trend, but I certainly could not trade it.

Time by Degrees

Gann had made various references to astrology, but once again, I had to work these things out on my own. Sometimes he mentioned looking for a change in trend in 182 days and on other occasions he spoke about 180°. I had to work out what he meant. I found that 182 days equaled 180° in the cycle of the year. Somewhat reluctantly, I bought an ephemeris, which is a table that gives the coordinates of celestial bodies during given periods. This enabled me to work out the degrees of each star sign and proved to be a more accurate way to expect a change in trend. I had a name for this style of technical analysis. I called it Time by Degrees™ because that did not sound as wacky as astrology. I found that 90°, 180°, and 360° worked on all time frames, from a quarter-hour to a monthly chart. It was also a common denominator between Gann and R.N. Elliott.

Here's what Elliott had to say about it, according to Robert Prechter in his book *The Major Works of R.N. Elliott*: "[Three hundred and sixty] degrees divided by two continuously will produce a number whose units always add up to 9 or multiples of 9.... Each degree is composed of sixty minutes, and each minute is composed of sixty seconds. The circle is subdivided into six equal segments, that is, 60°, 120°, 180°, 240°, 300°, and 360°. The digits of each of these add up to nine or multiples of three. The circle was also divided by the Babylonians into four segments or seasons: from 0 to 90, 90 to 180, 180 to 270, and 270 to 360. The digits in each of these add up to nine. Further subdividing the circle into eighths gives degrees as follows: 0°, 45°, 90°, 135°, 180°, 225°, 270°, 315°, and 360°; the digits of all add up to nine." For example, 4 + 5 = 9; 1 + 3 + 5 = 9, and so on.

Although Time by Degrees was not a stand-alone indicator at that stage of the game, it backed up my work on ranges and time frames. I started to count everything. At this time, all of my charts were done by hand and many of my calculations were written on them. I started the company called Safety in the Market™ in 1989 because everyone wanted to know how I was doing my calculations. Originally, the company was no great money-making idea. But at least I was getting my trading organized. The lessons I learned from Gann's work were based on everything I have put into this chapter.

If you want to get this right, the first thing you must accept is that there is an order to everything, wars, weather, politics—the lot. But there is no money in wars or weather and I cannot stand politics, so I stuck to the markets. I started to see that on one side of the markets everything seemed to revolve around 90°, 180°, and 360° and time frames. Everything. You just have to look hard enough. I found the market was ever expanding. I hasten to add that I was not always in front of it. But neither was W.D. Gann. I found that a one-hour chart was like a sixty-year cycle. One hundred eighty-two days were like 180 months, which in turn were like 180 years. All of this is very relevant both to the market and to the current war cycle, as I'll explain later.

Forecasting

The chart shown in **Figure 6.1** is the point at which I started trading in 1985. The yearly top came in on October 24. That was the day I took my first trade under my own steam. You can see, as I did, that a couple of the market turns figured through Time by Degrees worked quite well. From the November 19, 1985, low the market ran up exactly 168 days to May 6, 1986. The market then did a 50 percent retracement in time by running down for eighty-three days to July 28, 1986. (Eighty-four days would have been an exact 50 percent retracement, but that would have put the market out of whack with the important dates.) That is when I first came across the date of July 28, which is one of my "war dates." The number of hours in a week is 168. It's said that God made the world in six days and on the seventh day He rested. Six days represent 144 hours. Fourteen years equal 168 months. All of this has meaning in terms of minutes, hours, days, and weeks. In any case, the market got itself back into balance by running up 169 days till January 13, 1987. This was the first major top that I had both forecast and traded. The chart in **Figure 6.2** shows equal time frames of eighty-three days and 201 days working in 2006 and 2007.

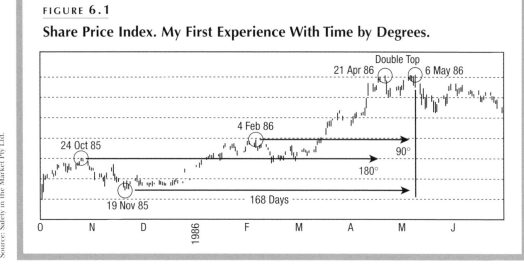

FIGURE **6.1**

Share Price Index. My First Experience With Time by Degrees.

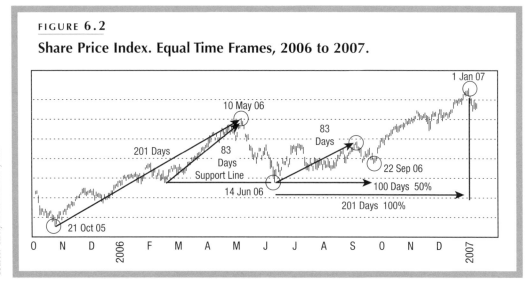

FIGURE **6.2**

Share Price Index. Equal Time Frames, 2006 to 2007.

The chart in **Figure 6.3** shows us Time by Degrees working after the Crash of '87, which was probably the most volatile market we'll ever see. I actually raised the money to buy a new house, the first since I had gone broke in 1986, by trading into that low on February 10, 1988. It was one of the few times I found trading easy. I had picked the top in 1987 and traded it. A few traders and my broker were aware of this. I used to give all of the credit to W.D. Gann, but I was using a lot of market smarts that I had picked up in any number of places.

Source: Safety in the Market Pty Ltd.

FIGURE **6.3**

Share Price Index. Time by Degrees From November 11, 1987.

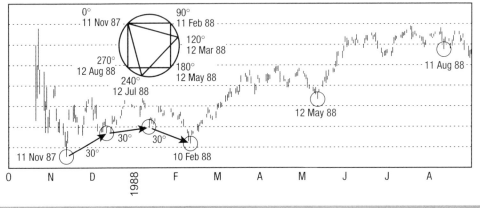

FIGURE **6.4**

Share Price Index. Time by Degrees in 2006.

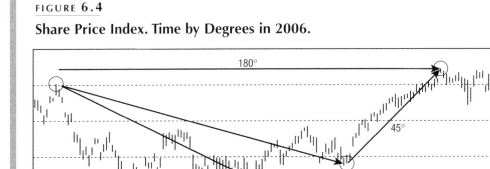

Source: Safety in the Market Pty Ltd.

A fair proportion was my own, but I must give thanks to all of the masters who, along with Gann, came before me. Thankfully, they left a path, which I was able to recognize and follow. As can be seen in the chart in **Figure 6.4**, the technique is every bit as relevant in 2006 as it was in 1987.

Even after the '87 Crash there were some traders still knocking Gann—and me, for that matter. You might think that people would just rejoice in their good fortune and keep trading the market. But real life is not that simple. People often don't see things that clearly—especially when things are not all black and white and especially when ego and emotions are involved. But I was learning by doing. I had all of the cycles for the Share Price Index, from the birth of the contract in 1983, marked on my charts, and in most cases I knew when, where, how, and why they would repeat. There is no doubt that the trick is to identify the cycle before it happens. A well-trained monkey on a stick can do an adequate job of describing something after it has happened.

A trading sequence isn't always as simple as in 1987–88, but this was when everything came together for me. I had not yet started writing articles or doing presentations at that time, but traders were beginning to look over my shoulder and, in many cases, follow my every move. More than a little bit irritating were the phone calls I'd get when I was wrong, telling me how dumb I was and how this Gann stuff did not work. When I was right, there would be no calls.

I was living more than well from my trading, so I decided to put a Gann article into a financial newsletter, just to prove how all this stuff worked. I sent off a one-page article titled "Safety in the Market" to *Research Technology*, which was the biggest supplier of market data in Australia at the time. Plenty of traders knew that I had picked various tops and bottoms in the markets, but I had no real proof except for my trading statements. I was not publicizing my work for the money. In the article, which I wrote late in 1988, I decided to go out on a limb and nominate the day of the top for the Australian Share Price Index contract in 1989. I was willing to put myself to the test. In the article, I explained how the yearly top for 1988 had occurred by squaring time in price. I have already said that a well-trained monkey on a stick can describe events after they happen. So we can put my 1988 call in that basket. But for 1989, I said, "So, of course, the next question is what is going to happen in 1989. I see a volatile year ahead, similar to 1988, with a major top due on October 3, with the reversal and panic in the market. Short positions should be covered on about November 16 and December 18." This forecast, along with some notes on the Dow Jones Index, was published in the United States in the February edition of the *Gann and Elliott Wave* magazine. How did I do? You can bet I did pretty well, or I would not be writing this chapter. The high of the year in Australia came in on October 4, 1989, at a price of exactly 1855, which was exactly what I had calculated twelve months earlier. That price was the highest our market traded for a number of years. It was followed by what was called "the crash of 1989," not to be confused with the real Crash of 1987. My dates for November and December also came in very close. By that time, I was doing a few seminars, called "Safety in

Source: Safety in the Market Pty Ltd.

FIGURE 6.5

Share Price Index. My Call for the Top of 1989.

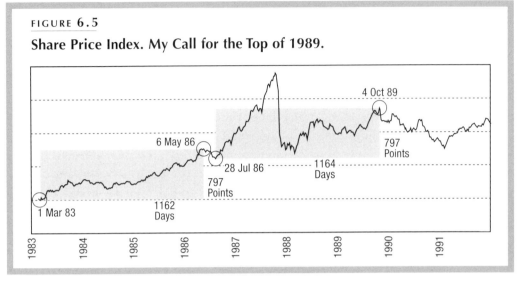

the Market™." After the low of the year came in on April 7, 1989, it reinforced my forecast top of October 4, 1989 (see **Figure 6.5**). This was presented to the attendees of my seminar and was recorded on video.

My method for predicting the tops and bottoms was simple and consistent with how I made my trading decisions, as I've already outlined. I don't regard either Time by Degrees or price action/reaction as a stand-alone indicator. But as can be seen here, when they independently agree, there can be a window of opportunity.

My decision was based first on my Time by Degrees theory. October 4, the actual day of the top, came in 180 days from the low of the year, April 7, 1989. It was also 180 weeks from the high on April 21, 1986. That was the first of the double tops and it came in at 1254.5. It was 180 months from the major low on September 27, 1974, which was felt worldwide. These time frames indicated a major change in trend.

The process was also based on the theory that time and price ranges repeat. The all-time low of our Australian Share Price Index contract came in on March 1, 1983, at a price of 458 exactly. The first major top came in 1,162 days later on May 6, 1986, at a price of 1255 exactly (half a point higher than April 21, 1986, the other date in the double top). The market at this time was trading in decimal points. So we had a time frame of 1162 days and a price range of 1255 minus 458, which is 797 points. The next major low, as I've already mentioned, occurred on July 28, 1986, at a price of 1058. So if we are looking for a future price target, we add the range of 797 to the price of 1058, to get 1855 exactly. If we use the length of the previous time frame, we will go out 1162 days from July 28, 1986, to October 2, 1989. I was one day out on time in my published forecast for October 3, 1989, but I got the price right on the button.

This style of analysis is also one of the tenets of the Elliott Wave Principle as described by Prechter and Frost in their book of that name. In the 1990 edition, under the heading "Wave Equity," they quote the relevance of the 0.618 ratio to the Elliott wave theory, but they also give the following example: "Thus, in the year-end rally of 1976, we find that wave one traveled 35.24 points in 47 trading hours while wave five traveled 34.4 points in 47 trading hours. As can be seen, the guideline of equality is often extremely accurate." Here, they are quoting the equality in both time and price of wave one compared with wave five.

I followed up this analysis in my next article for *Research Technology* by calling for a major change of trend on January 16, 1991. As it turned out, that day became better known for the start of the Gulf War. But it was also the end of the rundown from the 1989 top. This time, in *Research Technology*, I nominated exactly 4:00 p.m. as the time for the low. The publication's records show the low occurring at exactly 3.59 p.m., so I was one minute out. I should add that the Gulf War started officially at 4 p.m. Australian Eastern Standard Time, which is midnight in Washington, D.C.

At this stage of my career, I had been trading for only about five years. I was self-taught and I did all my calculations by hand. It is fair to say that I used more than Time by Degrees and equal ranges and squares of price and time. But it is also correct to say that when these things aligned, I would make my move. This chapter attempts to give an Australian perspective on the relevance of the work of W.D. Gann in relation to the Australian market. I could have picked any time in the last twenty years, but I chose the time when I was learning. To make things easier, I am including some current charts. My methods seemed to work equally well on the Swiss franc contract and on May soybeans, one of Gann's favorites.

My health started to fall apart in 1994. By 1998, those around me knew that I was a long way from well. For the first time since 1988, when I started Safety in the Market, I had to restrict what I did. But I have stuck to my research, because I love it. By 2000, I thought it was wisest to step back from running Safety in the Market. Most of the work on the markets, which I used to do by hand, was computerized at about this time.

War and Market Cycles

Throughout this chapter, I have made references to wars and their relation to Gann's work. I first became interested in the war cycles after reading Gann's 1927 novel *Tunnel Thru the Air*, or *Looking Back From 1940*, in which he wrote that the United States was about to be involved in an Armageddon-style war, starting in April 1930. He described the Japanese planes bombing the American fleet in the Pacific as the start of the war. More than a decade before December 7, 1941, this is how he portrayed the United States being dragged into the war:

> The United States government fearing that Japan would make the first attack on the Pacific coast, either around Los Angeles or San Francisco, rushed the battle fleet to the Pacific. As soon as the battleships cruised into the Pacific, Japan attacked from the air with the noiseless airplanes and began dropping deadly bombs from great heights. The antiaircraft guns from the decks of the battleships were powerless to reach the bombing planes at such great heights. Defeat was swift and severe and only a few of the battleships escaped complete destruction from the first attack.

His timing was off, but I can understand that because I know how he did his calculations.

This book compelled me in 1988, sixty years later, to look at the relationship between the United States and Japan and see if this knowledge could give me an advantage in trading. In 1986, *Tunnel Thru the Air* led me to natural time because the book contained a lot of trading examples. I found that the United States led Japan by an exact time frame. This time frame varied with different situations and industries. For example, in the auto industry, Japan trails the United States by about twenty years and Taiwan follows Japan. The American stock market seemed to lead its Japanese counterpart by an approximate time frame of sixty years. My theory was that after the '87 Crash, when all of the markets worldwide looked shaky, Japan still had a little more than two years left in the bull market. As I was doing my work, the Japanese market kept defying the trend and going up. The Japanese market topped on December 27, 1989. Once that top was in place, I could expect the same rundown that the United States had experienced between 1929 and 1932. The American market had run up 95 points in ninety-five days to top out on September 3, 1929; then it ran down for a period of 1,039 days to July 8, 1932. According to what I had learned from Gann's book, when the Japanese market topped on December 27, 1989, it seemed to make sense that the Japanese market would not bottom out until

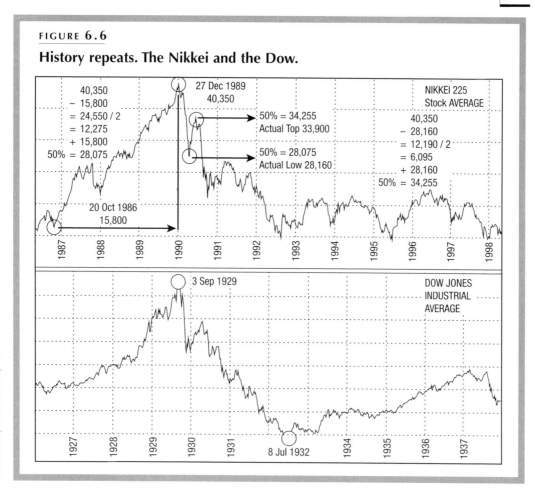

FIGURE 6.6

History repeats. The Nikkei and the Dow.

Source: Safety in the Market Pty Ltd.

sometime around October 31, 1992.

I did not trade either side of my call on the Nikkei 225 Stock Average. But I overlaid the 1929 weekly chart of the Dow Jones Industrial Average with the 1989 chart of the Nikkei, shown in **Figure 6.6**. In real time, the Nikkei ran down for 966 days to bottom out on August 19, 1992, whereas the Dow ran down for 1,039 days in 1932. The relevance of all this becomes apparent when you look at the overlaid charts.

The Theory in Practice

Let's take this theory a little further and see what economic advantages we can derive from some of this knowledge. From 1998, under doctor's orders, I needed to ration my time and spend less time working. I had been publishing forecasts since 1988. Often this included drawing up road maps for the stock market. Now that I had some time on my hands, I decided to focus on an aspect that had interested me—an analysis of cycles in the history of the twentieth century—using my own methods and in my own time. The results are astounding.

I participated in a worldwide trader's teleconference on September 7, 2002, which involved approximately 500 traders. I spent about an hour and a half answering questions. Early in the conference, I was asked by one trader where I believed the next pressure point would be on the road map. The first pressure point I mentioned was July 28, 2004. I also said there was a pressure point somewhere around August 2–5, 2004. I based this on historical war dates and the fact that 2004 was an election year in the United States.

In November 2002 and again in 2003, I was guest speaker at the annual traders' conference run in Sydney by Hubb Limited, a trading software developer who was granted a license to sell my courses after I retired in 2001. At these seminars, I mentioned the date of May 17, 2004, as a major pressure point on the stock market and referred to this and the previous pressure points I'd mentioned as "war dates." This took place years after I had completed my final Safety in the Market trading seminar, and the dates were based on the research I was conducting on the history of the twentieth century.

The first week of August has often been a critical day in world history—and so it has been a significant week for the stock market. On July 31, 1914, the London and New York stock exchanges closed to avoid panic trading. That was almost the case again in 2004, when an immediate security clampdown occurred in New York and Washington on August 2, 2004. The buildings affected were the New York Stock Exchange and Citigroup Center in New York as well as the World Bank and the International Monetary Fund in Washington. Britain declared war on Germany on Tuesday, August 4, 1914. The United States dropped the first atomic bomb on Japan on August 6, 1945. (It had been scheduled to be dropped on August 3.) On August 1, 1941, President Roosevelt stopped the export of oil and aviation fuel from the United States to Japan. Japan had the choice of either changing its foreign policy or gaining access to the East Indies oil by force. On August 2 and 5, 1964, two U.S. destroyers were attacked in the Gulf of Tonkin, and they in turn sank two North Vietnamese patrol boats—leading the United States into the Vietnam War.

To fully illustrate the scope of the pattern, I would need to trace early-August events through the whole century and give you the time frames, but I think I've made the point. Here is the main thrust: Britain entered World War I

FIGURE **6.7**

History repeating fourteen years (168 months) later – August 3 and 4.

Published on August 4, 1990
in the *Courier Mail*

Published on August 3, 2004
in the *Australian*

on August 3, 1914. The United States originally planned to drop the first atomic bomb on August 3, 1945. Forty-five years later, Iraq invaded Kuwait on August 3, 1990 (see **Figure 6.7**).

I had already recognized the pattern by the time it repeated itself in 1990. When I saw the same cycle repeating in 2002, I could make the call for 2004 just as if I were reading it from a book. I knew what effect the war would have on the price of oil, because I had seen it all happen on the same day and in the same way in 1990. I hope I've made clear that cycles do repeat and that second time around, they give you an edge in the market.

I believe there are times when forecasting the future is just as realistic as reading the past, because the future is just a repetition of what has previously occurred. Hindsight becomes foresight if you use it often enough.

CHAPTER 7

Options-Based Technical Indicators for Stock Trading

BERNIE SCHAEFFER

Equity options have come a long way since they were first listed on exchanges in 1973. Beyond the explosive growth in the volume of options trading during this period, which speaks for itself, options have become a risk-management tool as well as a tool for speculation for a broad spectrum of market players, from modestly capitalized individual investors to hedge funds.

In basic terms, the world of listed options consists of call options and put options. The buyer of an equity call option has the right but not the obligation to buy shares of a company, referred to as the *underlying stock*, at a specified price (called the *strike price*) for a specific period of time, at the end of which the option "expires." The call option buyers are bullish—they're hoping to profit from a rise in the stock price over the life of the option.

Why Options?

Why would a bullish investor choose to pay for a call option with a limited life instead of buying the underlying stock? The short answer is leverage—the ability to participate in the upside movement in the underlying stock for a relatively small initial investment. The price of a call option is most dependent on the price of the underlying stock relative to the strike price, the stock's volatility, and the amount of time remaining until the option expires. But in all cases, the call option price will be a fraction of the stock price, and in many cases, this fraction will be very small indeed.

To illustrate, let's assume Stock A, which does not pay a dividend, is currently trading for $50 and an investor is expecting the stock to move to $60 during the next three months. If the annualized volatility of the stock is 25 percent—typical of many of the blue chips—a three-month call option with a strike price of $50 will trade for about 5 percent of the share price, or $2.50 in this case. If the stock should in fact reach $60 by the time this call option expires in three months, the $50-strike call option will have a value of $10 in the listed options market.

So, in this case, the call option will have quadrupled from $2.50 to $10 on a move by the underlying from $50 to $60, and thus a gain of 300 percent could have been realized by the option buyer on just a 20 percent gain in the stock. And the leverage in this case would have been 15 to 1 (300 percent/20 percent). Put another way, the option holder achieved a profit of $7.50 with an investment of just $2.50, whereas the $10 gain realized by the stock holder required a $50 investment.

Needless to say, the scenario described above was on the best-case end of the spectrum for the call option buyer. Note, for example, that if the stock does not rise above $50 during the life of the option and the position is held until expiration, the call buyer will lose 100 percent of his investment. And in the case of the on-the-money option—when the stock price is equal to the strike price—such total losses can be expected to occur 50 percent of the time.

Based on this quick risk-reward profile, one can reasonably conclude that call option buyers (those who are said to have long call-option positions) are rather aggressively bullish in the pursuit of leveraged profits—bullish enough to be risking a total loss of their investment if they're wrong.

The buyer of an equity put option, however, has the right but not the obligation to sell a stock at a specified price (the strike price) for a specific period (at the end of which the option expires). The put option buyer is as aggressively bearish as the call option buyer is aggressively bullish.

So in its purest form, the options world consists of two constituencies: the aggressively bullish call option buyer and the aggressively bearish put option buyer. In addition, the listed options market provides a treasure trove of information about the activity of call and put buyers in each of the thousands of underlying stocks on which options are traded. Trading volume data are available for calls and for puts, as well as option open interest, which represents the number of option contracts open at any time.

Gauging Investor Sentiment

It should be no surprise, therefore, that technical and quantitative analysts have made ongoing efforts over the years to measure the relative intensity of put and call activity as a gauge of the sentiment of aggressive investors. Stocks on which these investors are very bullish—as indicated by greater call activity than put activity—could be deemed by contrarians to be vulnerable. An excess of bullish options sentiment could be an indication of investor exuberance and overcommitment, and the resulting dearth of sideline buying power could pave the way for a major pullback. Similarly, stocks on which investors are very bearish—as indicated by greater put activity than call activity—could have significant upside potential. An excess of bearish options sentiment could indicate investor pessimism and capitulation, and the resulting buildup of sideline buying power could pave the way for a major rally.

Surprisingly, the focus on put and call option activity over the years has been pretty well restricted to:

1.   *Aggregate options data across all equities rather than an equity-by-equity analysis.* A series commonly quoted by analysts is the "CBOE Equity Put/Call ratio," which represents the trading volume of all puts and calls listed on the Chicago Board Options Exchange. This aggregation of equity options data may have made sense decades ago, when few individual equities had robust markets in their options. But these days there are many equities with options that trade thousands of contracts each day and with option open interest equivalent to millions of shares of stock.

2.   *Option volume, as opposed to open interest.* Option open interest is a much more stable series than option volume. Option volume can vary very significantly from day to day, whereas open interest adjusts incrementally each day based on the number of positions that were opened or closed the day before. In addition, option volume can be subject to all manner of intraday "noise," including the activities of day traders who hold no position at the end of the day.

Schaeffer's Open Interest Ratio

Schaeffer's Investment Research has attacked the deficiencies of traditional put/call ratio analysis on each of these two fronts by developing a ratio of put open interest to call open interest for every optionable stock. This ratio is referred to as the SOIR (Schaeffer's Open Interest Ratio), and it is updated daily in the data presented on www.SchaeffersResearch.com, as well as for the company's internal analysis. A graph of the SOIR can tell a very interesting story of the option trader sentiment toward a particular equity, and this unique perspective can add considerable value to an analysis of a stock's technical picture. Before delving into some compelling examples of SOIR analysis, consider the potential pitfalls of this approach.

Again, in its purest form the options world consists of two constituencies: the aggressively bullish call option buyer and the aggressively bearish put option buyer. For purposes of maximizing the value to contrarians of put/call ratio analysis, there would be another element to this "purity," namely, the participants in the options market would be confined to relatively unsophisticated individual investors. In such a pure options world, we would know that heavy call activity (or heavy put activity) would be the result of a strongly bullish (or strongly bearish) view held by the unsophisticated crowd, and, as such, traders should consider taking the contrarian approach of fading this activity.

But the real world of options differs significantly from this pure world that would delight the contrarian.

1. Options market participants include professionals such as large money managers and, particularly in recent years, hedge funds that trade very actively. Many of these larger investors are quite sophisticated and have access to valuable information well beyond the scope of the smaller individual investor. To automatically take a position counter to the option activity of this contingent would be foolish indeed.

2. Option activity is by no means always initiated by buyers. For example, there is quite a large constituency that sells call options against stock they own as a tool for generating additional income, and others who seek a similar objective by selling puts against cash. And some traders sell uncovered (or "naked") calls, which is a bearish bet that a stock will not rise above the call strike price. If heavy call activity is the result of a surge in covered or naked call writing, it certainly would not indicate a wildly bullish investment view.

3. Option activity can occur in conjunction with trades (or positions) in the underlying stock. One example would be when a covered call position is initiated. Another would be the purchase of put options to protect a long stock position from a major decline, perhaps ahead of a critical earnings report. Option activity that results from strategies that involve the underlying stock (or strategies that involve the buying and selling of other options on that stock) can dilute the value of put/call ratio analysis.

4. Hedge funds in particular use options as part of "pairs trading" strategies. For example, a put option on an energy exchange-traded fund (ETF) might be purchased in conjunction with a long position in Occidental Petroleum (OXY) if the manager feels that the stock will outperform its sector. So the purchase of the puts in this case is not a reflection of a bearish view on energy but rather a hedge for a bullish view on a particular energy stock.

Considering the Extremes

So the perception of a put/call ratio as a clear indication of the bullish (or bearish) sentiment of a crowd of unsophisticated traders is certainly a flawed one. But there is still substantial insight to be gained from this information—insight that can add value to an investor's stock trading. And this insight can be especially valuable when focusing on extreme situations.

It has been a fact of life that there are more trades in call options than in put options. The facile explanation is that investors tend to be more bullish than bearish, even when they have trading vehicles that allow them to exploit their views in either direction. That's true, but another factor that tilts that option activity equation to the call side is the popularity of covered call writing as an investment strategy.

Since 1990, the put/call ratio (put volume divided by call volume, excluding index options) for all equity options has averaged about 0.50. In other words, equity call volume tends to be twice that for puts. This ratio will likely hold over the long term, but it can vary substantially during particularly strong or particularly weak periods in the market. During the bubble years in the late 1990s, when investors tilted very strongly to the bullish side, the equity put/call ratio dipped to about 0.44, or about 2.27 calls traded for every put. But since 2001, the equity put/call ratio has averaged about 0.64, or about 1.56 calls traded for every put, as investors have become more concerned about downside risk.

One fruitful technique in the quest for bullish contrarian ideas is to filter for stocks whose SOIR (put/call open interest ratio) exceeds 1.00, that is, stocks for which put open interest exceeds call open interest. Over time, call volume will be about twice put volume, so a stock that develops put open interest that exceeds its call open interest is exhibiting quite an unusual tilt by its option players to the put side. In fact, over the years at any given time, only about 15 percent of the optionable stock universe has an SOIR that exceeds 1.00.

For the reasons cited—the growing professional contingent that trades options, the fact that many options trades are seller-initiated or part of a stock/option combination—one must be careful before concluding that an SOIR that exceeds 1.00 is a clear-cut indication of strong bearish sentiment on the part of unsophisticated speculators. In other words, one needs to be careful before adopting the contrarian approach of fading such a situation by taking a bullish position on the underlying stock.

But filtering for stocks whose put open interest is clearly on the outlier end of the spectrum—particularly if this condition persists over time—does bring to light many stocks that are in fact being viewed bearishly by option speculators. And by further narrowing the SOIR filter to emphasize those stocks whose price action has been strong relative to the market, one can develop a list of potential bullish contrarian plays that is turbo-charged from two standpoints:

1.   A trader will bolster the effectiveness of his contrarian conclusion. The major conundrum of sentiment analysis results from situations in which the sentiment simply confirms the price action in the stock. So a stock that doubles in price during a one-year period is very likely to be the object of a fair amount of bullish sentiment simply because the gains it has registered are likely to have attracted major attention among investors, because everybody loves a winner. Technical analysts will be drawn to the stock based on the notion that "the trend is your friend," and even those with a fundamental bent will likely be swayed by the strength in the shares and will tend to view the company's prospects more positively. And, as technicians well know, such a powerful move by a stock often indicates that there have been (or are about to be) some major positive developments in the company's business. So the task of the contrarian in these situations becomes the extremely difficult one of attempting to determine whether this bullish sentiment has reached a euphoric extreme that indicates a serious depletion of sideline buying power and thus a potential top.

But if a stock is exhibiting strong price action and the sentiment remains skeptical or outright bearish, the task for the contrarian is much easier. Bearish sentiment combined with strong price action is an unusual situation, indicating with great regularity that an uptrend in a stock is relatively early in the game because there remains major sideline buying power that can fuel substantial additional gains.

2.   A trader will have "structural buying" working for him because of the buildup in put open interest and its subsequent unwinding. When puts are accumulated on a stock, those who are on the other side of the trade (those who are selling these puts to the put buyers) must protect themselves from the open-ended risk they'll incur should the stock decline substantially. And they generally hedge their short put exposure by shorting the underlying stock. But should a strongly performing stock continue to post outsize gains, these short positions will begin to be covered as the put buyers begin to capitulate and close their positions. And even if the put positions remain open, there will be short covering because the hedgers need to be short fewer and fewer shares as the puts they've sold move farther and farther away from the strike price and (as time passes) thus have a smaller and smaller chance of ever attaining value.

Here are some detailed examples of stocks that exhibited outlier put open interest in combination with strong price action. **Figure 7.1** charts the price

FIGURE 7.1

Chart of AMR With 50-Day SOIR Moving Average

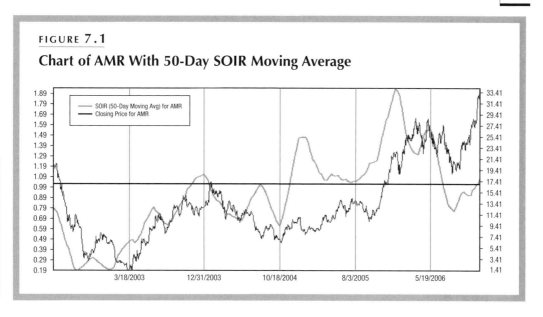

action in AMR Corporation (AMR) along with the 50-day moving average of its SOIR. Note the powerful rally in AMR from late 2004 through mid-2005, along with the skeptical option trader sentiment as reflected in the 50-day moving average of its SOIR as it crossed above the 1.00 level (as indicated by the horizontal line). This juxtaposition of strong price action and bearish sentiment provided a very bullish backdrop for the shares during this period.

The SOIR line crossed with authority above 1.00 in November 2004 and remained in this zone until June 2006. During this period, AMR shares rallied from the $9.00 area to a high of $29.32. For more than eighteen months, while the shares were more than tripling, skeptical option traders were accumulating more AMR put contracts than call contracts.

In addition to the bearish sentiment of option traders, AMR was being played very heavily on the short side in late 2004. Short interest in excess of 50 million shares equaled almost 25 percent of the company's total float. Although some of this short interest could be attributed to the heavy put option buying, there was a clear overall pattern of negative expectations for AMR shares.

When might a technician have felt comfortable with buying AMR as a bullish contrarian play, given this backdrop of bearish sentiment? **Figure 7.2** charts the weekly price action of AMR along with its 40-week moving average and provides a good backdrop for an answer. The 40-week moving average is a widely used barometer among technicians of whether a stock is in bullish or bearish territory.

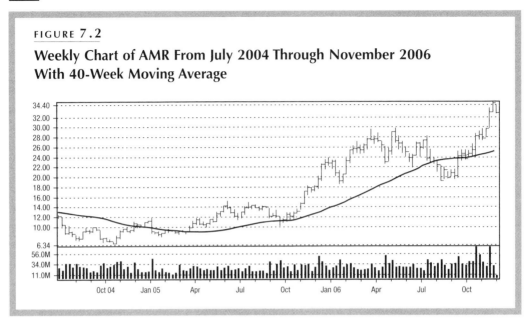

FIGURE 7.2

Weekly Chart of AMR From July 2004 Through November 2006 With 40-Week Moving Average

Source: Thomson/ILX

Figure 7.2 indicates there were a number of junctures in late 2004 and early 2005 for entering an AMR long position based on a move above the 40-week moving average. Some of these moves were followed by pullbacks that may have stopped the trader out, but an entry in the $9 to $10 area in late March 2005 or perhaps an entry in October 2005 in the $12 area on the successful retest of the 40-week would each have been quite legitimate.

Using a move back below the 40-week moving average as an exit criterion, the trader would have exited in July or August 2006 in the $21 to $22 area. So a technician trading AMR off the bearish sentiment could have achieved something in the area of a double based on a simple 40-week moving average cross criterion for entry and exit.

Figure 7.3 presents a second example, which charts the price action in Yahoo! (YHOO) along with the 50-day moving average of its put/call open interest ratio (SOIR). The SOIR for Yahoo! remained above 1.00 for most of the period from mid-2003 through the end of 2004, during which the shares tripled from $13 to $39. This is once again a juxtaposition of strong price action and bearish sentiment, and it provided a very bullish backdrop for Yahoo! shares during this period. What's more, Yahoo! was among the most heavily shorted Nasdaq shares during this period, with short interest in the neighborhood of 100 million shares.

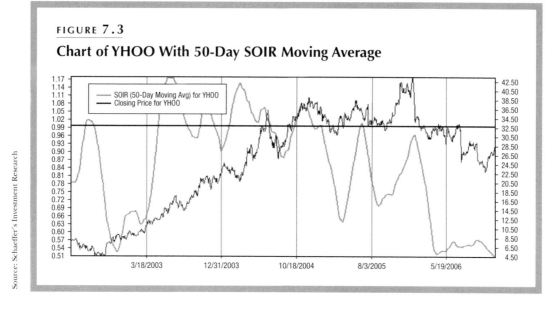

FIGURE 7.3

Chart of YHOO With 50-Day SOIR Moving Average

Source: Schaeffer's Investment Research

Figure 7.4 charts the weekly price action of Yahoo! along with its 40-week moving average and shows the powerful uptrend in Yahoo! shares during the entire period of excess put activity from mid-2003 through the end of 2004. A contrarian trader could have felt comfortable in entering a long position at the

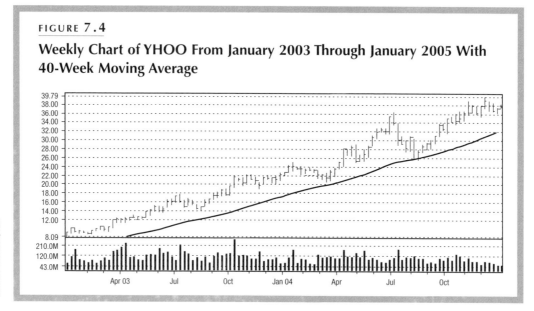

FIGURE 7.4

Weekly Chart of YHOO From January 2003 Through January 2005 With 40-Week Moving Average

Source: Thomson/ILX

beginning of this period and holding it for the entire 200 percent gain, but a few caveats are in order.

Note in Figure 7.3 that the SOIR for Yahoo! did move below 1.00 for several brief periods. And although one could argue that Yahoo!'s strong price action would have been more than sufficient to justify retaining the long position in the shares, there was the potential for a trader to exit the position based solely on the SOIR above the established 1.00 parameter. Also, the shares did move briefly below the 40-week moving average in August 2004, although not on a weekly closing basis. Again, there would have been the potential for a shakeout, but nonetheless at a very hefty profit level.

Immeasurables

The put/call open interest ratio (SOIR) is one of a number of ways of slicing and dicing the information a trader can glean from the ebb and flow of option activity. A put/call open interest ratio that's a consistent outlier may indicate tradable extremes in sentiment on a particular equity, but there are limitations to the scope of what the ratio can measure.

The SOIR is calculated using a ratio of put to call open interest for the three front expiration months. A stock may exhibit a very high SOIR, but if the level of option activity on that stock is modest—relative to average trading volume or to share float—the significance of a high ratio of put to call open interest is radically diminished and may in many cases be of zero consequence. This option activity would be described as being of "low intensity."

Option pricing would be yet another measure of the intensity of option activity. Options are priced based on a probabilistic model whose major inputs include the share price, the strike price of the option, the time remaining until option expiration, and the assumed future volatility of the underlying stock. Within a group of on-the-money options (options for which the stock price equals the strike price) on various nondividend-paying stocks with a common expiration date, the differences in option pricing levels can be explained almost entirely by the differing assumptions for future volatility.

Although the assumed volatility (known as *implied volatility* among options traders) does not coincide precisely with the recent volatility of each stock, it is usually close enough so that the following example of how option prices can vary more than suffices. Hansen Natural (HANS) is an energy drink manufacturer whose stock has alternated between very hot and very cold. The wild gyrations in the share price translate at this stage into an annual volatility of about 70 percent.

Cisco Systems (CSCO), on the other hand, has become a steadily growing blue-chip company in the technology space with a market capitalization in excess of $150 billion. It is widely covered on Wall Street and widely held by institutional investors. So it should be no surprise that the annual volatility of Cisco shares is modest and in the neighborhood of 25 percent.

How do these varying volatilities translate into the pricing of Hansen and Cisco options? A three-month, on-the-money call option on Hansen would trade at approximately 14 percent of the share price; a similar option on Cisco would trade at approximately 5 percent of the share price. In other words, the options are priced in direct proportion to the assumed volatility of the underlying stock.

The Fear Factor

But volatility assumptions are constantly changing for every optionable stock. Sometimes this is simply the result of a change in the recent volatility of the stock. Sometimes it's in anticipation of an upcoming event—such as an earnings report—that is expected to result in increased share volatility. And sometimes it's the result of intense option buying prompted by greed or, more often, fear. Fear is a potentially strong directional clue for the trader. At Schaeffer's Investment Research, an "equity VIX" is calculated for every optionable stock in order to sharpen the focus on such situations.

Most traders are probably familiar with the CBOE Volatility Index (VIX), calculated by the Chicago Board Options Exchange to measure the implied volatility of the options on the S&P 500 Index (SPX). The VIX is often referred to as a "fear gauge," because a rising VIX is almost always associated with increased demand for index put options due to increased investor fear of a market decline. In fact, major spikes in the VIX have been associated with major market bottoms, as extremes in fear invariably indicate massive investor capitulation and liquidation, which denotes that the selling pressure has lifted. Of course, the difficulty lies in determining when the fear level has reached a true extreme, because taking a bullish position before the fear has truly peaked is extremely risky and potentially disastrous.

The equity VIX calculated at Schaeffer's is designed to focus attention on stocks experiencing unusual swings in the implied volatility of their options, and, just as with the CBOE VIX, spikes in volatility are of particular interest as a directional indicator for stocks. No stock in recent years has provided traders with more in the way of volatility spikes than General Motors (GM).

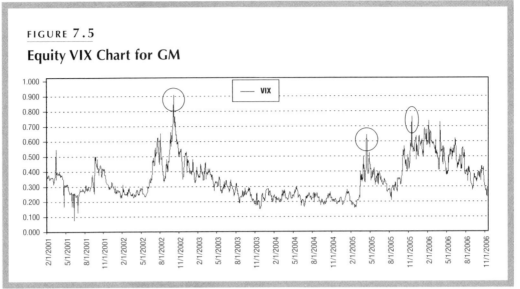

FIGURE 7.5

Equity VIX Chart for GM

Source: Schaeffer's Investment Research

Figure 7.5 displays the VIX for GM options since 2001. Note that the first major volatility spike occurred in the fall of 2002. This was not a company-specific spike, because option volatility was surging across the board in a climax of investor fear as the market plunged into its major bottom in October 2002, and GM shares bottomed along with the broad market (see Figure 7.6).

The next major spike in GM option volatility occurred in the second quarter of 2005, as serious concerns about the company's financial viability began to reverberate through Wall Street. Huge positions in long-term GM puts were being accumulated, some as outright bets on the company's demise and some as part of hedged positions with GM debt. Accompanying this volatility spike was a pullback in GM shares to the $25 area, a level not seen since the major bottom in the second half of 1992 (see Figure 7.6). The stock lifted off these long-standing support levels, and by July 2005, it had rallied by about 50 percent to just shy of $38.

This combination of a pullback to a well-defined support level and an extreme in investor fear as evidenced by a major volatility spike created a good buying opportunity for nimble contrarian traders.

In terms of the bigger picture, the GM story illustrates the pitfall of trading off sentiment extremes—that is, taking a bullish position before the true peak in fear. **Figure 7.6** shows that GM's share price proceeded to get cut in half during the six months following July 2005, to a low of $18.33 by year-end 2005, while a spike in the VIX for GM comfortably exceeded the second-quarter 2005

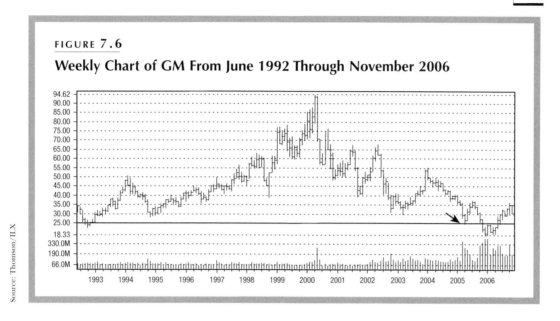

FIGURE 7.6

Weekly Chart of GM From June 1992 Through November 2006

Source: Thomson/ILX

spike (see Figure 7.5). By the start of 2006, the chances of a GM bankruptcy had reached coin flip levels, according to many analysts.

By February 2006, a mind-boggling three million put contracts had been accumulated on GM, equal to 300 million shares, or more than half the company's outstanding shares. Of course, most of these options were out of the money so this comparison is somewhat misleading. Still, the sentiment on GM in the options market was extremely bearish, whether measured by put/call ratios, the intensity of put open interest, or by option volatility levels.

The Contrarians Weigh In

But sometimes the strongest confirming evidence that the bottom is truly in place comes from outside the quantitative world. From a contrarian perspective, this evidence arrived in the form of a cover story on GM in *Fortune* magazine by Carol Loomis in the issue dated February 20, 2006. Below is an excerpt from my commentary of February 13, 2006, on www.SchaeffersResearch.com regarding this cover story:

> It is the instinctive wish of most American businesspeople, even those unlikely to be directly affected, that General Motors not go bankrupt. True, some people will say, "They had it coming to them." But the majority will be more practical, telling themselves that the company is so central to the economy, so sprawling in its commercial reach, that bankruptcy—"going into chapter" as restructuring folks say—is ominous

almost beyond contemplation. And yet the evidence points, with increasing certitude, to bankruptcy. Rick Wagoner, GM's 53-year-old chairman and CEO, may say, as he did in a January interview with *Fortune* in his aerie of an office high above the Detroit River, "I know that things will turn around." But he cannot know that. He may not, deep down, even believe it himself.

—("The Tragedy of General Motors," *Fortune*, February 20, 2006)

Schaeffer's addendum (February 13, 2006): The words quoted above were emblazoned on the cover of one of America's most popular business publications. It is the second major negative piece on General Motors from *Fortune* in less than a month ("Detroit's Endless Winter," January 30, 2006).

I point this pattern out not to proclaim that GM does not have the problems that have been well documented in these articles. But I'll also note that, in my opinion, there is absolutely nothing that was revealed in this somber and extensive cover piece that has not been thoroughly documented and discussed on numerous occasions in numerous other media forums.

Calling a bottom in a troubled company is always supremely difficult (I've been thus far way too early [read: "wrong"] in calling one for GM), as much of the negative sentiment is well deserved and the weak price action does not provide the "contrarian contrast" between negative sentiment and strong technicals that is at work in the best of contrarian buy situations. It is only when the sentiment becomes over-the-top gloomy and almost inescapable in its pervasiveness and totally dismissive of current and potential positive developments that one can feel somewhat safe in making the bottom call. And I think with the arrival of this latest GM cover story, we're there, just as we were in November 1992, when *Time* magazine's cover asked, "Can GM Survive in Today's World?"

This does not mean that GM stock has no additional downside. It is certainly possible, even if bankruptcy were not at all a concern, for the shares to retest the recent lows in the 18 area. And one cannot completely rule out the worst case. But investing is a probability game and a game of comparing potential rewards and risks, and in GM's case here and now, I believe the potential upside is well worth the risk of the potential downside.

The Volatility Payoff

If an options trader takes away just one concept from this chapter, it would be the following: When buying options, the trader *pays* for volatility but the *payoff* is in directional price movement. In other words, options are priced from a statistically based model keyed to the variability of a security's price movement (its volatility) without regard to the direction of that price movement or, in fact, without regard to whether there has been any net directional price movement at all.

This fact can be very useful to the option buyer, but one will see a bit later that tracking volatility can lead to a timing tool for trading stocks or futures that can be quite effective. Schlumberger (SLB) had very little net directional price movement from June through November 2006. Yet it gyrated rather wildly within its trading range, and its 30-day volatility during this period averaged about 40 percent (see **Figure 7.7**).

Harley-Davidson (HOG), on the other hand, rallied steadily during this period, gaining about 50 percent from trough to peak. Yet its 30-day volatility was quite low, averaging in the neighborhood of 25 percent, as seen in **Figure 7.8**.

Based on the standard options pricing model, on-the-money options for non-dividend-paying stocks are priced in proportion to the volatility of an asset. On this basis (ignoring the fact that both Schlumberger and Harley-Davidson paid small dividends), options on Schlumberger were priced about 60 percent higher than options on Harley-Davidson (45 percent/25 percent) during this period. So call buyers on Schlumberger were doubly penalized: They paid up for the stock's relatively high volatility and received no payoff in directional movement.

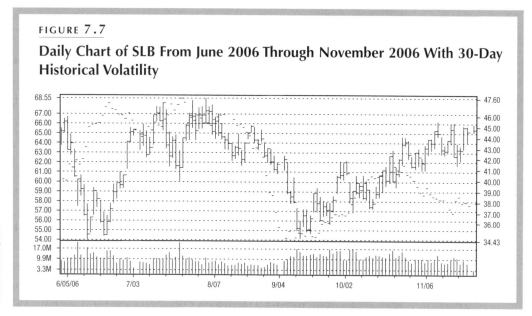

FIGURE 7.7

Daily Chart of SLB From June 2006 Through November 2006 With 30-Day Historical Volatility

Source: Thomson/ILX

FIGURE 7.8

Daily Chart of HOG From June 2006 Through November 2006 With 30-Day Historical Volatility

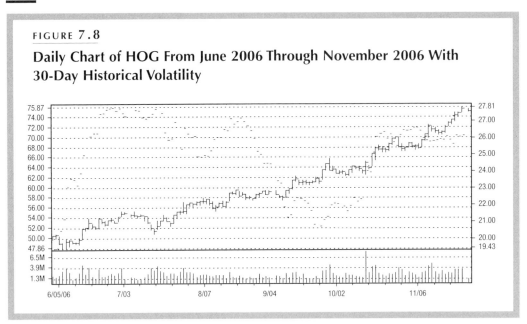

Source: Thomson/ILX

But Harley-Davidson call buyers received a double benefit: They paid relatively little for their options because of the stock's modest volatility and their payoff was huge on the big rally in the shares.

The point here is that there is a sweet spot for the option buyer—a period during which volatility is low, option prices are cheap (due to the low volatility), and directional movement is robust. Steady-as-she-goes rallies such as that experienced by Harley-Davidson in Figure 7.8, perversely enough, register as a low volatility input to the option pricing models, which then spit out low option premiums. In such an environment, the leverage offered to option buyers for the risk they assume increases substantially, often skewing the risk-reward equation dramatically in their favor.

In the Harley-Davidson example (assuming a 25 percent annual volatility), a six-month, 50-strike on-the-money call option would have been priced at about $3.50 when the shares were trading near the $50 level in June and July 2006. Harley-Davidson proceeded to trade as high as $75 by November 2006 (see Figure 7.8), and this 50-strike call option would have had a value of $25 ($75 – $50) at that time. The call buyer thus achieved a profit of $21.50 on a $3.50 investment, for a 614 percent gain, and the option's leverage in this example on the 50 percent gain in the stock was 12.3 to 1 (614 percent/50 percent). But if the options on Harley-Davidson were priced at the 40 percent volatility level (comparable to those of Schlumberger during this period), this leverage would have been significantly reduced to about 7.5 to 1.

Before the Storm

But does the fact that low volatility can turbo charge the leverage of option buyers have significance for the stock trader? It does in the sense that major troughs in volatility are often a signal of the calm before the storm, the storm being a major directional move for an asset.

A funny thing happened in July 2006 as crude oil futures (CL/) were pushing through the $80 mark amid talk of ever-rising energy prices—the four-week historical volatility for crude oil reached a three-year low (see **Figure 7.9**). In fact, crude oil volatility had declined by 60 percent from its pinnacle in late 2004 and by 50 percent from its September 2005 peak. And this trough in volatility was quickly followed by a 20 percent decline in crude oil prices.

The collapse of Amaranth Advisors (which lost half its asset value in September 2006 as a result of trading blowups in the natural gas market) was a tough lesson on the volatility of natural gas prices. But in yet another instance of the calm before the storm (see **Figure 7.10**), by early September 2006 the 10-day historical volatility of natural gas futures (NG/) had declined to less than half its level of just a month earlier. And natural gas futures then

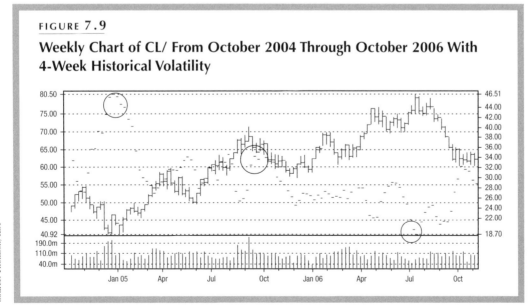

FIGURE **7.9**

Weekly Chart of CL/ From October 2004 Through October 2006 With 4-Week Historical Volatility

Source: Thomson/ILX

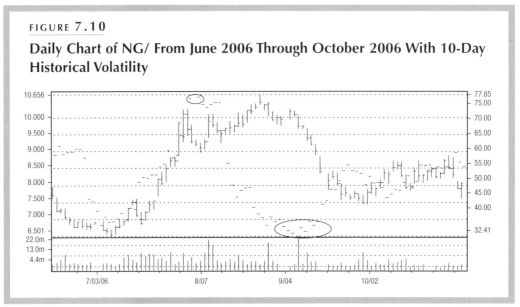

FIGURE **7.10**

Daily Chart of NG/ From June 2006 Through October 2006 With 10-Day Historical Volatility

Source: Thomson/ILX

proceeded to tank to the tune of about 25 percent during the two weeks that followed.

But major troughs in volatility can also be followed by moves to the upside, such as that which occurred with the stock market in 1995 at the inception of a multiyear bull market. Note in **Figure 7.11** how the 3-month volatility for the S&P 500 Index (SPX) hovered at very low levels from 1993 to 1995, with most readings below the 10 percent mark. The powerful bull market that began in 1995 and ended in early 2000 was characterized by steadily rising volatility.

Note as well that during the period from 2004 through late 2006, the market was characterized by low volatility readings similar to those registered a decade earlier at the beginning of a multiyear bull market. Yet what's particularly interesting is the nearly unanimously bearish conclusion by the investment community regarding the implications of these low volatility levels. The low VIX has been professed to be an indicator of increasing investor complacency, which is consistent with a stock market that is fast approaching a major top.

Troughs in volatility often indicate an upcoming acceleration in directional movement. In the examples from the crude oil (Figure 7.9) and natural gas (Figure 7.10) markets, this acceleration was to the downside. In the case of the stock market from 1993 to 1995 (Figure 7.11), the acceleration was to the upside. It appears that the odds favor a similar resolution of the 2004–2006 low volatility

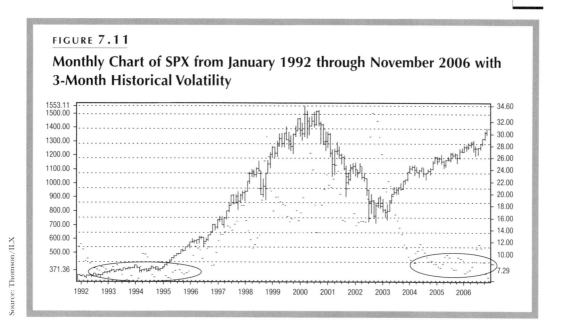

FIGURE 7.11

Monthly Chart of SPX from January 1992 through November 2006 with 3-Month Historical Volatility

Source: Thomson/ILX

situation, but at the very least, it is by no means certain that this low volatility period will be a harbinger of a bear market.

As of late 2006, the ultimate resolution of the 2004–2006 period of low volatility in terms of market direction has not been played out. But ultimately such periods prove to be unambiguously positive for the option buyer, who is paying very modest premiums for options that will provide him with turbo-charged leverage in the event of a major directional move, even as the chances for such a major move are heightened by the natural tendency for periods of low volatility to be followed by periods of increasing volatility.

Finding the Middle Ground

Much has been written about the choice that traders face between discretionary trading and systems-based trading. This is a false dichotomy in the sense that there is a middle ground that captures the best features of each approach.

Discretionary traders face the pitfall of too much subjectivity, which can lead to a lack of trading discipline that can include a sloppy entry-and-exit process, as well as potentially entering positions that do not result in an edge for the trader based on objective criteria. Systems-based trades can better meet the standards of discipline and objectivity, but they can suffer from a rigidity that leaves them vulnerable to failure when market environments change or when some or all of their trading criteria lose effectiveness, often from overuse by competing traders.

One compromise is to use a screening process to identify potentially tradable opportunities based on a set of objective criteria. A trader then drills down to extract much more detail on each name generated by the screen to determine which of these stocks might be tradable. The operative concept here is that it is impossible to screen for all the criteria necessary to generate a trade, but without the screening process one will fall prey to becoming "objectivity challenged" and insufficiently disciplined, and the breadth of ideas suffers, as well.

What follows is an illustration of a screening process that used criteria based on the principles discussed in this chapter. The screen is for potential buy candidates and is based on the general principle that stocks with strong price action combined with evidence of skeptical or bearish sentiment have a greater-than-average likelihood of posting additional gains. This approach combines the best features of "trading with the trend" and "avoiding the crowded trade," that is, the trade that might look good on the chart but is dangerous because too many players have already committed too much money, causing the stock to be excessively vulnerable to a reversal.

Our screening criteria are as follows:

- Put/call open interest ratio (SOIR) is in excess of 1.00 (open put positions exceed open call positions)
- SOIR is in the 75th percentile or greater of all SOIR readings taken during the past year
- The stock has outperformed the SPX by at least 10 percent during the past fifty trading days
- The short-interest ratio (short interest/average daily trading volume) is above 3.00
- Less than 50 percent of analysts rate the company a buy

This screen returned 28 names, and **Figure 7.12** displays a subset of seven names.

FIGURE **7.12**

Table of Filtered Stocks

DATE	COMPANY TICKER	PUT/ CALL RATIO	PUT OPEN INTEREST	CALL OPEN INTEREST	PERCENTILE RANK	RELATIVE STRENGTH	SHORT- INTEREST RATIO	ZACKS BUY/HOLD/SELL PERCENT
11/24/06	The DIRECTV Group (DTV)	1.59	26010	16398	84.86%	110%	5.3	13% / 69% / 19%
11/24/06	Eastman Kodak (EK)	1.18	193805	163995	76.10%	114%	15.66	0% / 33% / 67%
11/24/06	The Goodyear Tire & Rubber Company (GT)	1.47	140113	95149	75.70%	113%	5.2	0% / 100% / 0%
11/24/06	Gymboree (GYMB)	1.91	8485	4437	90.04%	111%	3.26	40% / 60% / 0%
11/24/06	JetBlue Airways (JBLU)	1.3	110316	84851	99.60%	135%	10.53	33% / 44% / 22%
11/24/06	Krispy Kreme Doughnuts (KKD)	1.53	147988	96942	86.06%	120%	53.15	50% / 0% / 50%
11/24/06	Lear Corporation (LEA)	1.61	142506	88387	84.86%	135%	7.83	7% / 64% / 29%

Source: Schaeffer's Investment Research

Investors often fear that focusing on strongly performing stocks on which expectations are modest or downright low might generate too few actionable trading ideas. After all, they argue, stocks that have been clearly outperforming the market will very likely have attracted significant call buying, the shorts will have covered their positions, and Wall Street analysts will surely have fallen in love with them. But, in fact, such low-expectation situations are rather plentiful, as negative opinions often die hard despite being regularly invalidated by strong stock performance. And the bonus for buying such stocks is that the uptrend is unlikely to end before there has been at least some capitulation by these skeptics.

Just how persistent a negative sentiment backdrop can be despite powerful price action is illustrated in **Figures 7.13** and **7.14**, which show the performance of DirecTV Group (DTV) and Gymboree (GYMB), respectively, for year-to-date 2006.

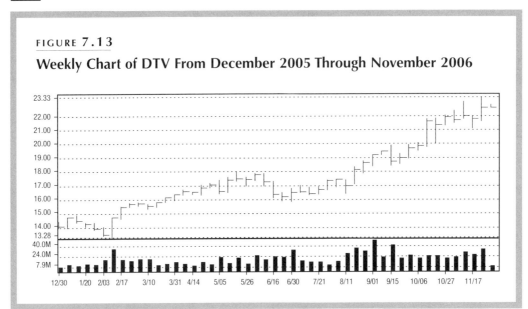

FIGURE **7.13**

Weekly Chart of DTV From December 2005 Through November 2006

Source: Thomson/ILX

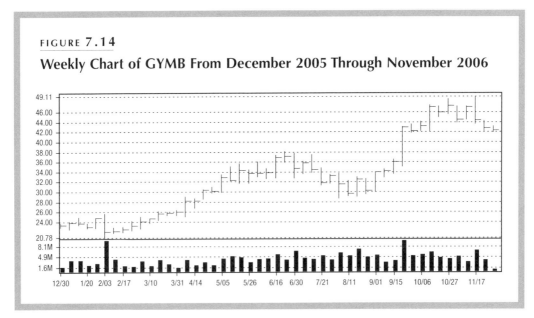

FIGURE **7.14**

Weekly Chart of GYMB From December 2005 Through November 2006

Source: Thomson/ILX

As of late 2006, DirecTV had gained 59.9 percent in 2006 and had reached an all-time high. Yet only 13 percent of Wall Street analysts had buy ratings on the stock, short interest was 5.3 times the stock's average daily trading volume, and put open interest exceeded call open interest by nearly 60 percent.

GYMB had posted an 83 percent year-to-date gain for 2006 and had also traded at all-time highs. But there was 80 percent more put open interest than call open interest on GYMB, short interest exceeded three times daily volume, and just 40 percent of analysts had buy ratings on the stock.

According to Humphrey Neill—the market analyst for whom I have the greatest respect and from whom I've learned the most over the years—in his classic work, *The Art of Contrary Thinking*, "No problem connected with the Theory of Contrary Opinion is more difficult to solve than: (a) how to know what prevailing general opinions are; and (b) how to measure their prevalence and intensity."

This chapter on options-based indicators in conjunction with other relevant sentiment indicators will help traders attack Neill's admittedly difficult problem and lead to more robust trading results. Being a successful contrarian investor is not about buying at low prices and buying cheap stocks; the successful contrarian investor is instead a buyer of low expectations on strong stocks. In fact, as Neill states in *The Art of Contrary Thinking*, "The 'crowd' is most enthusiastic and optimistic when it should be cautious and prudent, and is most fearful when it should be bold."

CHAPTER 8

Point and Figure Analysis: Modern Developments in an Old Technique

JEREMY DU PLESSIS

O ne can hardly describe the point and figure chart as a "breakthrough in technical analysis," but in its 130-year history, this measure of price changes has had many breakthroughs. That's because, unlike other chart types, point and figure analysis has not stood still, but has adapted to the changing times and technology. Even its name changed during its early development. This chapter highlights the changes to point and figure charts during their first one hundred years and discusses the new thinking and interpretation of this veteran strategy.

Point and Figure Charts: One Hundred Years of Change

Point and figure analysis started life on the trading floors and bucket shops of the late nineteenth and early twentieth centuries, where traders needed a method of recording prices. They simply wrote down the traded prices in columns; a rising column of numbers as the price rose and a falling column as the price fell. It served simply as a price record and ignored any fractions. Eventually traders began to notice patterns in their price records, and the record became known as a *figure chart*.

Writing down numbers was a tedious business, so traders began to use a vertical scale and inserted Xs instead of numbers. The resultant chart became known as a *point chart*. For thirty years, figure charts and point charts coexisted, with chartists referring to their point charts and their figure charts, or their *point and figure* charts, the name we use today. Figure charts were eventually dispensed with in the 1930s, and in the late 1940s, a new method of plotting the charts was proposed, using Xs for the rising columns and Os for falling columns. **Figure 8.1** shows this evolution.

FIGURE **8.1**

The Evolution of the Point and Figure Chart

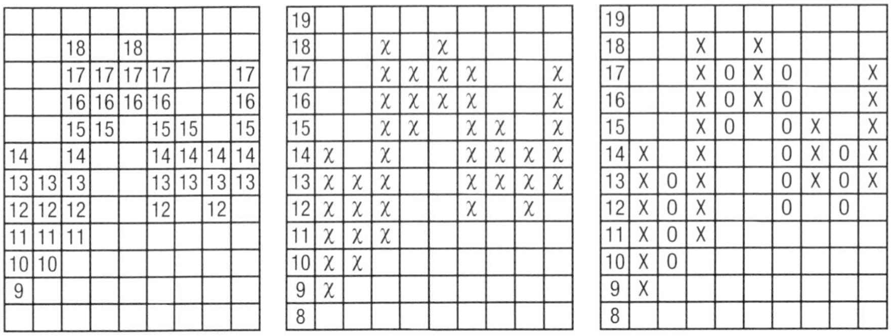

Figure Chart

	1	2	3	4	5	6	7	8	9	10
18		18		18						
17		17	17	17	17					17
16		16	16	16	16					16
15		15	15		15	15				15
14	14		14			14	14	14	14	
13	13	13	13			13	13	13	13	
12	12	12	12			12		12		
11	11	11	11							
10	10	10								
9	9									

Point Chart

	1	2	3	4	5	6	7	8	9	10
19										
18		χ		χ						
17		χ	χ	χ	χ					χ
16		χ	χ	χ	χ					χ
15		χ	χ		χ	χ				χ
14	χ		χ			χ	χ	χ	χ	
13	χ	χ	χ			χ	χ	χ	χ	
12	χ	χ	χ			χ		χ		
11	χ	χ	χ							
10	χ	χ								
9	χ									
8										

Point and Figure Chart

	1	2	3	4	5	6	7	8	9	10
19										
18		X		X						
17		X	O	X	O					X
16		X	O	X	O					X
15		X	O			O	X			X
14	X		X			O	X	O	X	
13	X	O	X			O	X	O	X	
12	X	O	X			O		O		
11	X	O	X							
10	X	O								
9	X									
8										

The plotting method has not remained constant either. As markets and data availability have changed, so too point and figure construction has adapted and changed. Originally, point and figure charts were constructed from the tape using every trade. The Xs were assigned a value—called the box size—of one point, and any price change less than one point was ignored. When the price reversed by one point, a new column was started. This became known as a 1-box reversal chart. Because these charts were very sensitive, a more condensed version was sought, and many traders transferred the data from their 1-box charts to their 3-box charts, where the column did not change unless the price reversal had the value of three boxes. Some even drew 5-box reversal charts to show the longer-term view, although these are rare nowadays, but 2-box reversal charts are popular. **Figure 8.2** shows charts drawn with four different box reversals. Notice how the look of the chart is transformed as the reversal is changed.

Originally, all these charts were constructed with tick data, which meant that the trader had to have access to every trade every day. This task was not a problem for anyone updating a small set of charts by hand each day, but it was an impossible one for anyone who wanted to start a new chart showing five years of tick data. In the late 1940s, therefore, A.W. Cohen of Chartcraft proposed a new construction method that ignored the tick data, taking instead the daily high or low to construct the chart. His method ignored 1-box reversal charts completely in favor of 3-box, and so 1-box fell out of favor. Because end-

FIGURE **8.2**

1-Box, 3-Box, 5-Box, and 2-Box Reversal Charts

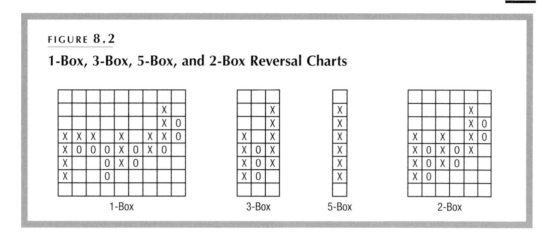

of-day data were being used to construct the charts, this change turned point and figure into a method for longer-term analysis.

Today, end-of-day point and figure charts are constructed with either the high or the low at the end of the day (Cohen's method) or with the close at the end of the day. What's more, the ability of computers to store vast amounts of data has allowed charts to be constructed using data at the end of every minute, every hour, or any intraday timeframe desired. Easy access to tick data has resulted in the original style tick point and figure charts making a comeback as well, although it is still not practical to draw a five-year point and figure chart using tick data for the simple reason that there is now too much data to store. All these changes, however, have made point and figure charts suitable for all time horizons, from very short term to very long term.

With the popularity of 3-box reversal charts, many common patterns have been identified and named. Space here precludes a full discussion of point and figure signals and patterns, but it's important to note that they are mostly based on breakouts. If a column of Xs rises above the previous column of Xs (see the 3-box chart in Figure 8.2), that is a basic point and figure buy signal. If a column of Os falls below the previous column of Os, that is a basic sell signal. All point and figure patterns are built from these two basic patterns. The wider they are and the more times the price reaches the equilibrium level before breaking out, the stronger the subsequent signal. Simple patterns combine to make more complex ones, and point and figure analysts always look to see whether these defined patterns exist and if a smaller pattern is part of a larger one.

Time Horizons

Before describing some new and innovative point and figure techniques, it's important to review how time horizon works in point and figure charts. Changing the box size effectively changes the time horizon of the chart without actually changing the underlying data. To understand this, imagine you are day-trading the Dow Jones Industrial Average. Would you draw a point and figure chart with a 50 point box? This would mean 50 points in the direction of the column produces a new box and 150 points against the direction produces a reversal and a new column. A day trader could not possibly make money with such an insensitive chart, but a medium-term investor may be quite happy with a chart drawn with those parameters. A short-term trader would be looking at perhaps a 5 point or 10 point box size. Thus, changing the box size does change the time horizon—though not the time frame—of the chart. The smaller the box size, the more sensitive the chart, and the shorter the time horizon. Typically, a point and figure analyst will look at two, perhaps three point and figure charts of the same instrument but with different box sizes and/or reversals to get a clearer picture of what is happening.

Internal 45° Trend Lines

Trend lines may be drawn in two ways on point and figure charts: either subjectively by connecting higher lows for an uptrend or lower highs for a downtrend, or objectively by drawing trend lines at 45° from highs or lows. These objective lines are most effective on 3-box reversal charts and are rarely used on 1-box charts. It's a unique feature of point and figure charts because only point and figure charts are drawn on a squared grid allowing the 45° lines to be drawn in the same position no matter what the aspect ratio of the chart.

The lines are drawn through the corners of the boxes from bottoms and tops, providing what are called bullish support and bearish resistance lines. They are the lines that show the last level of support in an uptrend or resistance in a downtrend. Evidence shows that the price behaves extremely well with these 45° lines, which are therefore used to determine major trend changes. Consider what is required to remain above a 45° trend line: The price must rise by at least five boxes for every three that it falls, and if it can't do that, it can't maintain a bull trend. Similarly, to maintain a 45° downtrend, the price must fall by at least five boxes for every three that it rises.

One problem with traditional 45° bullish support and bearish resistance lines, however, is that in strong bull and bear trends, prices move away from the 45° line, making them less significant for determining trend changes. To resolve this problem, new lines, called internal 45° lines, are drawn from reaction points during the trend to provide additional support or resistance lines closer to the price action.

The chart in **Figure 8.3** is a 10 × 3 point and figure chart of the S&P 500, showing the main bullish support and bearish resistance lines marked 1, 2, and 3. When price action moves away from these main lines, a series of 45° internal trend lines closer to the price action are drawn from reaction points during the trend. The importance of any internal line is reinforced if it is touched again when internal line 4 is at point (a), and internal line 5 is at point (b). Clustering of the internal lines is also important when a number of them drawn from differ-

FIGURE **8.3**

10 × 3 Point and Figure Chart of S&P 500, Showing 45° Trend Lines and Internals

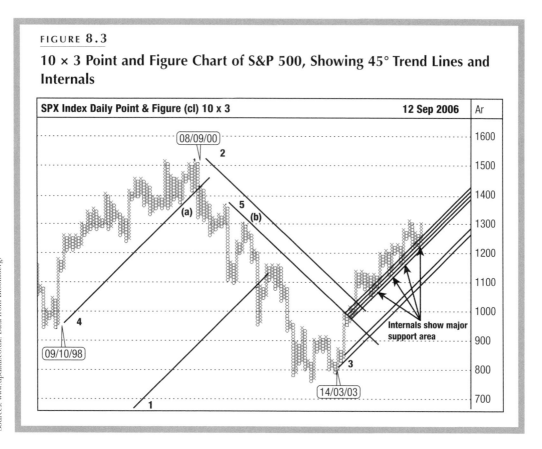

ent reaction points cluster together. This is clearly seen in the current uptrend, in which four internal lines run close together. This provides a significant and important support area for the uptrend, which becomes just as important as the main 45° uptrend line 3, if not more so. The more times an internal line is touched, the more important it becomes. This is because the starting point of the line and the 45° angle, not the price action, determine a 45° line position.

The main advantage of 45° trend lines is that they are objective, and no amount of subjective interpretation or positioning can influence them. As you can see, they carve up the chart into bull and bear trends and are very effective in showing areas of support and resistance.

Using Point and Figure Price Targets Effectively

From the earliest days of point and figure analysis, analysts have been establishing price targets from the charts derived from the width of congestion areas. Initially, the targets were on 1-box reversal charts, but 1-box price targets are less objective than those obtained from 3-box charts, which are therefore more popular today.

There are two ways to establish targets with a 3-box reversal chart. The vertical count is based on the thrust off a low or a high, and the horizontal count is based on the width of a top or bottom pattern. The vertical count is three times the length of the thrust column, whereas the horizontal count is three times the width of the pattern. Because computers now perform these calculations, the temptation is to count every column and pattern until one produces the required result. Certain rules, however, should be adhered to. Vertical counts should be established only from the first thrust off a low or a high, or the thrust off an intermediate mini-bottom or mini-top, or the breakout column from a pattern. Horizontal counts, however, may be established only from a top or bottom pattern where there is a clear column moving into the pattern and then some sideways congestion and a clear column moving out of the pattern.

Remember that these are potential targets and cannot be achieved with precision. Some may not be achieved at all; in fact, the last target in a trend seldom is. However, the achievement or non-achievement of a target gives important information about the strength of the trend. In bull trends, all upside targets should be achieved or exceeded, whereas downside targets should not be reached. In downtrends, all downside targets should be achieved or exceeded, whereas upside targets should not be reached. So assessing trends becomes an evidence-gathering process. If, during a bull trend, an upside target is not achieved or is negated, that is evidence that the uptrend is weakening. If at the same time, downside targets start to be reached, this is further bearish evidence and an indication that the uptrend is ending. The converse is true for downtrends, where evidence that a downtrend is deteriorating can be seen when downside targets are not achieved or canceled. Combined with the break of internal 45° lines, using point and figure targets this way allows you to see trend deterioration before the main trend line is broken.

The chart in **Figure 8.4**, showing the top in the Nasdaq, is a good example of how targets can provide evidence about the strength of the trend. Upside count (a) of 3,400 from the July 1999 low was exceeded as was count (b) of 4,920 from the October 1999 low, indicating a strong bull trend. At this stage, everything is in place for the achievement of the new target (c) of 5,640 from the January 2000 low. The Nasdaq turned, however, and allowed the establishment and acti-vation of downside count (d) of 3,720 from the February 2000 top and another count (e) of 3,460 from the second top in March 2000. At this stage the bull trend is still in place and there seems little likelihood that these downside counts will be achieved. But in April 2000, both downside counts were achieved, negat-ing the upside count (c) of 5,640 by passing through the bottom of the column from which that count was established. Although the main 45° trend line (1) is still intact at this stage, the evidence for a continuing bull trend is decreasing. An upside count has been negated, two downside counts have been achieved, and some internal 45° lines have been breached.

Following the price action, notice that two more upside counts (f) and (g) of 4,660 and 5,100 were not achieved but all the downside counts (h), (i), and (j) of 3,280, 3,660, and 3,620 were, which further adds to the bearish evidence. So, long before bullish support line (1) was breached, there was sufficient bearish evidence available to make a decision about the end of the bull trend.

Again, you should not expect targets to be achieved with precision, but that does not mean that targets from important patterns should be ignored if they seem improbable at the time. For example, horizontal count (k) taken across the large top between the October 1999 column going into the top and the October 2000 column coming out of the top gives a target of 1,080. When this target was established in October 2000, it seemed unlikely that it would be achieved; still, it should not be ignored, because the pattern from which it was established is an important pattern in the chart. In any case, before 1,080 can be achieved, many other smaller targets will have to be achieved first, helping to reinforce the like-

Sources: www.updata.co.uk. Data from Bloomberg.

FIGURE **8.4**

20 × 3 Point and Figure Chart of Nasdaq Composite Index, Showing Targets

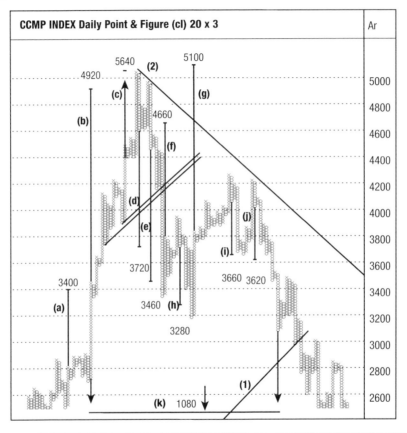

lihood that 1,080 will be achieved. In fact, the October 2002 bottom was within 30 points of the target.

There are, therefore, two reasons for establishing and analyzing targets, a trend-evaluation element, determined by the achievement or non-achievement of a target, and a prediction element, which helps to assess the potential price move. Combining the two is important. Moreover, clustering targets—when two counts from two different columns or patterns come in at a similar level—reinforces both the chances of a count in that region being achieved and the importance of the information, if it is not.

Risk-Reward Ratios From a Point and Figure Chart

The ability to obtain objective targets from a point and figure chart makes the calculation of risk-reward ratios—or, as some term them, reward-to-risk ratios—much easier. They are calculated by dividing the potential reward by the known risk, thereby providing a figure that tells you the number of points of reward for every point of risk you take on. The risk is the easy part of the calculation; calculating the reward has always been more difficult, causing many to ignore the ratio completely. The risk is the difference between your entry price and the price at your proposed exit. In point and figure terms, the exit price is the level where the first, or sometimes second, point and figure sell signal will be. The reward in point and figure terms is the difference between the point and figure target and entry price.

Risk-reward ratios are calculated at the time a trade is entered. Not only do they tell you whether the trade is worth taking, on point and figure charts they also tell you where to place your stop and what the risk-reward ratio is of using that stop. The upper section of **Figure 8.5** shows a progression of charts for Bank of America. The first panel shows a double-top buy signal at point A activating an upside vertical count of 43. If you place your stop at 28, the first point and figure sell signal, your risk-reward ratio is 5. If, however, you prefer to place your stop below the bottom of the pattern, your risk-reward ratio is only 1.7. The risk-reward ratio therefore helps you to decide where to place your stop.

The second panel shows the chart a few columns further on. A second pattern breakout occurs at point B, allowing you to decide the risk-reward ratio of adding to your position. Stops at 28.5 or 28 give acceptable risk-reward ratios of 3.8 or 3.3, respectively. The third panel progresses further with another pattern breakout at point C. The risk-reward ratios of entering a trade at this point are an unacceptable 1.2 and 0.7. The final panel shows the chart up to date. The breakout at point D activates another vertical count of 46. The risk-reward ratios of acting on this are 3.4 and 1.5 based on stops at 35 and 32, respectively. The initial target of 43 is reached, as is the 46 target a few columns later on. Another vertical count is activated with the breakout at point E. Risk-reward ratios are 2.3 and 1.6 based on stops at 41.5 and 39.5, respectively. Once again, these help you to assess whether the trade is worth taking and which level you will use for your stop.

Risk-reward ratios work for down counts as well. The lower section of Figure 8.5 shows a progression of charts for Home Depot. The double-bottom sell at point X activates a vertical down count of 32.75. The risk-reward ratios are 3.9 and 1.7, indicating that if you place your stop at 41.25, the trade is worth taking,

Sources: www.updata.co.uk. Data from Bloomberg.

FIGURE 8.5

0.5 × 3 of Bank of America & 0.25 × 3 of Home Depot, Showing Risk-Reward Ratios

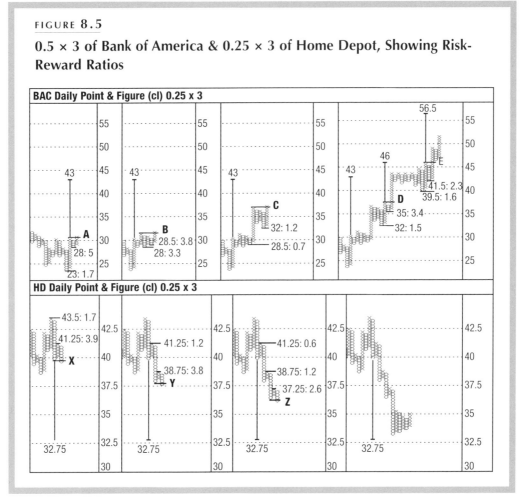

but at 43.5, it is not. The next panel shows another sell at point Y, with a new stop level at 38.75, yielding a risk-reward ratio of 3.8. Notice the risk-reward ratio based on the old stop of 41.25 is now only 1.2, indicating that it is too far away to use. The next panel shows another sell at point Z, with a risk-reward ratio of 2.6 if the stop is placed at 37.25. The final panel shows the target being reached and a point and figure buy signal to close the short trade.

The addition of objective risk-reward ratios to point and figure analysis has improved the decision-making process considerably. It has helped analysts to decide not only whether a trade is worth taking but also whether the stop they're considering is too far away from the entry price.

Log Scaling

One of the greatest innovations in point and figure charting has been the development of log scale point and figure charts. They were introduced in the early 1980s, when technical analysis software for PCs made the calculations possible. Using a fixed box size of 1 point or 10 points is fine if the price remains within a reasonable range, but it's of little use when the price rises or falls by large percentages. To accommodate increasing prices, point and figure analysts used to (some still do) change the box size—the value of the Xs and Os—at specific price levels. For example, when the price is between 0 and 5, a box size of 0.25 is used; when the price is between 5 and 10, a box size of 0.5 is used, and so on, with the box size changing at certain price levels. Between 50 and 100, the box size would be 1, and between 100 and 200, it would be 2. This design has the effect of producing a pseudo log scale chart, but at the same time, it creates problems. First, 45° trend lines, which must pass through these box size step-up points, are compromised; second, point and figure targets become more difficult to establish if the box size changes part way through the counting column.

The computerization of point and figure charts enables true log scale point and figure charts to be drawn by increasing the value of each box by a fixed percentage. This means the percentage change throughout the chart is constant, but the box size at each level varies. So instead of a box size measured in the traditional fixed number of points, the box size is measured as a percentage. For example, if a box size of 1 percent is chosen, the size of the box above is 1 percent larger than the box below, or 1.01 times the size of the box below.

Point and figure construction is about setting a scaling framework before the chart is drawn. With fixed box size (arithmetic scale) point and figure charts, the box size determines the chart grid. So a box size of 5 points results in grid values of 5, 10, 15, 20 points, whereas a box size of 10 points results in grid values of 10, 20, 30, 40 points. With a percentage box size (log scale) chart, however, the grid is determined by increasing the value of each grid point by the percentage. Mathematically, it's easier to do this by taking the natural log of the starting price, as well as the percentage increment, and adding the logged increment to the logged starting price to achieve the new grid. Once the grid has been obtained, the chart data are logged as well and the chart plotted using the logged values. Finally, the logged values and grid levels are anti-logged to bring the chart back to real prices. The result is a true log scale point and figure chart in which the box size grows smoothly as the price rises, thereby catering to the

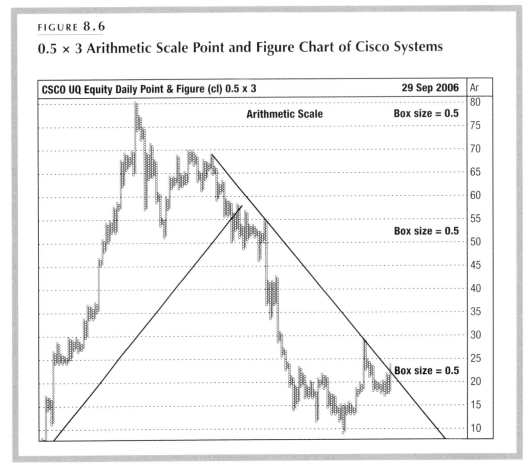

Sources: www.updata.co.uk. Data from Bloomberg.

FIGURE 8.6

0.5 × 3 Arithmetic Scale Point and Figure Chart of Cisco Systems

change in price volatility. This approach has brought a new dimension to longer-term point and figure analysis, and accommodates sharp rises and declines in price by constantly adjusting the box size.

Figure 8.6 shows an arithmetic scale point and figure chart of Cisco Systems, Inc. Each box throughout the chart is 0.5 points (fifty cents), but the price range is between $10 and $80, making 0.5 an unsuitable box size for most of the range. The size is too small and therefore too sensitive when Cisco is at $80 and too large and insensitive when Cisco is at $10. The solution to this dilemma is to log scale the chart, making the box size a percentage instead.

Figure 8.7 shows a log scale chart of Cisco Systems. Each box throughout the chart is 2 percent of the latest price, and the value of each box is 2 percent larger than the box below, so the value of the box increases as the price rises. For

FIGURE 8.7

2 % × 3 Log Scale Point and Figure Chart of Cisco Systems

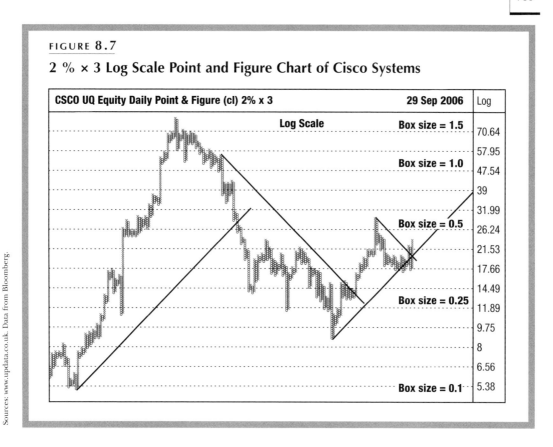

Sources: www.updata.co.uk. Data from Bloomberg.

example, at $75, the box size is 1.5, whereas at $5 it is 0.1. There is a smooth, not a stepped, increase in the box value as the price rises and falls.

In comparing the two charts, notice the large swings in the arithmetic chart around the 75 level, indicating that the box size is too small. Notice the lack of sensitivity around the 10 level, indicating a box size that is too large. The log scale chart adjusts for this automatically, because it is a chart of constant percentage change rather than constant point change. Trend lines are valid on both charts, but they pass through different points. Point and figure targets (not shown) will also be different because the column lengths and pattern widths are different as are the values of the boxes within the columns.

The decision whether to use log or arithmetic scale is no different from that with bar or line charts. Log is better for longer-term analysis and when the price has risen exponentially. Arithmetic is better for the shorter-term and when the price is within a range. Some instruments have linear trends, and some have exponential trends. The simple rule is to look at both, and you will soon see which is better. Notice, for example, the last pattern in both charts. They are almost the same, showing that the box size on the arithmetic chart is similar to that on the log scale chart. So if you're analyzing just a small section, there is virtually no difference between log and arithmetic.

Point and Figure Charts of Indicators

Point and figure is simply a method of displaying price data without regard to the passage of time. This means that the point and figure method can be used to plot any series of numbers including calculated indicators. This is done for all the same reasons that point and figure analysis of price is used: objective trend lines, objective targets, clear-cut signals, and generally easier analysis. In theory, any indicator can be plotted in point and figure style; however, smoothed indicators such as a moving average or MACD should be avoided because they result in long, uninterrupted columns without reversals and provide no useful information to a point and figure analyst. The most effective use of point and figure indicators is relative strength and accumulation/distribution lines like on-balance volume (OBV), although oscillators such as RSI, momentum, and overbought/oversold also work well in point and figure format. Here we'll concentrate on relative strength only, but the implementation and analysis is the same for other indicators.

Relative strength is the simple division of the price of one instrument (usually a stock) by the price of another (usually an index). Most people use relative strength in this form, but the problem is that the scaling numbers are just ratios and therefore mean nothing, so it is difficult to compare the relative strength of one stock with the relative strength of another. It is better to normalize the data by setting it to 100 at a benchmark date so that the scale reflects the over- or underperformance of the stock to the index. This makes the comparison of one relative strength chart with another easier, and it's easier to choose point and figure box sizes, as well.

The normalization process is as follows:

● Calculate the relative strength ratio throughout the time series
● Choose a benchmark date such as the beginning of a year
● Divide all the relative strength ratios by the ratio on the benchmark date
● Multiply all by 100

This calculation has no effect on the shape of the relative strength chart, but it becomes far more readable.

Figure 8.8 shows a normalized relative strength chart of Anheuser-Busch against the S&P 500, with the data normalized to 100 on January 2, 2000. Notice first that the scale has meaning. The last value on the chart is 168, which means that Anheuser-Busch has outperformed the S&P 500 by 68 percent since January 2000 despite underperforming the index since the break of the relative strength uptrend in August 2003. Notice also how well the 45° trend lines define the up and down trends in the relative strength chart, providing support at point (a) and resistance at points (b) and (c), with further resistance looking likely at point (d).

Point and figure targets can also help you to determine how far the relative strength can go and whether the trend is deteriorating. The numbers themselves

FIGURE **8.8**

Normalized Relative Strength Chart of Anheuser-Busch Against the S&P 500

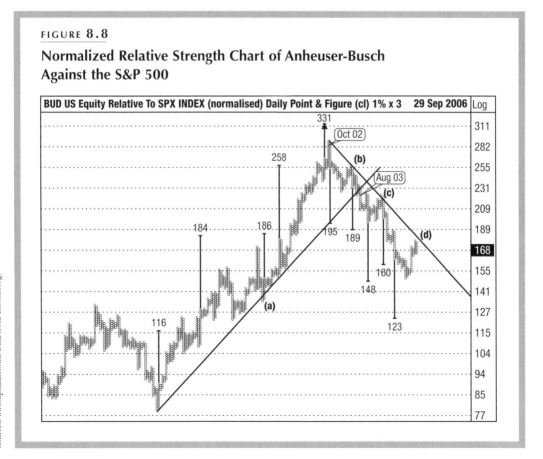

Sources: www.updata.co.uk. Data from Bloomberg.

are not important, but the level of the target is. A number of targets have been placed on the chart so you can see the levels predicted and how these help to confirm or reject the trend. Notice during the uptrend in relative strength that all upside counts are exceeded and no downside count is achieved until the top in October 2002, when the upside count of 331 is negated and downside counts are achieved. There is one outstanding downside count of 123, indicating that there is more downside potential on the relative strength.

The chart in Figure 8.8 is a log scale chart using a box size of 1 percent. It is suggested that you use log scale charts for relative strength so you can match these with the same percentage box size on the price chart, ensuring that you're looking at the same time horizon. You may look at a shorter time horizon by changing the box size to 0.5 percent or even 0.25 percent.

Moving Averages, Parabolic SAR, and Bollinger Bands

Another recent development in point and figure charts is the addition of moving averages following the technique discussed by Kenneth Tower in his chapter on point and figure charts in *New Thinking in Technical Analysis* (Bloomberg Press, 2000). Tower suggests that the length of the moving average be measured in columns rather than in days or weeks, allowing moving averages to be used effectively on point and figure charts. The purpose of using moving averages on point and figure charts is to assist in defining the trend and therefore in accepting or rejecting point and figure buy and sell signals. Because signals are more objective on 3-box charts, the use of moving averages tends to be easier, although there is no reason why 1-box charts can't be used just as effectively. Trend direction is best defined by two moving averages of different lengths. When the shorter length crosses above the longer length, the chart is placed on a buy alert. The buy signal occurs on the next point and figure double-top signal.

Determining the best lengths to use is a trial and error, or optimization process. A good rule of thumb is to use lengths that are half those you use on line charts, because in calculating moving averages on point and figure, the average of each column is calculated before the moving average is calculated. Average lengths can be close to one another because a crossover is not a signal but rather an alert. Crossovers have to be reconfirmed by the point and figure signal.

Panel A in **Figure 8.9** is a 2% × 3 log scale chart of the Walt Disney Co., with 5- and 8-column exponential moving averages. When the 5 crosses below the 8,

Sources: www.updata.co.uk. Data from Bloomberg.

FIGURE 8.9

2% × 3 Log Scale Chart of Walt Disney, With 5- and 8-Column Exponential Moving Averages (Panel A) and Wilder Parabolic SAR (Panel B); 0.5% × 3 Log Scale Chart of DuPont, With 10-Column Bollinger Bands (Panel C); and 1% × 1 Log Scale Chart of MedImmune, With 10-Column Bollinger Bands (Panel D)

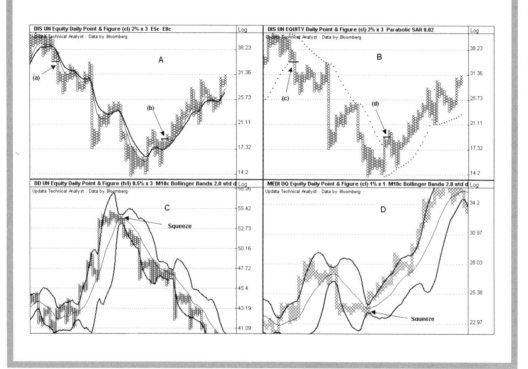

you're placed on sell alert to take the next point and figure double-bottom sell signal, marked (a). When the 5 crosses above the 8, you're placed on buy alert to take the next double-top buy signal, marked (b). Notice that a number of false buy and sell signals against the flow of the moving averages is avoided by using the crossover as the alert trigger.

The use of calculated lines on point and figure charts is not limited to moving averages; Wilder's parabolic SAR (stop and reverse) may also be calculated based on columns and used in a similar way.

Panel B in Figure 8.9 is the same log scale chart of Walt Disney but with a Wilder parabolic SAR with an acceleration factor of .02. The parabolic is a stop-and-reverse system, in which the parabolic line starts away from the price but then accelerates toward it as the trend matures. Its use with point and figure is the same as that for moving averages: The parabolic switch from long to short places you on alert, and the next double-bottom sell signal is taken at point (c). The parabolic switch to long places you on alert to take the next double-top buy at point (d). Notice that immediately after the buy at point (d), the price retraced but did not trigger the parabolic.

Another innovation in point and figure charts has been the use of Bollinger bands, because they show a number of things that are not immediately apparent from the plain point and figure chart. These are trend strength, overbought and oversold situations, as well as areas of low volatility. The standard Bollinger settings are 20 days and 2 standard deviations, but with point and figure charts it is suggested that 10 columns and 2 standard deviations be used.

Panel C in Figure 8.9 shows a 0.5% × 3 log scale of DuPont, with a set of 10-column Bollinger bands. The strength of the uptrend is indicated by the price remaining above the moving average and continually touching the upper band. In the same way, the strength of the downtrend is indicated by the price continually touching the lower band. Failure to cling to the outer bands is a signal that the trend is weakening as seen at the top when the column of Xs fails to reach the upper band. Point and figure shows accumulation or distribution by congesting sideways. The Bollinger bands emphasize this by converging into what Bollinger calls "the squeeze," indicating very low volatility and the probability of a sharp move. The width of the bands during the squeeze is easy to see on a log scale point and figure chart because the number of boxes between the bands is the percentage difference. In the chart in panel C, you can clearly see the squeeze occurring during the congestion after the uptrend, where the bands converge to four boxes, or 2 percent apart.

Sometimes, however, the squeeze is difficult to see in 3-box reversal charts, so if you see a potential congestion pattern and you're not sure whether a squeeze is taking place, it's worth looking at it in a 1-box reversal chart. Panel D is a 1% × 1 chart of MedImmune, Inc. The squeeze of three boxes, or 3 percent, before the sharp uptrend is easy to see. It's worth noting that 1-box reversal charts are clearer and easier to analyze if they're drawn using the point method of Xs only.

Indicators of Point and Figure Charts

One of the traditional disadvantages of point and figure charts is that they can't be used with indicators such as MACD, stochastic, or OBV, and the like, because they don't have a time scale and consequently won't match up with the indicator. If, however, the indicator is calculated based on columns rather than time, any indicator can be used with a point and figure chart. In fact, the indicator becomes an indicator of the point and figure chart, not of the raw price data. The difference is that the indicator "period" (length) is measured in columns rather than days or weeks. This approach opens up a host of new point and figure analytical techniques because it allows you to look for over-bought or oversold conditions or for divergence in relation to point and figure charts using volume-based indicators such as OBV. Remember, however, that the indicator construction is based not only on the indicator length in columns but also on the number of columns in the chart, and that varies according to the box size and reversal used. An RSI calculated on a length of 14 columns can produce a dozen different RSI charts, depending on which box and rever-sal is chosen for the point and figure chart from which the RSI is derived. The analogy is to changing the time frame of your bar charts to produce different RSIs based on hourly, daily, or weekly data.

Indicators do not work well on fixed box size arithmetic point and figure charts because the sensitivity and hence the number of columns is not consis-tent throughout the chart. Log scale percentage box charts should, therefore, always be used.

Figure 8.10 is a $1\% \times 3$ log scale point and figure chart of Merck & Co., with an MACD using column lengths of 26 and 12, with a signal line of 9 columns. Notice how the MACD indicator adds information to the point and figure chart in a number of ways. It shows when the point and figure chart is overbought or oversold, when the MACD moves to extremes away from the zero line. It also shows divergence, or nonconfirmation. For example, the new price high, marked (a), is not matched by a new high in the MACD, which is bearish. Similarly, the new price low, marked (b), is not matched by a new low in the MACD, which is bullish. In addition, in the traditional way, the MACD issues buy or sell alerts when the MACD crosses above or below its trigger line (moving average). Because point and figure buy and sell signals come from the point and figure chart itself, the MACD signals put you on alert to look for the next point and figure signal.

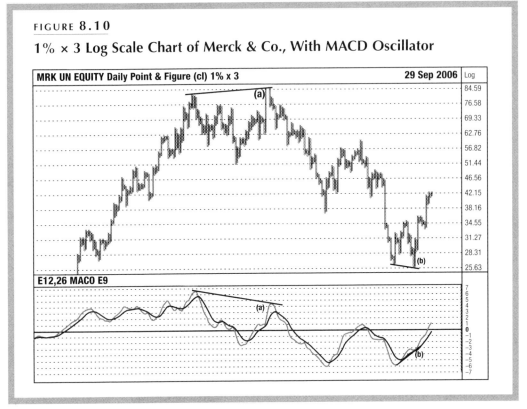

FIGURE **8.10**

1% × 3 Log Scale Chart of Merck & Co., With MACD Oscillator

Sources: www.updata.co.uk. Data from Bloomberg.

Almost any indicator, such as RSI, momentum, stochastic, or even directional movement, can be used in this way. **Figure 8.11** shows a 0.5% × 3 log scale point and figure chart of the S&P 500, with a 14-column directional movement below. Traditionally, a directional movement buy signal occurs when +DI crosses above –DI as it did in May 2003, shown by the vertical line on the chart. In point and figure terms, this places you on alert to take the next point and figure buy signal. Thereafter, the position remains unchanged, but notice that although +DI and –DI came close during the May 2006 correction, +DI remained above.

An oscillator isn't the only indicator that works well; accumulation/distribution lines such as OBV are also very informative. Many regard the lack of volume as a failing of point and figure charts, because it's important to know whether there is volume behind a point and figure buy or sell signal. Adding an OBV of a point and figure, therefore, not only helps you to decide whether to act on a point and figure signal but also gives you an overview for the volume flow within the point and figure chart.

FIGURE 8.11

0.5% × 3 Log Scale Chart of S&P 500, with Directional Movement Oscillator

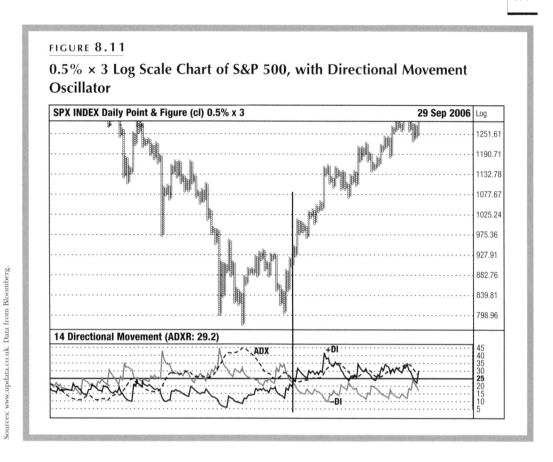

Figure 8.12 is a 1% × 3 log scale point and figure chart of Black and Decker Corp., with an OBV below. The important point and figure buy signal in May 2003 was accompanied by a sharp increase in OBV showing volume behind the price breakout, which is bullish. The price continued to rise, with OBV confirming the price moves. In January 2005, the point and figure gave a triple-top buy signal.

When a signal of this importance is seen after a long uptrend, it should be treated with suspicion; only an accompanying sharp move in OBV would confirm the signal to be significant. Although OBV rose, it did not spike, which places doubt on the strength of the signal. More important, though, is that when the price pulled back into the pattern, the OBV retraced more than it had gained, which has bearish connotations. After a period of corrective consolidation, the price made a higher high in July 2005, but notice that the OBV did not follow and peaked lower than the January peak, indicating no volume behind the

Sources: www.updata.co.uk. Data from Bloomberg.

FIGURE **8.12**

1% × 3 Log Scale Chart of Black and Decker, With On-Balance Volume Line

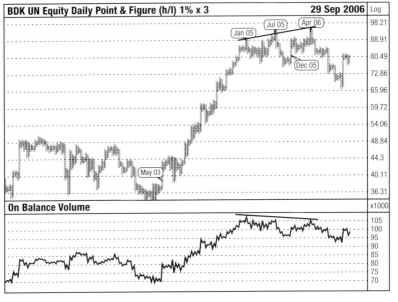

move to the July high. The price then corrected sharply followed by the OBV. In December 2005, it rose sharply, but although the OBV followed, it did not have the same impetus. The price consolidated again and broke out to a new high. Notice that the OBV did not do so. Looking at the OBV of a point and figure chart helps you to accept or reject point and figure signals because a good signal should have volume behind it.

Remember, when drawing indicators of point and figure, the box size, the reversal, and the indicator lengths are all input parameters. In the examples above, the standard indicator lengths have been used and the point and figure chart parameters have varied. The charts demonstrate what an important point and figure development this is. In most cases, the traditional periods can be translated into columns, although there is a fine balance between the sensitivity of the point and figure chart and the column length of the indicator.

Market Breadth Indicators

Point and figure also has its own measures of market breadth. The most common calculates on a day-to-day basis the percentage of stocks in an index for which the last signal was a point and figure double-top buy signal. The indicator is called bullish percent and has been in use for some fifty years. But there are other ways to calculate point and figure–based market breadth indicators; for example, the percentage of stocks for which the relative strength chart against the index is on a buy signal, or the last column is a column of Xs, or the last plotted box is above a chosen column moving average. These indicators are normally plotted as point and figure charts but can be plotted as line charts as well. They act like overbought/oversold oscillators and put you in the right frame of mind when assessing whether to accumulate or distribute stocks in the index.

Flipping Point and Figure Charts

Technical analysts have been turning printed charts upside down for years to remove any subconscious bias, but flipping a point and figure chart wasn't as effective because the columns of Xs and Os were the wrong way when turned upside down. Computers can, however, flip the chart and swap the Xs for Os and the Os for Xs to provide a perfect point and figure chart upside down and "fool" the brain into believing the chart is the right way up.

Most who analyze a chart have a bias. Some are constantly bullish and can't see tops; others are bearish and can't see bottoms. No matter what bias you have, flipping the chart tends to remove that bias even though consciously you know the chart is upside down. It's important that the flipped chart look as natural as possible, so maintaining the original price scale—even though the numbers don't match the flipped chart—adds to the deception. The eye and brain must be fooled into thinking that the chart is right side up.

There are two occasions to flip a chart: first, when you just can't make your mind up about the state of the chart, and second, when you're so blinded by extreme confidence in your analysis that you can't see any opposite signs. It's quite amazing how well it works. Even though you consciously know it's upside down, you'll analyze it as if it's right side up.

The chart in **Figure 8.13** is a 1% × 3 chart of the Dow flipped upside down. Notice the price scale is not flipped, thus aiding the deception, but the columns

FIGURE **8.13**

Flipped Chart of Dow Jones Industrial Average

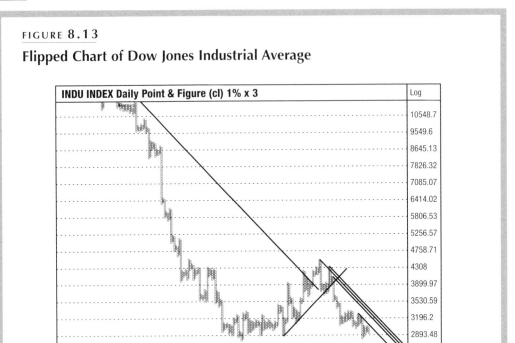

Sources: www.updata.co.uk. Data from Bloomberg.

of Xs have become Os and the columns of Os have become Xs. Some analysts may be looking for a top in the Dow; some may be talking about new highs. You make up your own mind by looking at the chart. Do you think it's making a bottom, or do you think it's a continuation of the downtrend? Whatever you think, the opposite is, in fact, your view, because the chart is upside down.

Flipping charts is one technique you should not overlook, and you will find the point and figure version works better than the version for candles or bar charts.

—⁓—

LIKE NO OTHER chart, the point and figure chart has evolved to maintain itself in the modern world, and there's no doubt that it will continue to do so. Not being bounded by time allows it to be adapted in more ways than any other chart. This chapter has covered a number of new and not-so-new point and figure techniques; from internal 45° trend lines to log scaled point and figure charts; from establishing point and figure targets to calculating risk-reward ratios from them; from the use of moving averages and parabolic curves on point and figure charts to the use of Bollinger bands; from point and figure charts of indicators to the newest technique of indicators of point and figure charts; and finally to one of the best techniques any technical analyst can use, flipping point and figure charts upside down. All these techniques have made an already superb technique even better and incorporated what were regarded as non-point and figure tools into the analysis of point and figure charts.

What's more, the clear-cut and unambiguous way that 3-box point and figure signals are generated, trend lines are established, and risk-reward ratios are calculated makes them one of the most powerful techniques for scanning universes of stocks to produce shortlists. For example, looking for stocks that have just given a double-top buy signal, are above their 45° trend lines, and have a current risk-reward ratio greater than 3 will produce a suitable shortlist of potential candidates for buying. Adding relative strength and/or on-balance volume to the scan narrows the field even further.

CHAPTER 9

Deconstructing the Market: The Application of Market Profile to Global Spreads

ROBIN MESCH

Deconstruction, a method of analysis that emphasizes the relational quality of meaning, involves discovering, recognizing, and understanding the underlying—and unspoken and implicit—assumptions, ideas, and frameworks that form the basis for thought and belief.

Most spread traders are accustomed to working with line charts that show the value of the spread at discrete points in time, connected by lines. For example, **Figure 9.1** is a daily chart of the 10-year U.S. Treasury notes versus the 10-year EuroGerman Bund spread with a ratio of 100:55.

This type of chart is not very conducive to technical analysis. There is a lot of information here, but it is not organized in a way that is accessible to the trader. How we organize the data determines how we see the market. **Figure 9.2** shows a Market Profile chart for the same period. (For details on how the Market Profile

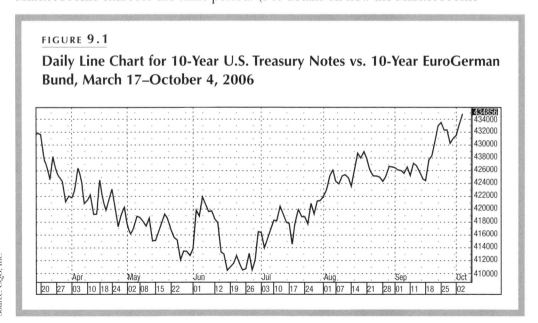

FIGURE 9.1

Daily Line Chart for 10-Year U.S. Treasury Notes vs. 10-Year EuroGerman Bund, March 17–October 4, 2006

FIGURE 9.2

Monthly Market Profile Chart for 10-Year U.S. Treasury Notes vs. 10-Year
EuroGerman Bund Spread, March 17–October 4, 2006

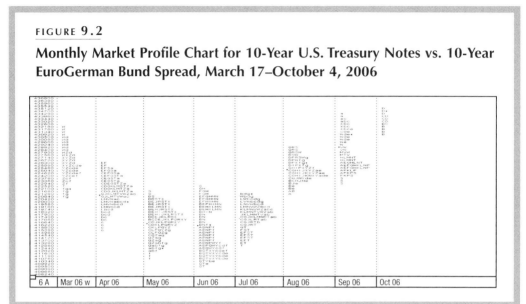

Source: CQG, Inc.

is constructed, see my chapter in *New Thinking in Technical Analysis*, [Bloomberg Press, 2000].)

We start with the basic understanding that the market is an auction. The progress of the auction and where the market spent time (and hence perceived value) become much clearer on this chart. But the real strength of Market Profile analysis, and the concept on which this chapter will focus, comes from reorganizing the profiles to reflect complete cycles of market activity and setting up a framework to guide the trader as the market progresses through its auction cycle.

Let's preview our approach by looking at a reorganized version of this same data (see **Figure 9.3**), showing a complete auction cycle followed by a new directional move.

This final version, created by combining monthly profiles from March through June 2006 and monthly profiles from July through October 2006, provides a structure and presentation of the data that, as we will see, gives a basis for determining strategy when trading spreads.

The strength of Market Profile is its organization of market data into a bell curve, revealing the underlying auction process that drives price fluctuations. In this chapter we apply Market Profile analysis to global spreads, as a tool to understand the relationship between two correlated markets. We'll start by reviewing the basic principles of Market Profile, and then apply those principles to some commonly traded global spread markets.

Source: CQG, Inc.

FIGURE 9.3

Combined Monthly Profiles of the 10-Year U.S. Treasury Notes vs. 10-Year EuroGerman Bund Spread, March–June 2006 and July–October 2006. Reorganized profiles from Figure 9.2 show a more complete auction cycle.

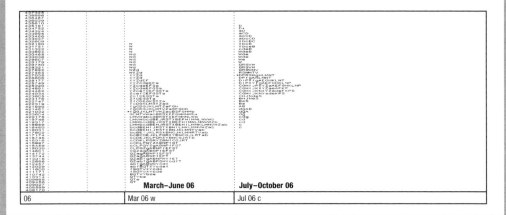

What you will learn in this chapter is a practical approach to using Market Profile to recognize underdeveloped bell curves, trade within the range they establish until they are complete, and establish a larger context for clarifying the next directional move.

Market Profile and the Bell Curve

How does Market Profile so clearly capture the auction process? When depicting the auction process in terms of how much time a market spends at a given price, it naturally organizes itself into a series of bell curves. The structure of the bell curve emerges out of the basic nature of the auction, where a negotiation between buyers and sellers explores the extremes before gradually settling down to a consensus price.

Let's start by looking at this process in an actual market, the S&P 500 futures. The chart in **Figure 9.4** is a snapshot of the S&P 500 futures between January 1999 and April 2003, depicted in Market Profile format. This format shows the prices at which the market spent the most time, not just the price range. You can see readily the shape of the bell curve emerge.

Figure 9.5 is a detailed view of the right-hand profile in Figure 9.4. This chart

FIGURE **9.4**

Market Profile Chart, S&P 500 Futures January 1999–April 2003. The auction process naturally organizes into a series of bell curves.

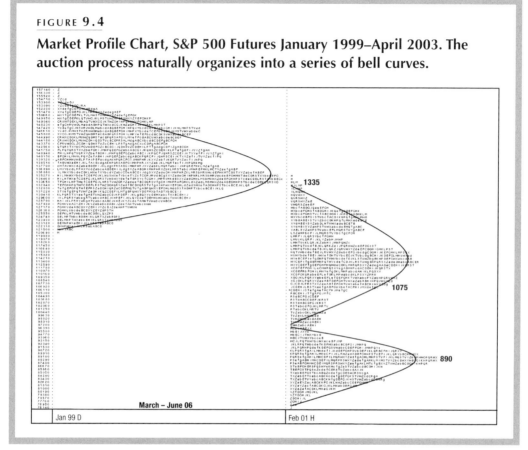

Source: CQG, Inc.

captures market activity from February 2001 through April 2003. Once the low was set, the S&P spent most of 2002 and up to April 2003 trading in the lower part of the new range, rotating around 890 as it negotiated a consensus price. At the end of this two-year period a completed profile (the lower part of Figure 9.5) was in place, forming the shape of a bell curve.

Based on this chart, I called for a rally out of the 890 mode that would fill in the underdeveloped pocket of low activity between the high volume ledges of 930 and 1075, constructing a bell curve over the entire range. (Bloomberg, Technical Analysis Roundtable 11.19.03.) This structure of smaller bell curves building into larger ones is typical of market behavior and is the key to using Market Profile to read markets.

There was also an alternative scenario in which a move would initiate to the downside out of the 890 consensus price. It's wise to have a contingency plan

FIGURE **9.5**

S&P 500 Futures, February 2001–April 2003. Expanded view of right-hand profile of Figure 9.4.

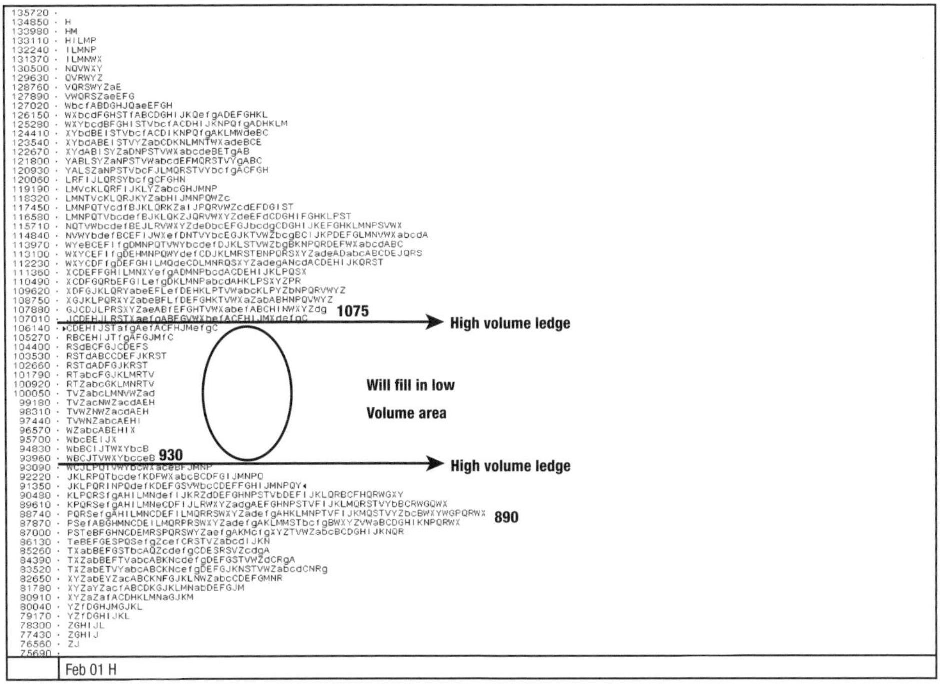

```
135720 ·
134850 ·  H
133990 ·  HM
133110 ·  HILMP
132240 ·  ILMNP
131370 ·  ILMNWX
130500 ·  NQVWXY
129630 ·  QVRWYZ
128760 ·  VQRSWYZaE
127890 ·  VWQRSZaeEFG
127020 ·  WbcfABDGHJQaeEFGH
126150 ·  WxbcdFGHSTfABCDGHIJKQefgADEFGHKL
125280 ·  WXYbcdBFGHISTVbcfACDHIJKNPQfgADHKLM
124410 ·  XYbcBEISTVbcfACDIKNPQfgAKLMWdeBC
123540 ·  XYbcABEISTVYZabCDKNLMNTWXadeBCE
122670 ·  XYdABISYZaDNPSTVWXabcdeBETgAB
121800 ·  XYeBCEIfgDEFMNPDMYderCDJKLMRSTBNPQRSXYZadeADabcABCDEJQRS
120930 ·  YALSZaNPSTVbcFJLMQRSTVYDcfgACFGH
120060 ·  LRFIJLQRSYbcfgCFGHN
119190 ·  LMVcKLQRFIJKLYZabcGHJMNP
118320 ·  LMNTVcKLQRJKYZabHIJMNPQMZc
117450 ·  LMNFQTVcdfBJKLQRKZaIJPQRVWZcdEFDGIST
116580 ·  LMNFQTVbcdefBJKLQKZJQRVWXYZdeEFdCDGHIFGHKLPST
115710 ·  NQTVWbcdefBEJLRVWXYZdeDbcEFGJbcdgCDGHIJKEFGHKLMNPSVWX
114840 ·  NVWYbdefBCEFIJWXefDNTVYbcEGJKTVWZbcgBCIJKPDEFGLMNVWXabcdA
113970 ·  WYeBCEIfgDMNPQTVNYbcgefDJKLSTVWZbgBKMPQRDEFWXabcdABC
113100 ·  WXYCEFIfgDEHMNPQMYderfCDJKLMRSTBNPQRSXYZadeADabcABCDEJQRS
112230 ·  WXYCDFfgDEFGHILMQdeCDLMNRQSXYZadegANcdACDEHIJKQRST
111360 ·  XCDEFFGHILMNYefgADMNPbcdACDEHIJKLPQSX
110490 ·  XCDFGQRDEFGILefgDKLMNPabcdAHKLPSXYZPR
109620 ·  XDFGJKLQRYabdeEFLefDEHKLPTVWabcKLPYZbNPQRVWYZ
108750 ·  XGJKLPQRSYZabdeBFLfDEFGHKTVWXaZabABHNPQVWYZ
107880 ·  GJCDJLPRSXYZaeABIEFGHTVWXabefABCHINYXYZdg    1075
107010 ·  JCDEHIJLRSTXaefgABFGVWXbefACEHIJMXdefgC
106140 ·  XCDEHIJSTafgAefACFHJMefgC
105270 ·  RBCEHIJTfgAFGJMfC
104400 ·  RSdBCFGJCDEFS
103530 ·  RSTdABCCDEFJKRST
102660 ·  RSTdADFGJKRST
101790 ·  RTabcFGJKLMRTV
100920 ·  RTZabcGKLMNRTV
100050 ·  TVZabcLMNVWZad
99180 ·  TVZacNWZacdAEH
98310 ·  TVWZNWZacdAEH
97440 ·  TVWNZabcAEHI
96570 ·  WZabcABEHIX
95700 ·  WbcBEIJX
94830 ·  WbBCIJTWXYbcB
93960 ·  WBCJTVWXYbcceB  930
93090 ·  WCJLPQTVWYDcKXabcBBFJMNP
92220 ·  JKLPRQTbcdefKDFWXabcBCDFGIJMNPQ
91350 ·  JKLPQRINPQdefKDEFGSVWbcCDEFFGHIJMNPQY·
90480 ·  KLPQRSfgAHILMNdefIJKRZdDEFGHNPSTVbDEFIJKLQRBCFHQRWGXY
89610 ·  KPQRSefgAHILMNeDFIJLRWXYZadgAEFGHNPSTVFIJKLMQRSTVYDBCRWGQWX
88740 ·  PQRSefgAHILMNCDEFILMQRRSWXYZadefgAHKLMNPTVFIJKMQSTVYZbcBWXYWGPQRWX
87870 ·  PSefABGHMNCDEILMQRFRSWXYZadefgAKLMMSTbcfgBWXYZVWaBCDGHIKNPQRWX
87000 ·  FSTeBFGHNCDEMRSPQRSWYZaefgAKMGfgXYZTVWZabcBCDGHIJKNQR
86130 ·  TeBEFGESPQSefgZcerCRSTVZabcdIJKN
85260 ·  TXabBEFG3TbcAQZcdefgCDE3RSVZcdgA
84390 ·  TXZabBEFTVabcABKNcdefgDEFGSTVHYZdcRgA
83520 ·  TXZabETVYabcABCKNcefgDEFGJKNSTVWZabcdCNRg
82650 ·  XYZabEYZacABCKNFGJKLNWZabcCDEFGMNR
81780 ·  XYZaYZacfABCDKGJKLMHabDEFGJM
80910 ·  XYZaZafACDHKLMNaGJKM
80040 ·  YZfDGHJMGJKL
79170 ·  YZfDGHIJKL
78300 ·  ZGHIJL
77430 ·  ZGHIJ
76560 ·  ZJ
75690 ·
```

1075 → High volume ledge

Will fill in low

Volume area

930 → High volume ledge

890

Feb 01 H

should the nonpreferred scenario unfold. But if the market was able to climb over the high-volume ledge of 930, it would confirm the bullish game plan that I was favoring at the time. Let's see what took place for the remainder of 2003.

For the remainder of the year, from April 2003 to December 2003, the market traded within the pocket of low volume left by the February 2001–March 2003 profile. **Figure 9.6** shows the resulting profile. This is what I would call a perfect fill.

This analysis exemplifies the strengths of Market Profile, which gives us the tools to:

- know market direction
- establish a target
- develop a timeline for the unfolding of our scenario
- identify the market activity pattern that confirms we're right, and know how to tell if we're wrong

FIGURE 9.6

S&P 500 Futures, February 2001–December 2003. Two composite profiles (February 2001–March 2003 and April 2003–December 2003) showing how larger profiles provide context for current development.

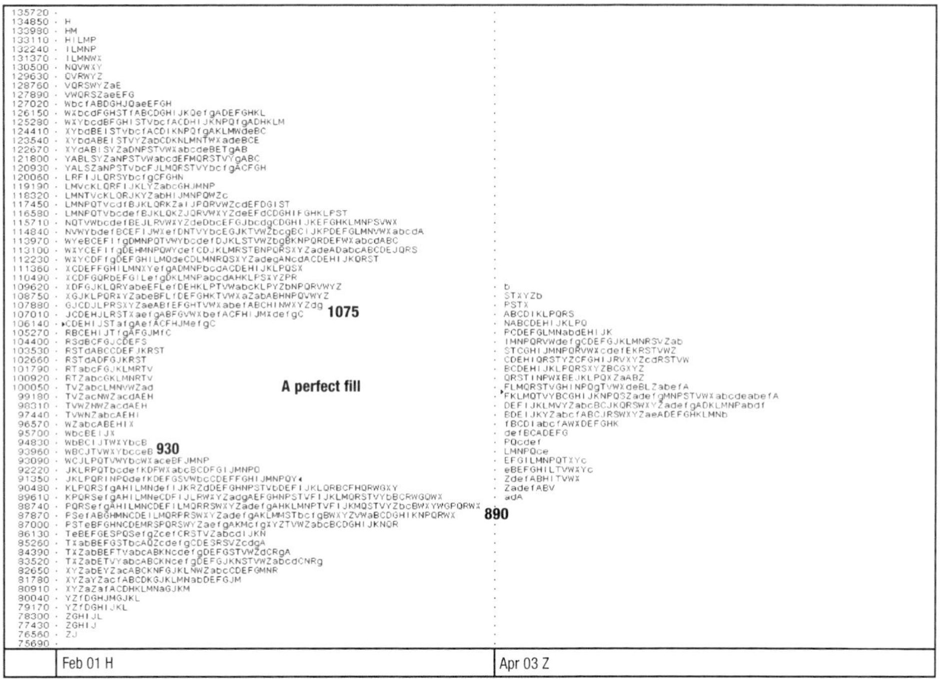

Source: CQG, Inc.

To recap our example in the light of these four elements of a trading strategy, we knew coming into April 2003 that the lower bell curve was complete and that the market was poised for a directional move. With the undeveloped area looming above the market, chances were good that the auction would return to that territory to fill in volume, and that the new auction extremes would be from 930 to 1075. This would make a buy over 930 a major directional play. Market Profile analysis gave us a direction and a target.

We also knew that if our favored scenario was unfolding, the market should not develop back below the consensus point (most traded price) at 890. Once we saw that the bullish scenario was under way, we knew a range would develop until the low-volume pocket was filled, at which point we would know the strategy had run its course, and the market was ready for a new auction to kick off.

The Four Stages of Sticker Shock

To develop a deeper level of understanding of the negotiation process, let's talk about the underlying psychology that drives the auction. As the great trader Jesse Livermore once said, "I absolutely believe that price movement patterns are repeated and appear over and over with slight variations. This is because humans drive the stocks and human nature never changes."

As it builds the bell curve, the auction process tracks the psychology of the negotiation process in four stages. With a nod to Elisabeth Kübler-Ross, I call it the four stages of sticker shock.

1. In stage one (shock/denial), a dramatic directional move beyond the well-accepted value area is halted by a feeling of "sticker shock" on the part of participants. The new price point stirs feelings of "I can't believe it; this won't last."

2. In stage two (anger), usage slows down as people search for alternatives or attempt to change long-standing patterns of behavior, triggering a counter-move that seeks an opposite end of value. In this stage the extremes of a trading range are first established. Normally the market retraces a portion of the initial dramatic directional range. The feeling here is "I won't buy/sell it. I'll take my money/product elsewhere."

3. Stage three (bargaining) ushers in the beginning of development, which explores value and builds consensus to determine what is acceptable and unacceptable within the range established in stage two. During this phase, participants grow used to the price as shock and anger wear off. (This phase usually creates either a lowercase *b* shape or an uppercase *P* shape profile.) "I'll just use/sell what I need to get by."

4. After a brief or protracted period of bargaining, stage four (acceptance or rejection) unfolds in one of two ways:

- *Acceptance.* This represents resignation to the new level of prices and acceptance that it is fair. The market breaths a sigh that says, "This is the new standard." At this point, the initial imbalance revives and the cycle begins anew.
- *Rejection.* The market ultimately rejects the new price and returns to where the move originated.

Let's look at the fourth stage and the transition to a new cycle in more detail. If the market truly accepts the new price level, it will continue in the direction of the initial dramatic move to stake out a further price territory. **Figure 9.7** shows

FIGURE **9.7**

S&P 500 Futures, October 2004–May 2006. Market Profile pattern of price acceptance (consecutive P-shape patterns that continue in the direction of the initial imbalance).

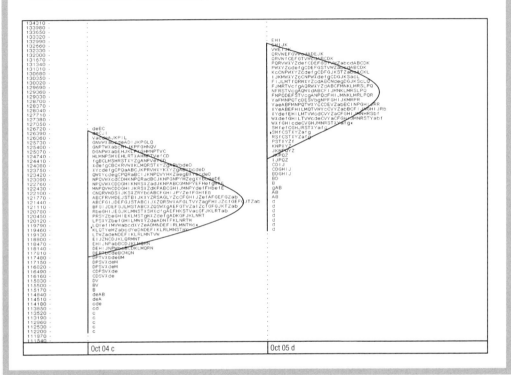

this scenario in action. After the completion of the bell curve on the left, which represents the market's progression through all four phases, prices continued in the original direction (upward) and a new curve developed on the right.

The profile at the left side of Figure 9.7 illustrates the typical profile shape after the four-phase process of negotiation. The bell curve on top of the tail created by the initial rally roughly resembles a capital *P* shape. If the initial phase had been a decline rather than a rally, then the profile would have the shape of a lowercase *b*. In an extended rally, the profiles would resemble a series of *P* shapes, with little retracement, a mark of price acceptance.

Alternatively, the market can ultimately reject the new price and retrace to where the move originated, as shown in **Figure 9.8**.

In the price-rejection scenario, the market often retraces its steps to fill in

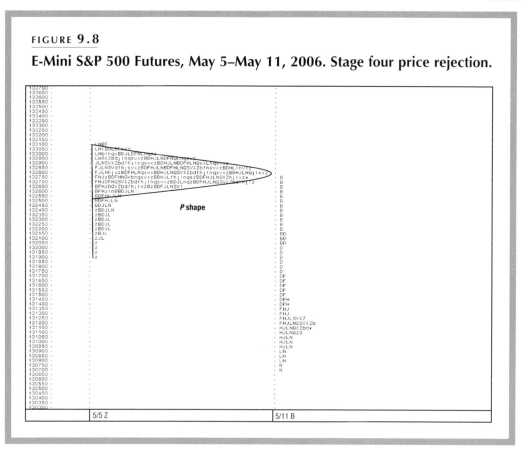

FIGURE **9.8**

E-Mini S&P 500 Futures, May 5–May 11, 2006. Stage four price rejection.

Source: CQG, Inc.

the narrow tail of the *P* or *b* shape. This creates a large bell curve, ultimately resembling a capital *D*.

Application to Spreads

Let's look at an example of this negotiation process as applied to a spread market.

Figure 9.9 is a chart of the 2-year Euro Schatz versus the 5-year Euro Bobl spread for the period July 25 through August 4, 2006, organized into the Market Profile format. Coming out of the mode (widest area) of a well-developed bell curve (*D* shape), the new auction process starts with an initiating directional move. Here, it's a sell-off that opens new territory to the downside.

As the negotiation (auction) begins, the first stage shuts off the selling, and then the later stages start to build volume toward the bottom of the dramatic directional move, forming the lowercase *b* shape (**Figure 9.10**).

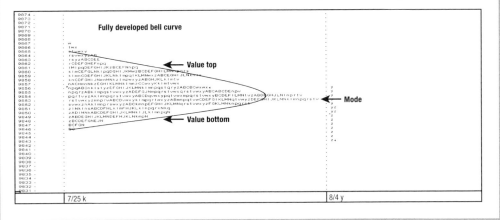

FIGURE 9.9

2-Year Euro Schatz vs. 5-Year Euro Bobl Spread, July 25–August 4, 2006. The start of a new auction process out of a completed D shape.

Source: CQG, Inc.

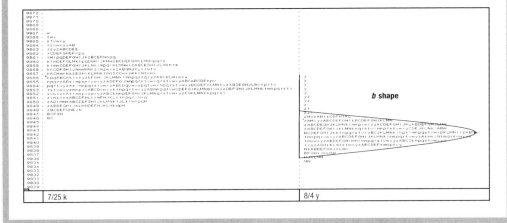

FIGURE 9.10

2-Year Euro Schatz vs. 5-Year Euro Bobl Spread, July 25–August 11, 2006. Formation of the bell curve, creating a b shape.

Source: CQG, Inc.

Once the *b* shape is complete, the market is ready for either price acceptance (a further move in the same direction) or price rejection (a return to the starting point of the decline). In this case, the market followed a price-rejection scenario, which resulted in a rally out of the high-volume level of the *b* back toward its ini-

FIGURE 9.11

2-Year Euro Schatz vs. 5-Year Euro Bobl Spread, July 25–August 14, 2006. Price rejection and the creation of the D-shape bell curve.

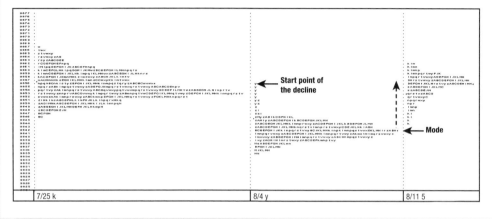

Source: CQG, Inc.

FIGURE 9.12

2-Year Euro Schatz vs. 5-Year Euro Bobl Spread, July 25–August 14, 2006. Composite profile of Figure 9.11, which creates a D-shape bell curve. The composite profile is still not complete.

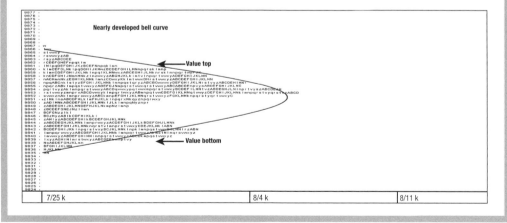

Source: CQG, Inc.

tiation point. The ultimate result was the creation of a *D*-shape bell curve.

Figure 9.11 shows how these events unfolded. In typical fashion the market sprang out of the developing high-volume area, or mode, as it made its way back

FIGURE **9.13**

2-Year Euro Schatz vs. 5-Year Euro Bobl Spread, September 2005– August 14, 2006. The greater context shows the larger-scale underdeveloped D shape.

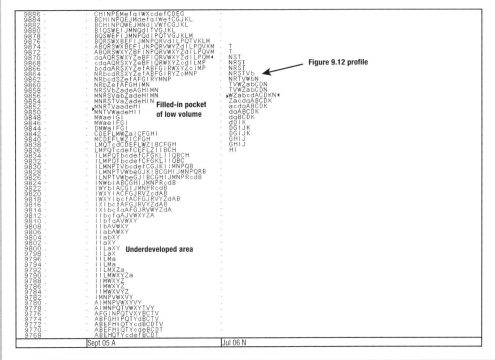

to the starting point of the decline.

Let's put these profiles together, as shown in **Figure 9.12**. On this composite profile, the 2-year Euro Schatz versus the 5-year Euro Bobl spread is showing a *D* shape that is close to completion of a fully developed bell curve. As often happens, the shape is not a perfect bell curve. It is rather wide and has a dent of low volume around 9847, between two completed bell curves. A market will sometimes fill in this type of low-volume area, but in this case the width of the profile suggests that the market is very near a new directional move. By putting this smaller bell curve into a larger context of development, we can determine the next directional move out of the high volume area of 9855.

In general, as a building bell curve nears completion, the trading strategy is to position oneself at one end of the developing value area in anticipation of the

FIGURE 9.14

2-Year Euro Schatz vs. 5-Year Euro Bobl Spread, September 2005–October 2006. Finding the context of a completed bell curve to determine the next direction suggested a new directional move to the downside to fill in the lower pocket of low volume.

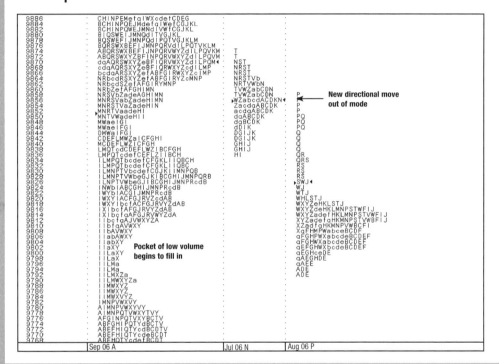

next direction as dictated by the larger context. This in essence means finding a bell curve on a larger time frame that our current, completing curve is helping to build. Let's look at how we determine the larger context for our example.

By combining the data going back to September 2005 (**Figure 9.13**), we see a larger underdeveloped bell curve in process of completion. The profile from Figure 9.12 is the separate portion toward the upper part of the figure. This larger composite profile informs us that the shorter-term profile of Figure 9.12 is filling a pocket of low volume. Now that the pocket of low volume is filled in and the short-term bell curve is "ripe and ready to spill," we look to this larger context to determine the next move and target. To determine a strategy and a directional bias, we look to where the context still needs development. In this case, we see a large underdeveloped area below the market and would begin to anticipate a new directional move to the downside.

Figure 9.14 shows the subsequent market action. The market did in fact follow our expected scenario and begin to build volume in the formerly underdeveloped area. In the next section, we consider this in light of the four elements of a trading strategy.

Finding a Larger Context

The idea of a larger context is critical to using Market Profile effectively. Recall our four elements of a trading strategy: determining market direction; establishing a target; knowing how much time you have in a trade; and recognizing whether you're right or wrong. We now have tools to support each of these trading decisions. We'll illustrate this process with the 10-year U.S. Treasury notes versus 10-year EuroGerman Bund spread, using a ratio of 100 to 55.

Using the profiles in their default organization (by days) is not the best way to track the progress of the negotiation process. I like to combine the profiles, as we've been doing here, to bring out the bell curves. But how do we know what to combine? In an underdeveloped value area, the market can spend days trading back and forth within the established extremes of value. If the range is established in one day, the market might spend three or four days building volume in that range. We typically combine profiles that are building within the same value area until the bell curve comes close to completion. When the profile is ripe and ready to spill directionally, we start to put the nearly developed curve into a context.

We'll illustrate this with an example. In **Figure 9.15**, on August 23, the market established a fairly broad range, but one day was not enough time to fully explore the range or build consensus within that value area. For two consecutive days, traders could have taken advantage of that underdeveloped profile in the low-volatility environment of development. The strategy, then, for August 24 and 25, was to sell the top of value and buy the bottom of value. We thus have a trade location for modest directional moves within this bracket. This strategy is valid until the range fully develops a bell curve. The idea of range trading within the value area is confirmed if you see horizontal price prints (multiple prints at the same price) at the top and bottom of value, as opposed to single upward prints at the top or downward ones at the bottom, which would mean the market was no longer range trading, but initiating a new directional move.

FIGURE **9.15**

10-Year U.S. Treasury Notes vs. 10-Year EuroGerman Bund Spread Daily Profiles, August 23–25, 2006. Learning to combine profiles within the same value area.

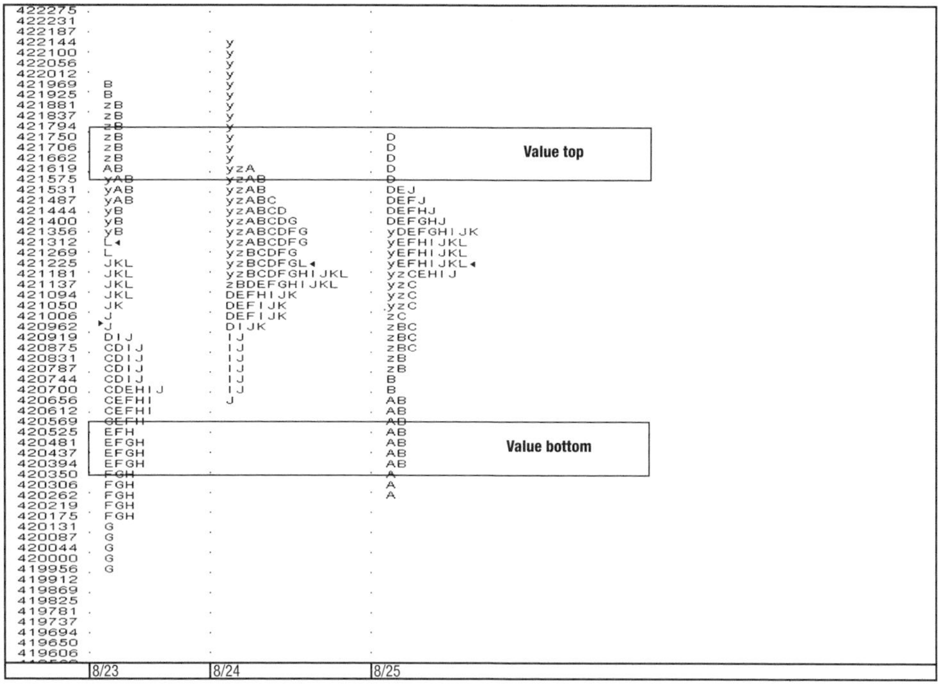

```
422275 .                .                .
422231 .                .                .
422187 .                .                .
422144 .                . y              .
422100 .                . y              .
422056 .                . y              .
422012 .                . y              .
421969 .  B             . y              .
421925 .  B             . y              .
421881 .  zB            . y              .
421837 .  zB            . y              .
421794 .  zB            . y              .
421750 .  zB            . y              . D
421706 .  zB            . y              . D        Value top
421662 .  zB            . y              . D
421619 .  AB            . yzA            . D
421575 .  yAB           . yzAB           . D
421531 .  yAB           . yzAB           . DEJ
421487 .  yAB           . yzABC          . DEFJ
421444 .  yB            . yzABCD         . DEFHJ
421400 .  yB            . yzABCDG        . DEFGHJ
421356 .  yB            . yzABCDFG       . yDEFGHIJK
421312 .  L◄            . yzABCDFG       . yEFHIJKL
421269 .  L             . yzBCDFG        . yEFHIJKL
421225 .  JKL           . yzBCDFGL◄      . yEFHIJKL◄
421181 .  JKL           . yzBCDFGHIJKL   . yzCEHIJ
421137 .  JKL           . zBDEFGHIJKL    . yzC
421094 .  JKL           . DEFHIJK        . yzC
421050 .  JK            . DEFIJK         . yzC
421006 .  J             . DEFIJK         . zC
420962 .  ►J            . DIJK           . zBC
420919 .  DIJ           . IJ             . zBC
420875 .  CDIJ          . IJ             . zBC
420831 .  CDIJ          . IJ             . zB
420787 .  CDIJ          . IJ             . zB
420744 .  CDIJ          . IJ             . B
420700 .  CDEHIJ        . IJ             . B
420656 .  CEFHI         . J              . AB
420612 .  CEFHI         .                . AB
420569 .  CEFH          .                . AB
420525 .  EFH           .                . AB       Value bottom
420481 .  EFGH          .                . AB
420437 .  EFGH          .                . AB
420394 .  EFGH          .                . AB
420350 .  FGH           .                . A
420306 .  FGH           .                . A
420262 .  FGH           .                . A
420219 .  FGH           .                .
420175 .  FGH           .                .
420131 .  G             .                .
420087 .  G             .                .
420044 .  G             .                .
420000 .  G             .                .
419956 .  G             .                .
419912 .                .                .
419869 .                .                .
419825 .                .                .
419781 .                .                .
419737 .                .                .
419694 .                .                .
419650 .                .                .
419606 .                .                .
        8/23            8/24             8/25
```

Source: CQG, Inc.

To continue with this theme of trading a broad initial range until the bell curve is completed, consider **Figure 9.16**. We combined two profiles to show the outcome of two consecutive days of rapid rallies. The result is an unexplored range that the market could spend multiple days developing. This sets up a framework for a trading strategy. It is very unusual for a market to sustain a separation from an underdeveloped value area. Based on our understanding of the psychology of the negotiation process, the market is going to want to build consensus before rejecting a value as too low or too high. This is the core principle of Market Profile trading. Traders can take advantage of this consensus-building phase. The premise is that the market will spend time trading between the projected value area top and bottom until consensus is reached toward the center of the range. The strategy would be to sell the top of value and play for a

FIGURE **9.16**

10-Year U.S. Treasury Notes vs. 10-Year EuroGerman Bund Spread, Composite Profile, August 15–16, 2006. Using the developing bell curve as the framework for our trading strategy.

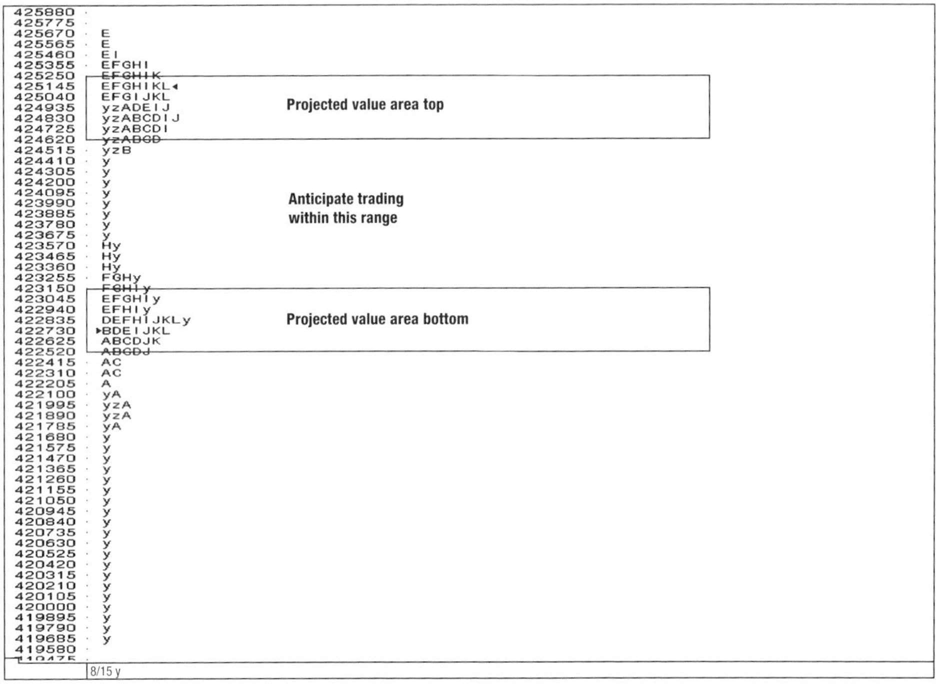

Source: CQG, Inc.

move at least to the bottom of the first pocket of low volume. Let's see how this strategy would have played out.

Figure 9.17 shows the market action for the following three days and how the market slowly declined into the bottom of the pocket of low volume.

A key question emerges from these examples: How do we know when to stop playing for development and start shifting our strategy to one of looking for direction? The key is to always be trading from a low-volatility context of development. This can be done by shifting to a larger context once a bell curve is completed or nearing completion. Let's look at how this might unfold on our current example.

Figure 9.18 shows the six days leading up to our example in Figure 9.17 as the market traded in an established range for several days, from August 7 to

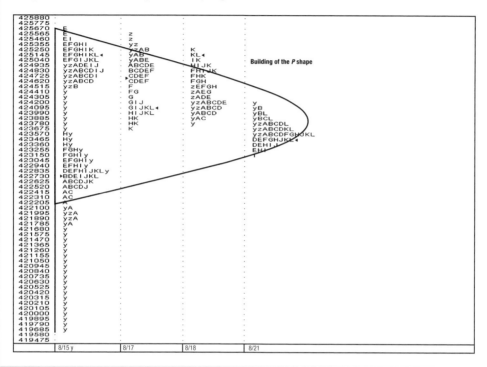

FIGURE 9.17

10-Year U.S. Treasury Notes vs. EuroGerman Bund (10-Year) Spread, August 15–21, 2006. Playing for the construction of the P shape by selling the value area top and buying the value area bottom.

Source: CQG, Inc.

August 14, 2006. A multiday strategy of selling the top of value and buying the bottom was appropriate.

As long as the market continues to spend time in the same value area, we combine those profiles into a larger developing bell curve. That process draws to a close once the combined set of profiles reveals a fully developed bell curve.

Figure 9.19 shows the result of combining the profiles in Figure 9.18. By the end of the six-day period, consensus has developed around a fair price, and the value area has been fully explored into a bell curve. This market is ready to move directionally. At this point, continuing to play for a range trade in the current range is a dangerous proposition.

When the bell curve is complete, the trader is driven to find a broader context to determine the next directional move. The context is a larger value area that

FIGURE 9.18

10-Year U,S. Treasury Notes vs. 10-Year EuroGerman Bund Spread, August 7–14, 2006. Combined profiles leading up to the scenario in Figure 9.17. A trading strategy of selling the top of value and buying the bottom of value was appropriate until a completed bell curve emerged.

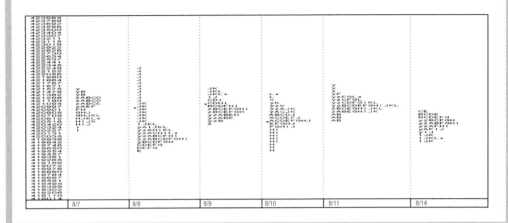

FIGURE 9.19

10-Year U.S. Treasury Notes vs. 10-Year EuroGerman Bund Spread, Combined Profile, August 7–14, 2006. Consensus has been reached. The bell curve is ripe and ready to spill directionally, but in which direction?

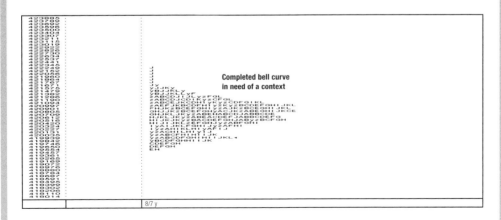

has not been completely explored. In this case, we have no idea of the likely directional move until we combine prior history with the current data for context.

Combining prior history with the data in Figure 9.19 shows an underdeveloped area resting above the completed bell curve. The combined profile in **Figure 9.20** indicates the likelihood that the next direction will be up. This suggests shifting to a strategy that anticipates the new upward move by buying the bottom of value. That is a low-risk buy because a move below the bottom of value would quickly tell you you're wrong, since it would signal that the next direction is down instead of up.

Figure 9.21 shows that the next direction was indeed upward, but the rally did not stop at the top of the low-volume area. In general, we let directional moves tell us when they're finished, by shifting into a development mode (that is, sideways activity). At this point our assumption is that the market is ready to develop the upper portion of the larger range.

Let's consider this move in a little more detail. When a bell curve is complete, there are two prime areas for the next move to initiate from: the mode or the extreme end of value. If we expect an upward move, we would try to buy either at the mode or at the bottom of value, if it is offered. In this example, the market

FIGURE 9.20

10-Year U.S. Treasury Notes vs. 10-Year EuroGerman Bund Spread, August 3–14, 2006. Combining prior history, or putting the building profile into a larger context to determine your directional bias, strategy, and targets.

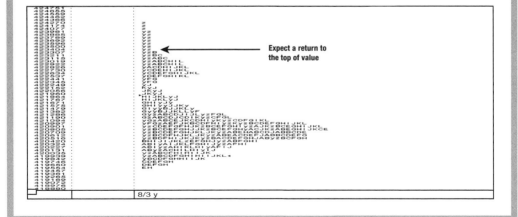

Source: CQG, Inc.

Source: CQG, Inc.

FIGURE **9.21**

10-Year U.S. Treasury Notes vs. 10-Year EuroGerman Bund Spread, August 3–15, 2006. Anticipating the directional move based on the context of the larger bell curve.

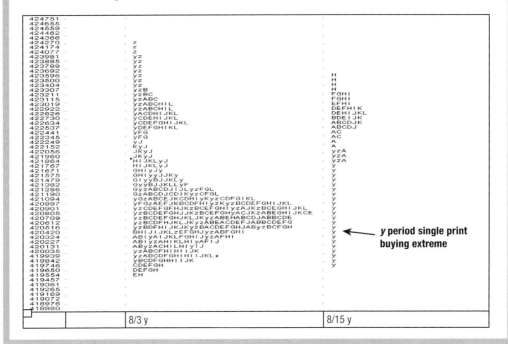

gave us one last chance to buy the bottom of value, and the rally in *y*-period came out of that point.

When looking for a directional move, the confirming price activity is a series of single prints. Anything short of that type of initiating activity tells the trader that the market is not yet ready to make its move. The typical target for a rally is the initiation point of the prior decline.

The alternative scenario in this example would have been an initiating move that went below the bottom of value. If that had happened, you would then have looked for a larger bell curve below the market that was underdeveloped and set your targets accordingly.

The amount of context to use would be just enough to return us to a situation of development as opposed to initiation. At times, a huge bell curve on the scale of months or even years will complete. Usually, though, we are working in a smaller time frame, and adding a few days or at most weeks of prior market activity will provide the necessary information. The basic premise is that large moves are built out of smaller bell curves. For a day trader, knowing what the market is likely to do for the year may not be helpful, because the price fluctuations in accomplishing the yearly scenario may be far too large for a short-term strategy to endure.

—⁓—

MARKET PROFILE IS a general tool that applies just as well to global spreads as it does to more traditional instruments. Because Market Profile captures the underlying structure of the auction, it is an effective way of analyzing any auction-based market.

The main principle is that the market is always building a bell curve on some time scale. By recognizing this and by matching the scale of the curve we're working with to our preferred trading interval, we can always be trading in a context of development, moving to a larger bell curve as a smaller one completes, and back to a smaller one once an initiating move has established a range for development. This gives us a framework to develop a trading plan involving the key elements of direction, target, timeline, and confirming events.

CHAPTER 10

The Ten Commandments

ROBIN GRIFFITHS

The Trader's Ten Commandments

Losing money is a sin. It means you have done what you should not have done, and you have left undone what you should have done. You must repent, and in future obey the rules. My rules. I call them the ten commandments.

None of these is original to me. The first is famously attributed to Warren Buffet.

1. Thou shalt not lose any money, as the probability is too high that you will never get it back again.

2. Don't risk money when you do not have to. You can beat any market by not being in the market all the time. If you can avoid the bad bits, it is better to do so; it can improve the risk-return ratio.

3. You can beat any index, or universe of stocks, by owning only part of it. It is easier to identify average and below than to find the best. What you do not own is more important, or at least as important, as what you do own.

4. When you do invest, only do so when the probabilities are on your side with odds of 60/40 or better. Even then you know it is not a certain outcome.

5. If you hold a position that is going wrong, cut it. At all times for all positions have a clearly identified level for exiting.

6. At all times own only the strongest actual and relative strength trends, or short only the weakest. If the trend is not strong, do not trade it.

7. Use a money management system that cuts out losses, exploits an uptrend, and changes unit size in proportion to the capital available.

8. Have reasonable but not excessive diversification. Typically this is the top quintile of any universe on our ranking order system.

9. Try always to deal in instruments, or use ways of activating investments, that reduce dealing and other costs to the lowest possible. This makes a good system better.

10. Set up your affairs in a way that minimizes, if it cannot eliminate, your tax burden. This makes a better system brilliant.

Of course my rules do not have the authority of the Divine. However, they were inspired by a logical, reasoned, and back-tested approach. This approach does not try to "forecast" the future. Instead, its goal is to achieve an edge by measuring the probability of certain outcomes and betting on them in a sensible way.

The product of this approach is a rules-based expert system, and my ten commandments are a by-product.

My approach to market analysis integrates technical and fundamental forces.

I see technical forces as global, macro, top down, and multi-asset-class. This is a direct result of the work of Harry M. Markowitz, 1990 Nobel Prize winner. He wrote a series of papers in which he demonstrated that the major part of all share price moves was due to these macro factors rather than stock-specific information. This is analogous to knowing that the tide is coming in and will float all boats, or it is going out and will leave them all back on the beach. This is more important than knowing that this boat is better than that boat. About 85 percent of the movement was due to the tide.

I am not alone in respecting the powerful influence of market trends. Years ago, however, most market participants believed in the Efficient Market Hypothesis, which gave rise to the more well-known Random Walk Theory. This theory asserts that market movements are random. Therefore there is no point in trying to comprehend market trends. Predictably enough, those who asserted the contrary view—technical analysts, also called chartists—were considered fringe players.

Nowadays, however, it has become more than respectable to dismiss the Random Walk Theory. Several Nobel prizes have been awarded to those who did just that. I offer less esoteric proof.

First, humans are irrational and exuberant, and have regularly overpaid for everything from tulip bulbs to dot-com stocks, and many things in between. Second, there are in practice real-world markets that are easily and demonstrably different from the markets that would be created were the organizing principle a random walk.

Professor Benoit Mandelbrot has a great way of demonstrating this. By plotting the deviations of actual prices around a moving mean and comparing them to a random walk generated by his computer, he can reduce the problem to a party game. A child with the mental age of four, and no previous training, can easily tell the difference. In essence, if the markets were really random, then the deviations would be in Normal, or Gaussian, distribution. In fact they are in skewed, heteroscedastic, leptokurtic distribution. This is the so-called fat-tailed pattern shown in **Figure 10.1**.

In a leptokurtic distribution, prices spend far longer than they should close to the mean. They remain mean-reverting and range-bound. Then, when they

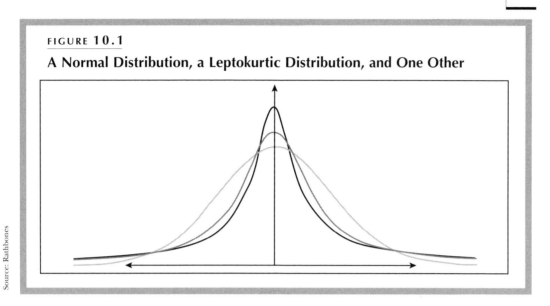

FIGURE 10.1

A Normal Distribution, a Leptokurtic Distribution, and One Other

start to trend, they move far more than they should. Deviations greater than three standard deviations are very common, and swings of seven to ten standard deviations, instead of occurring only once every other light year, occur regularly in a year of trading.

This—that market events fit the leptokurtic distribution and not the Gaussian—withstands all forms of back-testing. The fact is that in real-world stock markets trends appear more frequently, and persist for longer, than the laws of chance allow.

This is the justification for using technical analysis.

The second part of my analysis interrelates fundamental and technical forces. There is only one reality, and it is not helpful to divide it into parts. Concepts of value are just as relevant as those of price.

Analytics

The fundamentals that I use most are based on economics, and especially the model produced back in the 1930s by Joseph Schumpeter. I pay particular attention to economic cycles and annual seasonal deviation.

Economic Cycles

Schumpeter's model shows that economic cycles cause cycles in stock markets. The catch is that the market is a discounting mechanism driven by expectations.

It moves ahead of the real world. It sometimes makes mistakes, leading to the old quip that the market correctly identified all nine of the last four recessions.

Schumpeter's model included three cycles of different lengths: a very long one that he named after Kondratieff, a ten-year one named after Juglar, and a four-year one named Kitchin.

I use these in the following way. The long, Kondratieff waves I call secular trends, as they persist for longer than the short cycle. In practice they tend to run for multiples of the four-year wave, with sixteen to twenty being common lengths of time to be valid. All we need to know at any particular time is, are they going up or down? The sort of force that drives these trends can be technological innovation, a rapid rate of compound growth of GNP for a country, earnings growth for a stock, demographics, and expansion or contraction of valuation. All those forces themselves trend.

When Great Britain was a superpower, the Kitchin wave averaged 4.25 years, but it had considerable variation. An individual cycle could be as short as three years or as long as five. Since Roosevelt, however, the United States has been the superpower, and the cycle has become phase-locked to the presidential election cycle, which is mandated at exactly four years. It is the lows of the cycle that can be locked down accurately. The analogy is with a child's jump rope. He holds the ends of the rope in his hands, but the top of the loop moves around rapidly. In all that time there has been only one time so far when the lows of the cycle were

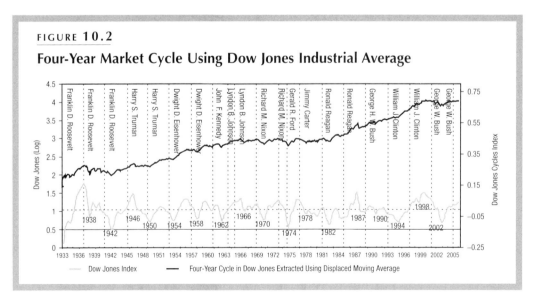

FIGURE 10.2

Four-Year Market Cycle Using Dow Jones Industrial Average

Source: Carnegie Mellon University

not exactly when they should be. The four-year low should have come in 1986, but the market did not fall until it crashed in late 1987. The next time that the cycle mistimed was in 2006, as the rhythm indicated a market low, not a high in that year (see **Figure 10.2**).

During the course of a normal four-year period there will tend always to be a rotation of the strongest trends from bonds, to equities, to commodities, always in that order. Within the equity market there will also be a rotation of sectors starting with interest rate–sensitive issues, to consumption-related, to cyclical laggards and resource-related issues. This has been well-illustrated by the work of Martin Pring, Ian Notley, and John Murphy. Following my system for these rotations will lead to moderately active investment, but not hypoactive. Typically I have found that for a large market like the United States or the U.K. the average holding period for a stock might be as long as nine months. There can also be times when it is nearer to three months. Total turnover is high compared with a normal private portfolio, but low compared with a hedge fund.

Figure 10.3 shows that a secular downtrend was in place from 1966 to 1982, an era for active management. From 1982 to 2000 a secular uptrend took place, when a more passive style worked well. Since 2000, however, active management has been required again.

Notice in **Figure 10.4** that, since 1968, when the S&P 500 index is plotted against gold bars it has performed badly. What this really emphasizes is the

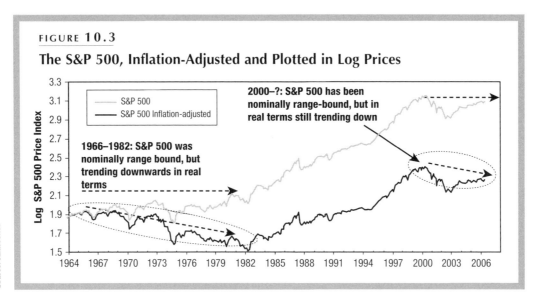

FIGURE 10.3

The S&P 500, Inflation-Adjusted and Plotted in Log Prices

Source: Rathbones

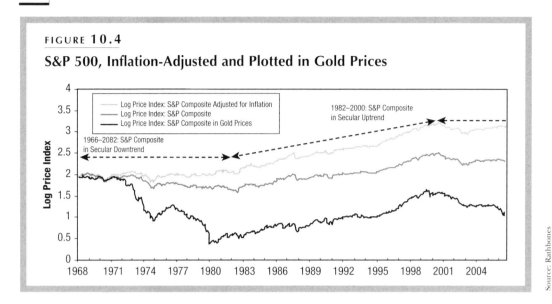

FIGURE **10.4**

S&P 500, Inflation-Adjusted and Plotted in Gold Prices

Source: Rathbones

importance of collecting dividends, which are not taken into account here. But for the growth in dividends the stock market has been a poor investment. Stocks are worse as a store of value than nondividend-paying gold.

Basically, all markets in secular uptrend are likely to be good buy-and-hold markets, and all those in secular downtrend will require active trading to survive. Commodities, as a major asset class, tend to be negatively correlated to stocks. **Figure 10.5** shows both the actual and inflation-adjusted performance since 1956. They were in secular downtrend until 2000, exactly out of step with the uptrend in the S&P 500 index. Ever since then, commodities and related share indexes and stocks have been in secular uptrend, and this is likely to persist until 2016 or even 2020. Do not forget, however, that they will still have the four-year corrective part of the cycle—in other words, a bear market. Once this is over, the secular trend should resume.

As a rule now the stock markets with the best secular uptrend will tend to be so-called emerging markets. The best of these will be China, India, Latin America, and economies dominated by a resource sector like Canada, Russia, and South Africa. The first two will probably eventually achieve superpower status. For 1,800 of the last 2,000 years, the two largest economies on the planet were China and India. They only missed out from 1820 onwards with the industrial revolution in the U.K., Germany, and the United States. If the world is now reverting to its mean, these markets should be top performers. Such a journey will not be linear, however, but a long and winding road, with many potholes.

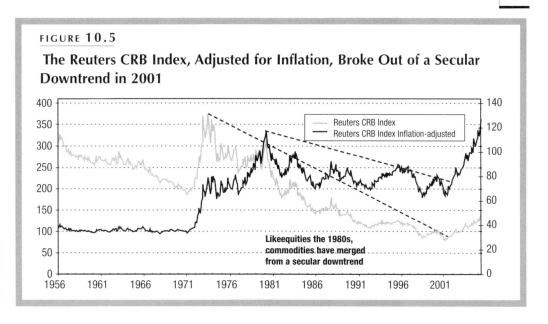

FIGURE **10.5**

The Reuters CRB Index, Adjusted for Inflation, Broke Out of a Secular Downtrend in 2001

Source: Rathbones

Because it is a democracy rather than a communist state, India will likely be the more rewarding stock market. Certainly any investors who ten years ago correctly identified the growth the Chinese economy was going to have and duly bought a China fund would by now have lost about 70 percent of their money. India, conversely, has done extremely well, as **Figure 10.6** shows.

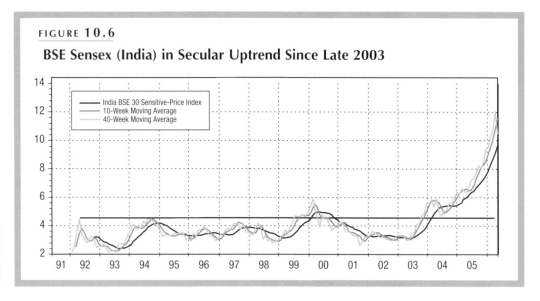

FIGURE **10.6**

BSE Sensex (India) in Secular Uptrend Since Late 2003

Source: Rathbones

Volatility is brutal in all these emerging markets. If you cannot take that heat, then stay out of the kitchen. If you have Teflon nerves, you will make a fortune. My best expectation is that the BSE Sensex of India can hit 40,000 in about ten years. It might just fall back to around 10,000 first. From May to July 2006, it did fall 36 percent with mercurial force. That is the nature of the beast.

The Juglar ten-year cycle dominates the four. The data reveal a very high probability of a recession in the early part of each decade. The first three years of any decade are normally the worst. A four-year downturn in mid-decade is seen as a mid-cycle correction from the ten-year perspective.

This example illustrates how to trade based on secular trends. When a market is in secular uptrend, an inactive buy-and hold-strategy is hard to beat. When it is in secular downtrend, only an active strategy can avoid losing money. After the end of World War II, the U.S. stock market rose dramatically to hit a high in 1966. From there it entered a secular downtrend until 1982. The prices went sideways in a trading range, while the valuation basis fell. Inflation-adjusted, a buy-and-hold would have been a disaster. Then, from 1982 to 2000, a new secular uptrend took place during which a buy-and-hold would have worked brilliantly. Since 2000, the picture is similar to that of 1966. Only active management is king. This is likely to persist until at least 2016 and possibly 2020.

Annual Seasonal Deviation

The next factor in my system is annual seasonal deviation. I first saw this form of back-testing done by Ned Davis Research (an independent institutional investment research and advisory firm), but to be thorough I have redone it myself on forty different world stock markets. The back data are examined and detrended to reveal the seasonal fluctuations. A selection is shown in **Figure 10.7**. There is only one market where it does not work, and that is New Zealand. (All the major economies are in the Northern Hemisphere where the land is, and Australia's sheep trade links it to the North, but New Zealand has a smaller sheep market.) In all the others you should sell in May and go away. Come back again on Halloween.

This example shows the power of annual seasonal deviation. A £10,000 investment made in 1962 in the U.K. market, to end 2005, would have seen buy-and-hold returns of 10 percent on average. However, just being in the market from late October to May during the forty-five years would have compounded to £470,485. The reverse strategy of buying in May and selling in October would have lost £4,325. You can increase returns dramatically by not being in the market

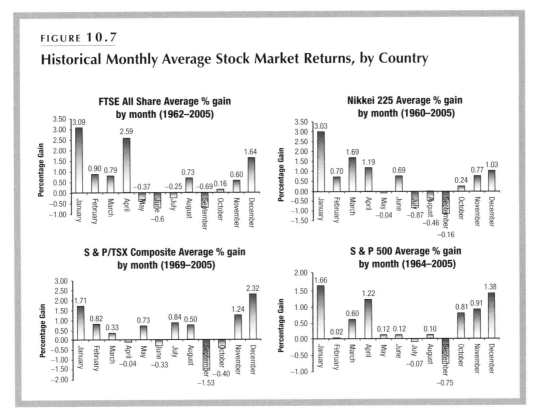

FIGURE **10.7**

Historical Monthly Average Stock Market Returns, by Country

at all for half of the time. The risk-reward ratio is improved beyond all measure.

Market Rankings

The next part of my process is a system for ranking markets against each other. The same methodology works just as well for ranking all the stocks within any particular index. Bear in mind that what is important is identifying the trends we want to back. Therefore we need to quantify the rate of rise of trends. To do so, I load the universe we are measuring into a spreadsheet and measure the rate of rise of the long-term trend, defined as the 200-day moving average. I do the same for the 25-day line, or short-term trend. Finally, I do the same for the 70-day moving average of relative strength to the benchmark. The results of this process are set out on the spreadsheet in **Figure 10.8**. At the macro level, the benchmark is the world index. In any given market it is the base index, such as the S&P or FTSE. Rank each column, add them together, and divide by three. The result is a composite ranking of the strongest and weakest absolute and rela-

FIGURE **10.8**

Global Stock Markets, Ranked by Quintiles, in Dollars

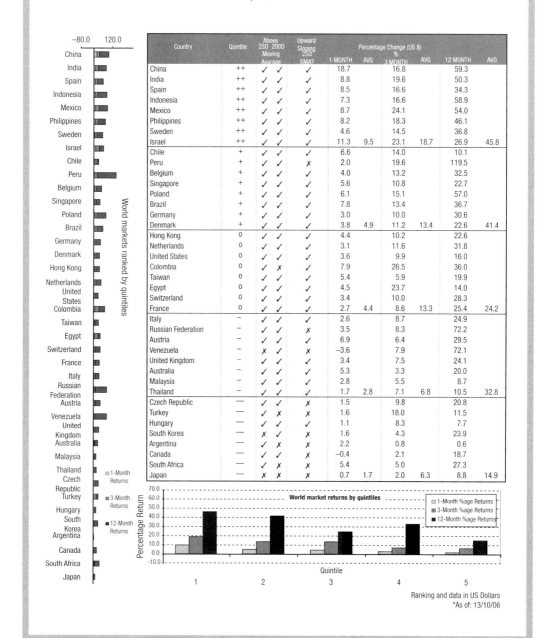

Country	Quintile	Above 25D 200D Moving Average	Upward Sloping 25D SMA?	Percentage Change (US $) %					
				1 MONTH	AVG	3 MONTH	AVG	12 MONTH	AVG
China	++	✓ ✓	✓	18.7		16.8		59.3	
India	++	✓ ✓	✓	8.8		19.6		50.3	
Spain	++	✓ ✓	✓	8.5		16.6		34.3	
Indonesia	++	✓ ✓	✓	7.3		16.6		58.9	
Mexico	++	✓ ✓	✓	8.7		24.1		54.0	
Philippines	++	✓ ✓	✓	8.2		18.3		46.1	
Sweden	++	✓ ✓	✓	4.6		14.5		36.8	
Israel	++	✓ ✓	✓	11.3	9.5	23.1	18.7	26.9	45.8
Chile	+	✓ ✓	✓	6.6		14.0		10.1	
Peru	+	✓ ✓	✗	2.0		19.6		119.5	
Belgium	+	✓ ✓	✓	4.0		13.2		32.5	
Singapore	+	✓ ✓	✓	5.6		10.8		22.7	
Poland	+	✓ ✓	✓	6.1		15.1		57.0	
Brazil	+	✓ ✓	✓	7.8		13.4		36.7	
Germany	+	✓ ✓	✓	3.0		10.0		30.6	
Denmark	+	✓ ✓	✓	3.8	4.9	11.2	13.4	22.6	41.4
Hong Kong	0	✓ ✓	✓	4.4		10.2		22.6	
Netherlands	0	✓ ✓	✓	3.1		11.6		31.8	
United States	0	✓ ✓	✓	3.6		9.9		16.0	
Colombia	0	✓ ✗	✓	7.9		26.5		36.0	
Taiwan	0	✓ ✓	✓	5.4		5.9		19.9	
Egypt	0	✓ ✓	✓	4.5		23.7		14.0	
Switzerland	0	✓ ✓	✓	3.4		10.0		28.3	
France	0	✓ ✓	✓	2.7	4.4	8.6	13.3	25.4	24.2
Italy	–	✓ ✓	✓	2.6		8.7		24.9	
Russian Federation	–	✓ ✓	✗	3.5		8.3		72.2	
Austria	–	✓ ✓	✓	6.9		6.4		29.5	
Venezuela	–	✗ ✓	✗	–3.6		7.9		72.1	
United Kingdom	–	✓ ✓	✓	3.4		7.5		24.1	
Australia	–	✓ ✓	✓	5.3		3.3		20.0	
Malaysia	–	✓ ✓	✓	2.8		5.5		8.7	
Thailand	–	✓ ✓	✓	1.7	2.8	7.1	6.8	10.5	32.8
Czech Republic	—	✓ ✓	✗	1.5		9.8		20.8	
Turkey	—	✓ ✗	✗	1.6		18.0		11.5	
Hungary	—	✓ ✓	✓	1.1		8.3		7.7	
South Korea	—	✗ ✓	✗	1.6		4.3		23.9	
Argentina	—	✓ ✗	✗	2.2		0.8		0.6	
Canada	—	✓ ✓	✗	–0.4		2.1		18.7	
South Africa	—	✓ ✗	✗	5.4		5.0		27.3	
Japan	—	✗ ✗	✗	0.7	1.7	2.0	6.3	8.8	14.9

Ranking and data in US Dollars
*As of: 13/10/06

Source: Rathbones

tive trends. Buys are selected from the top of the list and sells from the bottom. There will be a bunch in the middle that are neutral. I do not exert myself in trying to find the very best market or stock. That is obviously a difficult task. Instead I do the easy thing and identify the average or below average. And I don't own it. I define a good stock as one whose share price goes up while I do own it. The winners select themselves by going up and staying in the top part of the ranking list. Simple though this system is, it works very well. I have not found a universe of markets or stocks on which it does not work, even though the volatility of different universes varies widely.

Trading Rules

We now need to devise trading rules to get us in and out of our selected positions. I have not invented any new indicators. I did not invent the wheel either. It seemed to be there when I needed it, and I use the ones on my car because they work well. It is the same with indicators. We learn through back-testing that many indicators work well some of the time. A few work well a lot of the time. None work well all of the time.

In a leptokurtic distribution prices will spend about a third of the time in a narrow range, and about a third of the time each in an uptrend and a downtrend. Each situation requires three sets of indicators. What my method values most highly is not a range trade but a strong absolute and relative trend. We use the indicators (like RSI, MACD, OBV, Bollinger bands, and others) that are set up as standard defaults on the Bloomberg Professional® service. They are more than adequate for our needs. There is of course a built-in back-test facility.

Once the appropriate indicators have put us into the positions, we simply hold on until one of the prices drops enough to hit a stop-loss level. We then sell out and buy the next stock or market that has now been promoted up our ranking table. We always remain invested until the index itself gives a sell signal, by hitting its own stop-loss.

This level is a trailing percent behind the rising price. We do not use a fixed percentage trail but one that varies with the market or stock and is proportional to the volatility that is normal for that item. I call this the *volatility signature*, or sometimes I call it *beta with bells on*. For example, the number for the FTSE index is 7 percent (see **Figure 10.9**). In a bull market this index almost never has a setback bigger than 7 percent. Trailing up this much below the rising market index will keep you in a bull till virtually the end. However, a stock like BP is

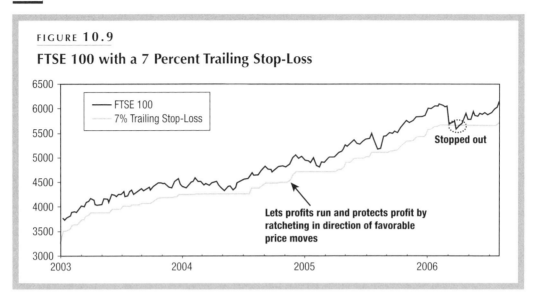

FIGURE 10.9

FTSE 100 with a 7 Percent Trailing Stop-Loss

Source: Rathbones

inherently more volatile, and the signature works out at 13 percent. The price regularly swings that amount while still in an uptrend. The signature for an index like the BSE Sensex (India) is 18 percent.

It is delusional to think that we can get away with very tight stop-losses and never lose money. As **Figure 10.10** shows, if the stop is too tight, you will over-

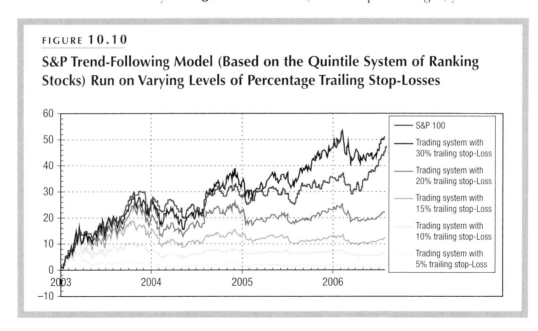

FIGURE 10.10

S&P Trend-Following Model (Based on the Quintile System of Ranking Stocks) Run on Varying Levels of Percentage Trailing Stop-Losses

Source: Rathbones

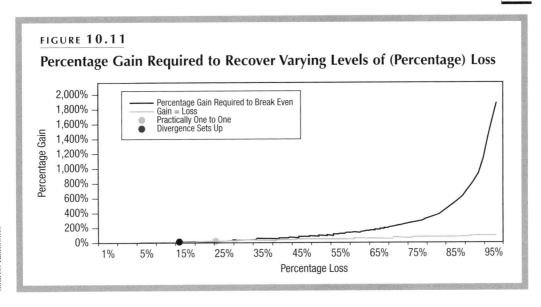

Source: Rathbones

FIGURE **10.11**

Percentage Gain Required to Recover Varying Levels of (Percentage) Loss

trade and make nothing. If you do not risk anything, you will not make anything. We can see that, over time, the more volatility we can accept, the more money we will make, within reason.

Of course, we do have to survive in the game. **Figure 10.11** shows how much we need to make to win back what might be lost on a very volatile swing. If we lose, say, 5 percent, we need to make just over 5 percent to get back onside. If we lose 10 percent, we need to make only 11 percent to be all square. If we go down 30 percent, we need 43 percent, a rather less probable outcome; at 50 percent we need to double just to get back onside. If we were ever to allow a drawdown much bigger than that, we would need to shoot the lights out just to get level. In other words, we would be eliminated from the game. In practice it is worth tolerating volatilities and the accompanying losses up to 25 percent for slightly greater profits. Our stops are normally taken within the range of 10 percent to 25 percent. The lower figure applies to big blue-chip situations and the higher one to smaller market capitalizations, either stocks or market indexes.

The next trading rule is to make sure the size of each investment unit is proportional to the capital available. Even using the ranking system and the correct stop-loss, it is possible to make wildly different amounts of money for a given amount of risk. There are essentially three ways to work this. One is to have equal-size units all of the time, or *unit position sizing*, the second is to use a *martingale*, and the third and best one is to use an *anti-martingale*.

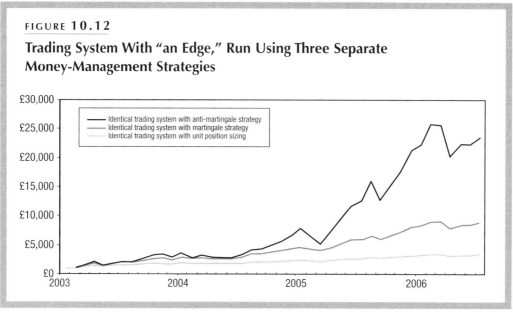

FIGURE **10.12**

Trading System With "an Edge," Run Using Three Separate Money-Management Strategies

Source: Rathbones

A martingale strategy is when a man playing roulette always bets on red. He knows red will eventually come up. Further, every time he loses, he doubles his investment. When red comes up, he gets all his losses back plus one. Unfortunately, if the wheel has a run against him, he will soon find that he is betting his whole wad just for the chance of getting a one-chip win. It simply is not worth it, and he risks getting blown away.

An anti-martingale is a better system. It works in reverse. The unit size is increased only if the position is winning. The unit is not actually a constant, but a constant proportion of the capital now available. If the positions are losing, the unit size is reduced accordingly. In this way downturns are survived and uptrends are more fully exploited. **Figure 10.12** shows that, using identical stock selection and entry and exit rules, a reasonable return can be transformed into an extraordinary performance with the help of an anti-martingale.

We can combine our analytics and trading rules to build a mechanical trading system that a computer expert would identify as a rules-based expert system. This means we can write algorithms for each part of the system. There are not that many rules and they are all simple, but their application leads to a sophisticated answer. They can all be back–tested, and we can put numbers on the probability of being right. We have an edge, and we know what it is. There is of course no such thing as absolute certainty. It is more like having a form book at a horse race. Heavily backed odds-on favorites do not always win, but it is the way to bet. For example, the normal seasonal setback in September to make a low in October is a 70/30 bet. It did not work in 2006. It did not work in 1986 either. On that occasion we had to wait until late in 1987 for a setback that then took the form of a crash. You do not have to be in this business very long before you will be wrong about something. Nobody knows what the future holds. We can speculate, and be right sometimes. Our system does not need us to forecast the future, but it does identify probabilities that we can bet on, and provides a way of exploiting the winners and minimizing the losers. With our system when we are wrong, we can be wrong with confidence.

—w—

IT PAYS NOT to be in the markets all the time. In any given year there are periods of up to six months when being out maximizes returns. This is usually between May and October.

In any four-year period there is likely to be a significant bearish correction phase during which swings down of between 20 percent and 40 percent are normal. Moves of 50 percent are rare, and moves greater than that are exceptional, epoch-making, and go straight into the annals of legend. These drawdowns do occur, however, and can exceed 80 percent. They require subsequent 400 percent gains to get back onside, which always take many years. They are essentially terminating experiences.

Once every ten years there is a very high probability of a recession, and this is at the very end or beginning of the decade. The ninth year of a decade is dangerous, and the first three years deeply disappointing.

Secular trends have a high probability of lasting for multiples of four years, with durations of sixteen to twenty being quite normal. These are periods when only active trading can survive (in a secular downtrend), or alternatively a buy-and-hold strategy is really hard to beat. Even within secular uptrends, when inactive styles are preferred, there is still a high probability of a fourth-year correction phase. This will typically retrace a significant major fraction of the entire uptrend to date, probably at least 20 percent and possibly as much as 50 percent.

The odds of winning are higher if we are long stocks or markets that are in secular uptrend. We must be willing to tolerate a certain amount of volatility but not more than 25 percent, or we risk being eliminated from the game. We always use stop-loss levels, but we do not leave such levels in the market as open orders.

We always aim to identify the strongest actual and relative trends. This achieves sufficient but not excessive dilution of risk. Not being in the market all the time and not owning everything is an important part of the entire process.

Finally, when investing we use an anti-martingale strategy, keeping our investment unit as a constant proportion of available capital. We adapt it actively up and down as events unfold. This makes a good system brilliant.

Index

About Bloomberg

Bloomberg L.P., founded in 1981, is a global information services, news, and media company. Headquartered in New York, the company has sales and news operations worldwide.

Bloomberg, serving customers on six continents, holds a unique position within the financial services industry by providing an unparalleled range of features in a single package known as the BLOOMBERG PROFESSIONAL® service. By addressing the demand for investment performance and efficiency through an exceptional combination of information, analytic, electronic trading, and Straight Through Processing tools, Bloomberg has built a worldwide customer base of corporations, issuers, financial intermediaries, and institutional investors.

BLOOMBERG NEWS®, founded in 1990, provides stories and columns on business, general news, politics, and sports to leading newspapers and magazines throughout the world. BLOOMBERG TELEVISION®, a 24-hour business and financial news network, is produced and distributed globally in seven languages. BLOOMBERG RADIO℠ is an international radio network anchored by flagship station BLOOMBERG® 1130 (WBBR-AM) in New York.

In addition to the BLOOMBERG PRESS® line of books, Bloomberg publishes BLOOMBERG MARKETS® magazine. To learn more about Bloomberg, call a sales representative at

London: +44-20-7330-7500
New York: +1-212-318-2000
Tokyo: +81-3-3201-8900

FOR IN-DEPTH MARKET INFORMATION AND NEWS, visit the Bloomberg Web site at **www.bloomberg.com**, which draws from the news and power of the BLOOMBERG PROFESSIONAL® service and Bloomberg's host of media products to provide high-quality news and information in multiple languages on stocks, bonds, currencies, and commodities.

About the Editor

David Keller, CMT, is a technical analysis application specialist with Bloomberg L.P. in New York and the chair of the New York region for the Market Technicians Association. Keller has conducted numerous seminars across North America on applying technical strategies to the equity, commodity, and foreign exchange markets. He has also presented sessions on combining fundamental and technical strategies for the CFA Institute, Canadian Society of Technical Analysts, and American Association of Individual Investors. He is the author and creator of the *Bloomberg Weekly Technical Strategy Report*, an exclusive newsletter for Bloomberg customers.